SEARCH FOR COMMUNITY
IN A WITHERING TRADITION

*This book is the
Institute for Christian Studies
choice as the*

1990 Robert Lee Carvill
Memorial Book

Permission was kindly given by
Marquette University Quarterly: Philosophy and Theology for reprinting "Kai
Nielsen's *Philosophy and Atheism"* as chapter 1 in this volume, and
The University of Ottawa Press for reprinting "On the Viability of Atheism"
from *God, Scepticism and Modernity* as chapter 2 of this volume.

SEARCH FOR COMMUNITY IN A WITHERING TRADITION

Conversations between a Marxian Atheist and a Calvinian Christian

by Kai Nielsen and Hendrik Hart

UNIVERSITY
PRESS OF
AMERICA

LANHAM/NEW YORK/LONDON

Copyright © 1990 by
University Press of America®, Inc.
4720 Boston Way
Lanham, Maryland 20706

3 Henrietta Street
London WC2E 8LU England

Co-published by arrangement with the
Institute for Christian Studies, Toronto, Ontario, Canada

Cover/Book design: Willem Hart
Willem Hart Art & Design Inc. Toronto

Library of Congress Cataloging-in-Publication Data

Nielsen, Kai, 1926-
Search for community in a withering tradition :
conversations between a Marxian atheist and a Calvinian
Christian / by Kai Nielsen and Hendrik Hart.
p. cm. — (Christian studies today)
"Co–published by arrangement with the Institute for
Christian Studies, Toronto, Ontario, Canada"—T.p. verso.
Includes bibliographical references.
1. Nielsen, Kai, 1926- . 2. Hart, Hendrik. 3. Atheism.
4. Reason. 5. Postmodernism. 6. Civilization,
Modern—20th century. 7. Faith and reason.
8. Calvinism. 9. Philosophy, Marxist.
I. Hart, Hendrik. II. Title. III. Series.
B995.N543S42 1990 211'.8—dc20 90–46385 CIP

ISBN 0–8191–7989–2 (alk. paper)
ISBN 0–8191–7990–6 (pbk. : alk. paper)

For Beyers Naudé
voortrekker
in the
battle against barriers
with gratitude for unmonitored
conversations each of us had
in his backyard

CONTENTS

INTRODUCTION

After the collapse of foundationalism and the rise of post-modernism an intensive and widespread inquiry has centered on Western philosophy's preoccupation with reason. Many questions have been asked: What sort of preoccupation has our focus on reason been? Do we have a unitary concept of reason? What is meant by rationality? What do we mean by reasonable? How do these notions relate to reason? Is reason related to Reason as that has been discussed in metaphysical traditions of modern thought? Is the tradition of reason an Enlightenment heritage or does it go all the way back to the Greeks? Is it fair to say that without a tradition of Western devotion to Reason, present confidence in reason is no longer warranted after the collapse of foundationalism?

In Germany the names of Jürgen Habermas and Hans Georg Gadamer are associated with this inquiry. In France the work of Jacques Derrida and Michel Foucault sets the tone. In the United States Richard Rorty and Richard Bernstein place the issues on our agenda. And in Canada Charles Taylor and Kai Nielsen lead the way.

Nielsen publicly announced his fascination with this set of problems in his presidential address to the *Canadian Philosophical Association* in June of 1984 in Guelph and in the last five years he has not left it alone. During the meetings of the CPA in Winnipeg in May 1986 a book recently published by Nielsen, *Philosophy and Atheism,* was the subject of a symposium. The book did not deal with these metaphilosophical issues, though their presence could be detected in the most recent essays in the book. Therefore, as one of the participants in the symposium, I tried to connect Nielsen's defense of atheism with issues of the current postfoundational and postmodern climate. I specifically argued that Nielsen's atheism was covertly sup-

VIII

ported by a religous appeal to reason and rationality. Nielsen strongly demurred. The first set of essays in this book are modified versions of our prepared exchanges at the 1986 symposium.

I felt that the 1986 discussion had hardly begun to deal with these issues and thought that a continuation might engender some progress. Since the 1984 presidential address, Nielsen had written extensively on the relevant issues and thus provided a more explicit record of his thinking on these matters. So I continued the exchange in May of 1987 with a CPA paper in Hamilton. I argued on the one hand that Nielsen displayed an allegiance to a reason that could double as a god—Reason—in spite of his wanting to avoid this, and that on the other hand Nielsen shared Rorty's radical rejection of god's-eye-views, though without wanting to end up with a debilitating relativism. Nielsen participated in the session but did not then prepare a written response. He again took issue with my analysis of his views and denied being a rationalist in any interesting sense of that appellation. But in a lengthy conversation over dinner that evening, we agreed that we shared significant concerns and that, in many ways, we also shared approaches to these concerns in contemporary culture. My paper—slightly modified again—together with Nielsen's response written newly for this volume follow as the third and fourth chapters.

As that second exchange was going on, Nielsen had come to appreciate Rorty's historicism more positively. In a new flurry of metaphilosophical papers he tried to take a position that would combine a normative approach to human issues with a thoroughgoing historicism. Taking his cues from Habermas and John Rawls, he launched his approach as Critical Theory (CT) in Wide Reflective Equilibrium (WRE). He came closer to Rorty, but made sure he would keep his distance from Derrida and Foucault in spite of certain limited sympathies for the latter's work. I admired the new turn, but continued to detect allegiances to reason that seemed out of keeping with Nielsen's deepest intentions. So a third discussion took place at a session of the Society for Christian Philosophers during the May1989 CPA meetings in Quebec City. Trying yet another angle, I again argued that reason, perhaps in hiding, still filled a religious function in Nielsen's thought. Again, he demurred. The somewhat modified exchanges of that session are chapters five and six in this volume.

The day before the third exchange, Nielsen's work in Marxist moral analysis was the subject of a CPA symposium in which both Evan Simpson (McMaster, Hamilton) and Derek Allen (University of Toronto) called attention to Nielsen's privileged use of theory in human affairs. Allen did this in a way which made Nielsen reflect on the possible correctness of this observation and in a discussion of this point he stated: "I guess I do finally appeal to reason." Though this move in the discussion does not yet emerge clearly in Nielsen's third response to me, the move as well as that response, encouraged me to finish this volume with a final rejoinder at the gracious suggestion of Nielsen.

This does not end the discussion. But hopefully it shows that even on traditionally moot points in philosophical debate between widely separated, perhaps even incommensurate positions, discussion is by no means fruitless. At the very least it is possible to get closer in understanding one another's positions and language. If it is true that in today's global culture deeply alienated communities do not sufficiently share significant beliefs, while at the same time the tradition of reason as a tradition widely trusted for providing shared beliefs is withering, we are in serious trouble. For shared beliefs are crucial if divided communities are to live together. Our attempt to continue to talk together is, therefore, of great importance in a culture deeply attached to conversation as a vehicle of human flourishing.

Three points, really, are placed on the agenda by me. One is whether we all do or do not use (either personally or in communities and traditions) final or ultimate points of reference (unarguable absolutes for some, historical and provisional stances for others) to which we appeal in our debates, in making our decisions, in settling our lives. A second is whether at heart our relation to such a finality or ultimacy requires trust or faith and can appropriately be called religious. And a third is whether in our culture reason or rationality has played or still does play a role as final arbiter to such an extent that even in freeing ourselves from it, we still do appeal to it.

Nielsen and I disagree on all three points. We agree, however, that both in the Marxian and in the Calvinian heritage, the tradition of reason is withering. We also agree that precisely in view of this withering tradition our search for community may benefit from new perspectives and is an important endeavor. Hence it is gratifying to see that, as the discussion moves on, deeper mutual understanding of the positions develops and, as a result, greater clarity. What is more, mutual respect and a willingness to learn and listen emerge as possibilities between, on the one hand, a convinced atheist Marxian who admits to a rejection of all religious faith as much more than a philosophical position and, on the other hand, a deeply committed Calvinian Christian who does not shy away from the totality claims that come with religious confession.

Many modern philosophers who believe that reason will no longer be able to serve us as the undisputed point of entry to universal agreement are deeply concerned about the divided state of humanity, the alienation across ideological abysses, the bitterness between moral or political camps, our inability to live together in peace. Many of these same philosophers are also convinced that a continued conversation which aims at contributing to overcoming our predicament is important. It is our hope that this very small strand of conversation may in some moderate way be helpful to someone who is a participant in this conversation.

Hendrik Hart.
Institute for Christian Studies
Toronto, Spring 1990

1. THE RELIGION OF REASON IN NIELSEN'S ATHEISM
Hendrik Hart

Introduction

Kai Nielsen's *Philosophy and Atheism* manifests a shift from the clinical-analytic stance of the earlier essays to the humanity, concern, and open conversation of the later ones. Section VII of the "Introduction," for example, tells us that he especially wishes to converse with religious believers who struggle with modernity and that he will try to do this "with what I hope is sensitivity and understanding, ..." (1:25). This shift is likely related to his self-critical reflections on the philosophical enterprise as such. His own recent move into a confrontation with postmodernity was self-conscious and was the theme of his 1984 presidential address to the Canadian Philosophical Association. What has not changed, however, is Nielsen's thorough style of treatment. He listens and responds to a wide range of arguments against his own position, rationalistic atheism. I characterize his position as rationalist because, in spite of his acknowledgement of the collapse of foundationalism, he subscribes, in matters of belief, to the ultimate authority of the combination of rational argument and empirical evidence. And thus, not surprisingly, the core of his debate with religious faith is the validity of the *concept* of God.

When Nielsen regards rational argument and empirical evidence as the primary criteria for abandoning or adopting a stance, he takes this as an indication that he holds a nondogmatic position. I think that minimally it shows the ultimacy of rational authority for Nielsen. The belief that all of our beliefs must either be rational-empirical beliefs or else risk being incoherent is itself not obviously a rational-empirical belief. As a second order belief about beliefs it does not evidently meet its own criteria. Someone with a significant investment in reason should therefore reflect on the nature of

1

such a belief. Of course, among our beliefs we do and should find rational-empirical beliefs. But the belief that ideally all our beliefs should be of that kind is not itself of that kind. To believe that it is of that kind would be self-referentially incoherent. I do not mean to suggest that having beliefs which are not simply rational-empirical is a problem. I believe that we both have and should have trans-rational beliefs. But for Nielsen it should be a problem and I do not believe that he is sufficiently self-critical on this point.

In his rationalism, however, Nielsen is not hostile to believers. He *struggles* with them in as honest, sensitive, and respectful a way as is possible between people who hold what seem ultimately irreconcilable positions. A good example is the closing essay, "The Embeddedness of Atheism." In his *struggle* he disagrees with Christian believers. He even relativizes his own rationalism in that essay. He rejects "an empiricist myth" about holding beliefs "solely on the basis of evidence..." (1:222). But it is not clear that these (recent) relativizations function in the rest of the collection of (largely earlier) essays. It is therefore not surprising that from his *position* he also at times needs to *disqualify* religious believers. And in doing so he bases his case on nothing but evidence and argument. He himself speaks of "a strong and indeed embarrassing claim" in this context (1:202). In spite of his solidarity in many respects, his final view is that believers must be poorly educated or significantly irrational. If they are poorly educated they may still be rational, because they can't know any better. And instead of calling believers irrational, Nielsen might prefer his own term "poorly rational" as a designation (1:203, also 208/9).

Nielsen's rationalism leads him to reject irrationality with as much force as Christian faith leads me to disavow unbelief. Thus we both understand disputes between Christians and atheists to be ultimate and exclusive. Is a discussion possible between them? I will try. I will focus on one argument that runs through his essays and I will ask Nielsen to reflect on it in the light of some of his other arguments. This one argument is that religion must be related to a transcendental or spiritual reality, such as for example the God confessed in advanced forms of Christianity, Judaism, and Islam. There may be other forms of religion. But the ones he addreses, the advanced ones, all believe in a deity (1:217/18). He speaks of "belief in spiritual beings" as "definitive of what it is for a belief system to be religious..." (1:11; see also 1:15, 17, 45, 51, 84, 125, and 147). I note in passing that it seems characteristic for his rationalism that Nielsen deals with religion defined primarily as a "belief system" which stands or falls with the *cognitive* adequacy of its *concepts*. He grants that there is more to religion than this, but he does not question his assumption that the adequacy of a religion stands or falls with its ability to withstand an attack on this front.

It is worthwhile to note that one reason for Nielsen's restrictive attention to religion may be that it allows him to escape taking his own commitments to reason or humanity as religious. He calls them "naturalistic" commitments. Just the same, we could take naturalism to be a spiritual position, if we take a spiritual position to be one that commits us to a lifeguiding perspective, to a vision of our destiny that helps direct us to that destiny. Visions and guiding ideals are certainly accepted by Nielsen. He even admits to entertaining utopian hopes. And it seems to me that if some vision or ideal functions as both an ultimate authority and a destiny-guiding perspective, we may be talking about visions that can with good grounds be called divine and spiritual. Religious people certainly no longer all associate "spiritual" with such weird concepts as "immaterial substance" or the like. I also see no objections to calling such concerns religious. But based on his definition of religion Nielsen denies that he makes reason or humanity into divinities. "A commitment... need not be a religious commitment..." (1:126). Of course, I agree.

Perhaps in the interest of fairness I should also note that Nielsen does not object to ultimate concerns and fundamental commitments. He agrees he has them. "Commitment yes; ideology and religion no" (1:126). He is not a nihilist. He just insists that this does not make him religious. Religion for him is more than ultimate concern, God is not a name for everything ultimate. To use a phrase Nielsen borrowed from C.B. Martin: "If nothing more is involved ... all unbelievers can be led gently into belief" (1:218). (See also 20-21 and 122: "Atheism is not a kind of religion: ... it is a reasonable belief....") But Nielsen seems unaware of the Biblical usage of defining one's god by the attitude one has to something. His rejection of reducing god-talk to talk about atheistic substances is in itself no guarantee that naturalistic god-concepts are impossible. When Rorty explicitly rejects not only God, but also what "doubles" for God, he strongly suggests that our divinities acquire their status not so much in what we explicitly allow or self-consciously articulate, but in how we relate to something.

Reason against Religion

His rationalist atheism seems central to Nielsen's concern. It is therefore curious that what he means by reason, rationality, rational, and similar terms is hard to figure out. As hard, it seems to me, as he finds figuring out God; perhaps for the same reasons. If we lack the devotion to reason Nielsen has, it is less clear what such devotion comes to than if we shared it with him. He is aware of problems: "rationality is itself a deeply contested and context-dependent concept" (1:102). Yet he also posits "an established use and evident paradigm cases" (1:102). Sometimes his discussions are specifically focussed on rational as narrowly logical. Then we are in the realm of "only propositions" (1:84) or "only statements" (1:92) and apparently this area of rationality is "ideologically neutral" (1:100). At other times it seems the crucial terms can be taken to mean whatever anyone might mean by them. Reason, reasonable, and rational then seem to acquire the meaning of terms of approval for whatever is dear to Western people.

Thus, it is unclear to me why the six statements of common sense mentioned by Nielsen as "rational principles" (1:193). should at all be called rational. Why not sensible principles? Or meaningful principles? Or our ways to hope? Why is acting efficiently or effectively the same as acting rationally (1:193)? Outside of rationalism that usage is, apart from a long Western tradition in the use of "rational," puzzling. Only rationalism will acknowledge the deepest meaning of all meaning to be rational meaning.

If I am right about both the importance and the vagueness of Nielsen's rationalism, I believe that many of his objections to

4

religion are also applicable to ultimate positions such his own. At the same time I believe this is obscured from Nielsen by his own position. Thus, when he makes his objections *from* his own position, he does not see them as applicable *to* his own. But on close inspection Nielsen's commitment to a Western emancipatory concept of reason appears vulnerable to his own arguments against religion and God. He considers his commitment to be exempt from his objections precisely because *in* his commitment to reason, his position seems rational rather than creedal.

I will not explain or defend what I mean by creedal here. I have done so elsewhere (2). All I need say is that among our many beliefs we also find, as I see it, creedal beliefs. And I believe it is often typical of creedal beliefs *both* that they make the impression of being self-referentially incoherent from a rational-conceptual point of view *and* that they are held with great conviction. "There is no truth" is an example. So is the non-pejorative rationalist belief that rationalism is irrational at heart. I do not think all creedal beliefs are necessarily religious. But I think they do become religious when their authority is ultimate, and they may even be called spiritual when their role in life is destiny-directing.

Nielsen's commitment to rationality has definite emancipatory roots (see the closing paragraphs on 1:53, the description on 194-195, and his appeal, on 224, to "the thrust of the development of our intellectual [!] culture since the Enlightenment"). From the point of view of such a position, creedal beliefs about the transcendent and the supernatural, which call for an allegiance beyond the authority of reason and a reality transcending what we empirically comprehend, are easily understood to be offensive beliefs. The form which Nielsen's attack on transcendent religion and a spiritual God takes is via his assumption that religion in any case requires truth claims, which he views rationalistically as exclusively factual-propositional claims. The theistic creedal beliefs are treated *as if* they were a species of Nielsen's rational-creedal beliefs. Over and over Nielsen emphasizes that religions minimally contain conceptual belief systems. The opening paragraph of the introduction zeroes in on the conceptual system (1:9). We talk about how we "conceive" things (1:15). We talk about God in terms of his capacity to be "a rational object of belief" (1:21). These sorts of references abound (1:17, 18, 23-24, 34, 38, 42, 48, 93, 94, 123, 154, 217 ["conceptually fundamental"]). Nielsen deals with all truth claims in this context (1:13, 22, 38, 79, 110, 116, 226). Truth is confined to the logical-empirical area of concepts and facts (1:78, 91, 95, 98). In this context his rational objections to religion are that God is empirically inaccessible and conceptually incoherent. He sees no rational way to sort out the Christian-Jewish-Moslem truth claims from others (1:35, 47, 112, and 223). Even when he *states* that not all argument is rational, not all belief grounded, and not all evidence empircal, these statements do not refer to anything we see *happen* within his essays. No irrational, ungrounded, or unempirical factor in belief is ever *admitted* in the case of religion.

Religion is rationally examined and thus found rationally wanting. And since rationality is best represented by the scientist and the philosopher, the scientifically and philosophically educated person in Western culture is our final judge. Talk about this is incessant. This is the only dimension of the book which at first I could not resist finding unempirically naive and imperialistically irritating, until I concluded this is the talk of a believer about his saints, which invariably comes across as offensive to an unbeliever, in this case an unbeliever in the Enlightenment (see 1:23, 40, 41, 100, 126, 146, 151, 164, 184/5, 189, 195, 201-203, 219, 224/5).

Reason as Religion

I mentioned that some of these arguments Nielsen uses against religion are also applicable—from my point of view—to his position. If our ultimate position is Nielsen's rationalism, truth can only be truth empirically accessible to reason and whatever is not thus rational is not true. If his version of rationalism excludes the legitimacy of religion, I can well understand how my referring to such rationalism as religious would appear to be false to a rationalist of this kind. Such rationalism can recognize itself as ultimate, yet would not acknowledge this ultimacy as religious. But perhaps this is precisely because of the ultimacy of this rationalism. However, my claim that Nielsen's position

6

is vulnerable to his objections to religion does not depend on seeing that his position is religious.

I can begin by suggesting that not every view of reason demands that we make truth exclusively rational. What *appears* to lack coherence or correspondence or evidence *from an ultimately rational point of view,* that is, to a rationalist, does not necessarily seem so from another point of view. A Christian can intellectually follow Nielsen's argument of incoherence, but will never be concvinced by it, because *from an ultimately Christian point of view* that incoherence is simply never experienced. To a believer, the experience of incoherence, even rationally, just never materializes. Further, it is questionable whether an ultimately rational point of view can be rationally grounded without begging the question of its own ultimacy. If "religion without foundations" is "religion without rational grounds" (1:47), we may conclude that foundations are by definition rational grounds. But, equally by definition, that makes "rational" unfounded. When we make "rational" the ultimate ground, the ultimacy means that rationality is without grounds. For if it were itself grounded, either it would not be an ultimate or "final" ground, or it would be grounding itself. One need not be a Christian to see this. Some grasp of Heidegger will suffice.

Rational grounding as the final authority in the grounding of our beliefs is, on my view, *the religion* of the Enlightenment. Rorty's attack on the role of philosophy as "final-court-of-appeal-epistemology" in the West did not go as far as unmasking Enlightenment faith in reason as the root of all this. That faith remains even in Rorty, as it does in Nielsen. Nielsen deals with some of this in "The Burden of Proof and *The Presumption of Atheism"* and "The Embeddedness of Atheism" (1:129ff. and 211ff.). I think this makes it possible for non-rationalists to see Nielsen's position as a religious one. For I think it can be argued that what makes a position religious is that it *ultimately* judges *every belief* from that position, while never questioning the belief in that position without begging the question. But I will leave this religious question aside and I will explore whether Nielsen's arguments against religion are not also telling against any authentically *ultimate* position.

Indeed, why should Nielsen's claims not be subjected to

7

the criticism he has of Christianity, namely, that its truth-claim to being the only and final truth is not rationally defensible against other claims? Isn't Nielsen's version of what is rational just one version? Is it the true one? Do other believers in reason, say the god's-eye-view kind, find Nielsen's views even rational at all? Can he rationally defend himself to *their* satisfaction? Why do we need to accept a version of being rational that excludes religious faith on the ground that on *some* version of what it is to be rational, to have religious faith is irrational? I don't doubt Nielsen's version does exclude religious faith. But why accept his version? It is, after all, supported only by an empirical minority: the philosophically, scientifically educated champions of reason. Empirically, *most* rational beings (people!) seem comfortable with a combination of reason and religion. Empirically, going by (rational) people's experience, Nielsen's position on what is rational seems to be an unempirical one.

Nielsen well knows about these people (1:202-203, 217). But for him they constitute different evidence. So let me ask about the empirical status of his own "utopian hopes" as "realistic endeavors" (1:53)? Do these not involve "beliefs 'whose scope transcends the empirical world'"? Nielsen has written several papers recently in which he defends his hopes for a unified humanity through the use of a common reason against the relativism of the incommensurability claims of people like Richard Rorty. They show, beyond dispute in my opinion, that Nielsen's belief in reason—contrary to his hopes— is not ultimately grounded in reason, but rather in hope. His own rational-critical inquiries into the reasonableness of the authority of a common reason always come up short of solid rational-empirical grounding. And then what? Then "we may always reasonably *hope*..." (6:285). The ultimacy of hope in Nielsen's own views is in sharp contrast with the ultimacy of rational-empirical grounds he demands of religionists; even when he calls hope reasonable.

Nielson's position on rationality, besides seeming unempirical, also does not seem to be obviously rational. For there surely are no strictly logical-conceptual reasons for his version of rationality. He seems to understand this and so gives a broader view of what is reasonable. But his position requires

8

Nielsen to view rationality so broadly that it loses specific connections with reason and logic or with philosophers and scientists. "Rational" comes to mean simply: meaningful, sensible, hopeful. But most (rational) people, except rationalists of some kind, do not define hope or meaning as peculiarly rational. We can use "rational" as a specific term with a narrowly specific meaning. It will then have a sense closely tied to the properties of what is logical. In that sense many "moderns" (a beloved Nielsen category of people, though he approves of them primarily if they meet the qualifications of philosophers and scientists) probably believe that much of life is just simply outside of the rational ballpark. It is neither rational nor irrational. It is just other than rational, different. About most of life we need not care whether or not it is rational.

But Nielsen winds up using rational much more broadly. It simply becomes a term of approval, as I noted earlier. It means to him what "good" means to others. So even "irrational" can be "rational" for him (1:196-197). But that statement is creedal and, as far as I can determine, it does not—as is the case with so many Christian beliefs—function. However, if for the indiscriminate term "rational" Nielsen would substitute "good," his book would have to defend that religion is not good for us. Even he is not convinced of that. And for that reason rational then becomes rational narrowly defined again.

Nielsen's case is heavily dependent on argument and the argument heavily dependent on whether or not we shall accept a concept of rationality offered by certain philosophers and scientists. The actual role of empirical evidence in his book is practically non-existent. To the contrary, evidence against Nielsen's argument is that his concept of rationality is neither held by nor practically functional for most human beings. Most people do not in fact believe his case. Furthermore, it is highly dubious that Nielsen could make a solid case for the rationality of his own position if he submitted his belief in reason to nothing else but his own criteria of rationality. In that case, I conclude from his writings, he would grant that belief in reason cannot be rationally grounded beyond reasonable doubts and criticisms. So I conclude that Nielsen's rational (empirical-conceptual) grounds for rejecting Christianity are also plausible grounds for rejecting his atheism. Indeed, Nielsen's ultimate position causes him empirical difficulties with the Berrigans, Naudés, Kripkes, and van Fraassens of this world. He agrees they are well educated and seem rational. But they have gods (1:52, 224). Why does he object to that? I suggest that when the authority of reason itself has ultimate (divine?) status it makes sense to make the (religious-monotheistic?) move of forbidding (other) gods.

The Rationality of Reason
Nielsen argues against calling his position religious by saying this requires too broad a definition of religion. He thinks on such a view we all turn out to believe in the God of Christianity. Then, he believes, a Christian can no longer make exclusive claims for Christianity. As I have already indicated, Nielsen's own concepts of reason and rationality are open to this very objection of his. He cannot possibly claim that his position on rationality is the position of most writers on rationality. So he falls back on seeing rationality as common sense. But much common sense is comfortable with God; indeed, not to believe in God at all makes no sense to many people.

One might conceivably argue that, if Nielsen's definition of religion and his arguments against religion are vulnerable to his own arguments, his own position is plausibly religious. The above may be considered as hints in that direction. But his attack on theism is open to other objections. One of these is that there is more to atheism than being anti-Christian. Even the Bible does not dispute the existence of many gods. It claims that Yahweh is the only true god, but does not deny the existence of others. Nielsen is, of course, fundamentally mistaken when he charges that the perspectival position—we all have our gods and we all have our creeds—is relativistic. That we all have faith does not mean everybody's faith is equally good. And to say that the choice for a true faith commits us to a rational criterion of truth is no more than another imperialistic claim of rationalism. We cannot say anything about our position from outside of our position. I agree. But that does not imply we cannot say anything true about our position, nor does it mean that truth is just the position we take, nor does it mean truth is just the

10

many positions that are being taken. Once we abandon the correspondence theory's criteria for truth, we also need to stop *treating* truth *as if* it is still the outside observer's call, the referee's-eye-view.

Nielsen does not define in general what a god is, or what revelation is. He registers his objection to a specific God and to a specific revelation (1:212). This interesting move, which we may perhaps call Christian atheism, creates the impression that Nielsen may be suppressing his awareness of the—for him uncomfortable—possibility that, though rejecting the Christian God, he does have a religion and divinity. Why should we believe we must "define" God as a person. In Christianity that's a very late doctrine, if by person is meant what we mean by it today. Today many Christians believe that only humans are persons and that God is not a human being. And why must we think God as spirit is an immaterial entity? As I said earlier, that's not a typically modern Christian belief. I believe that I, too, am a spirit. And I know I am physical.

Suppose we relate to a divinity as that on which "all depends" without itself being in any way dependent, what would that make of Nielsen's rationality? His rationality, he claims, even incorporates rational irrationality. And, characteristically for a creedal belief, that inclusion makes reason more rational, rather than making it irrational. From a purely conceptual point of view, the joint presence of rationality and irrationality could make for irrational rationality as well as for rational irrationality. But from the perspective of creedal rationalism, the inclusion of irrationality only increases the rationality. The fact that he thinks of himself as a critical rationalist is just another way, for rationalists, of saying that to be rational is to be critical (rationally). So a critical rationalist is just a good rationalist, a really rational rationalist. But a believer nevertheless. There is, of course, no such thing as "plenty of empirical justification" for thinking reason is our only hope for finding our common ground. Two thousand years of Western faith in reason certainly today gives us the empirical counter-evidence that our arguments divide us. In the face of that, religions have always provided us with hope. Hope is the instrument we grab for when empirical evidence fails us. If reason gives us that hope, we make belief in reason religious.

I suspect that Nielsen may not take these objections seriously. But then what distinguishes his attitude from Plantinga's, who according to Nielsen holds his own position as fundamentally unproblematic (1:25-28)? Though I am sympathetic to Nielsen's objection that at times Plantinga's arguments can come across as "tricky" (1:213-215), Nielsen himself seems insufficiently aware that what is "serious" in philosophy of religion often depends on where one is "positioned" ultimately. *From* the point of view of belief in God, belief in God is not seriously problematic. In fact, from that point of view atheistic rationalism is seriously problematic. But that, in turn, does not seem serious to the atheist. These clashes are typical of (religious?) conflict between irreconcilable ultimate positions.

I believe Nielsen needs to take more seriously the question: Why should ultimate surrender to God and trust in God's revelation be submitted to criteria of rationality as ultimate and exclusive criteria of authenticity and truth? With the collapse of foundationalism we can no longer take all sorts of early vintage assumptions about reason for granted. Christians have seen that very quickly and have begun to revise all sorts of elements of Christian belief, attempting to rid them of traces of a foundationalist rationalism. A debate with Christian faith should today no longer be conducted with Christian philosophers of religion who are defending an old style rationalist Christianity. The old style concepts of faith—immaterial body and others like it—designed to fit criteria of rationality turned out to be weird on criteria other than those of reason as well.

Nielsen assumes that religious belief must still meet criteria of rational soundness. But he cannot and does not show on conceptual-empirical grounds that rationality is self-grounding. And that, I believe, makes his assumption vulnerable to his own critique of Christian faith. What is this self-grounding? When one believes that we ought only to believe what we have good ground to believe, we have problems with the good ground for this belief itself. Of course, we can believe this not so much *on* the good ground of other beliefs or evidence, but *as* a good ground for believing. Such a belief does not so much *have* grounds, but *is* a ground and is believed because we experience that it has done well as such. Beliefs like this are not normally conclusions of argument supported by evidence, but serve as grounds for having arguments at all. It is a matter of *trust in* argument. But that trust is not itself a matter *of argument.*

The Reasonableness of Rationality and Religion

So my claim is that we do not trust reason on rational grounds and no amount of rational effort will so ground reason. In short: nothing that needs a ground can be its own ground. But if rationality is held to be our only ground for believing, it can only have itself as ground. That, I would say, sounds irrational. Except that to a rationalist it will just sound matter of factly the case! That's how a rationalist will experience beliefs as normal. I, of course, believe nothing of the kind. And argument does not usually settle my sort of "unbelief." That's because argument is not the ground for argument's ultimacy. Rather, it is *fundamental trust* in argument. In the light of such trust, that is, in the course of living out of such trust, the trustworthy nature of argument usually reveals itself to those who have that trust. That's why I call beliefs of this sort creedal rather than rational.

I do agree, of course, that we do well to be rational. But is faith a species of reasoning, that we should test it for its rational coherence? I realize that as a philosopher Nielsen is busy with rational truth claims. But why must religion's truth claims be evaluated as though they were philosophical ones? Only if reason is ultimate in matters of truth does that make sense. But how rational is it to fix our hope for truth ultimately on reason? Or if we base our hopes on more than reason, does reason still function as criterion that makes other bases acceptable? Only for real believers in reason would such a supercriterion be acceptable. And their number is diminishing in our postmodern world. Nielsen's hopeful saints are but a "remnant" of the faithful: some philosophers and scientists. By now most other (still rational) people have given up hope in such saints. Those who nevertheless keep up this (ultimate) hope behave like they have a religious hope: capable of hope against hope. Such a hope, which guides us from "outside" our situation, can be called spiritual and transcendent. As spirit, we can say, a person is capable of being in touch, via hope and trust, with what lies

13

beyond our immediate environment. But rationalism, which since the Enlightenment grounds itself within the horizon of empirically accessible reality, thus staying "on the ground," closes the horizon of transcendence.

Nielsen's objections to spiritual and transcendent realities seem so firmly lodged within his empirical-rational or naturalist-emancipatory perspective that many of them seem pointless for religious people. He seems to skirt problems and realities with an ease he himself bemoans when he sees Plantinga do it to atheists. But if, for example, we would look upon notions like "spiritual" or "transcendent" not as "disembodied" or "outside of the universe" (both very problematic concepts indeed!), but rather as having to do with our future and destiny, with being "in touch" with these even though they are not here now, then a number of Nielsen's own utopian remarks could be perceived to be spiritual and transcendent.

Rationalism thus fails to see that we do not ultimately ground ourselves on grounds other than the ultimate. An ultimate is trusted *as* ground, but not *on* grounds. "Trusting in reason on rational grounds" is fundamentally a pleonastic expression, hiding the fact that it is trusting in reason *for its own sake* rather than *on* any grounds other than reason.

From the point of view of belief in God, reason grounded in belief in God perceives sufficient coherence and evidence in religion. Belief in God is reasonable to itself. Only if challenged to legitimate itself as *ultimately* rational within a framework of rationalism do problems arise. Most people are happy to accept the given limits of their rationality. They gladly accept something—such as love—they do not understand, or cannot grasp with full coherence, or are unable to observe as we observe evidence of theoretical entities. What they do understand is that their lives would be the poorer without love, even when true love truly transcends all our efforts. Perhaps in just this way, people understand our lives would be the poorer without God.

Religious faith is not irrational. But its rationality is that of faith. Just like leaves are colored, but if we would assess them as colors we would miss the point; so to treat religious belief as though it should be all rationality is beside the point. Perhaps Nielsen could at this point rethink possible parallels of his

14

concept of the relation between rationality and morality. To him—as to me—morality and religion are different. And to him this difference allows people who are not religious or who do not believe in God nevertheless to make (moral) sense of their lives. But he also sees being moral as different from being rational. And again, so do I. For both of us, rationality and morality are different orders of experience. But why not also explore this possibility for rationality and religion? Why not consider the possibility that believing or having faith are not first of all matters of rationality? Believers assess their religious beliefs from within their faith. No other avenue is open. Only if our faith is in reason does all of this get masked, for then being rational is all there is to being a believer of that sort. And then we miss the benefit of understanding we are believers.

It hardly seems necessary to go to the lengths Nielsen goes to get us to accept that he does not believe in the God of the Bible. It seems clear that he doesn't. But he seems to want more. He wants his faith in reason to be non-religious. He does not even want it to be a faith. And that, it seems to me, would require a rational demonstration of reason's being grounded in itself. But that sounds rationally impossible and thus irrational. If, on the other hand, he believes in reason not *on* rational grounds, but *as* ultimate authority of all experience, then his rationalist position on reason seems vulnerable to his own objections against what he sees as religious.

In conclusion: in this context I do not primarily want to object to Nielsen's religious attachment to reason. Whether or not reason deserves religious trust is a matter for debate. Here I have primarily wanted to establish parity between Nielsen and religious believers by saying that where belief in God functions, it functions in much the same way that belief in reason functions for Nielsen. The division of 20th century people into religious people on the one hand and rational moderns on the other is not, I believe, a helpful one. Religious people can be, as I see it, as fully rational as any. And rationalist moderns are, if I understand religion, embedded in real religious faith.

2. ON THE VIABILITY OF ATHEISM
Kai Nielsen

Introduction

I n arguments between belief and unbelief which are at all informed, it is agreed by almost all parties that religious claims are paradoxical and that, if there is a God, He is indeed a very mysterious reality. The God of developed Judaism, Christianity, and Islam, whatever else that God is supposed to refer to, is supposed to refer to an Ultimate Mystery. God is supposed to be the Incomprehensible Other, the Ultimate Mystery whose mysterious reality is beyond all ordinary knowing. A God who was not such an ultimate mystery would not be the God of Judaism, Christianity, or Islam.

This alleged ultimate reality, at least in tolerably orthodox versions of these sister religions, is taken to be a personal creative reality in the form of an infinite and eternal individual who exists beyond the bounds of space and time, and who, without ceasing to be infinite, transcends the world. This is what, most essentially, "God" is taken to refer to in such religions. What in my *God, Scepticism and Modernity* as well as in my *Philosophy and Atheism* and elsewhere I have probed is whether we have any good reasons at all for believing that there actually exists such a reality or whether it is even reasonable for us, standing where we are now and knowing what we know, to believe that such a reality could exist.[1]

I reject such a religious belief—the fundamental religious presupposition of these religions—because it seems to me that we have no good reason for believing that such a reality exists or indeed even could. It is not just that we cannot decide whether we can be justified in believing in such a reality and thus naturally gravitate toward agnosticism. Rather—or at least so I argue—the most reasonable thing for us to do is to reject such a belief because at best the probability that such a reality

16

exists is of a very low order and at worst such a belief is so problematic as to justify the claim that God, so conceived, connotes an illegitimate concept—an ersatz concept, if you will—that could never have an actual application because what we are saying in speaking of God is actually incoherent. Moreover, it seems to me that when we examine the matter carefully, we will come to see that the worst-case scenario from the point of view of religious belief is also the more likely case.

Such a rejection is, of course, a form of atheism. And it is that atheism that I try carefully to characterize and defend in *Philosophy and Atheism*. I argue there, and in *God, Scepticism and Modernity* as well, the strong thesis, some might even say the offensive thesis, that we cannot come to have a sufficient understanding of such perfectly orthodox talk of God such that the reality to which "God" purports to refer could be the object of a religious commitment that is both clear-headed and informed.

What I have sought to worry out and what seems to me to be plainly a central issue for a nonevasive consideration of religion, at least in cultures such as our own, is whether sufficient sense can be made of the key religious conceptions of the dominant religions of our culture to make belief in God a live option for a reflective and concerned human being possessing a reasonable scientific and philosophical understanding of the world we live in, or whether some form of atheism or agnosticism is the most nonevasive option for such a person. My argument has been that belief in God should no longer be a live option for us standing where we are and knowing what we know.

Suppose we say, in a properly orthodox manner, as Richard Swinburne does, that God is "a person without a body (i.e., a spirit), present everywhere, the creator and sustainer of the universe, able to do anything (i.e., omnipotent), knowing all things, perfectly good, a source of moral obligation, immutable, eternal, a necessary being, holy and worthy of worship."[2] What I call (perhaps tendentiously) *simple* atheism maintains either (a) that such a belief is false and that there is no such reality or (b) (more modestly) that there is no good evidence that there is such a reality and that the probability is so low that

17

we will ever come up with evidence sufficient to make such a belief even plausible that we cannot, if we know that, be justified in believing in God. The simple atheist will then add, as a codicil, that we should in a society such as ours know such things, if we are informed. In a parallel way a simple believer will say either that we have enough evidence to be justified in believing in God or, as an alternative fideistic view, that, evidence or no evidence, we are justified in living by faith. We are justified, the simple believer claims, in taking belief in God to be a basic belief for which we do not seek evidence. And again, in a parallel manner, simple agnostics will say that we do not have evidence or more generally reasons here and now either to justify belief in God or to justify the belief that God does not exist or probably does not exist. So, in such a circumstance, the agnositc will say that the reasonable person should suspend any committing belief one way or the other; the reasonable person should neither accept religious beliefs nor reject them.

My argument is that, given a reasonable understanding of the development of Jewish, Christian, and Moslem belief systems, we should no longer, if we are so informed, be either a simple atheist, a simple agnostic or a simple believer. Such positions are no longer justified and the reasonable thing to do is to abandon them. Whatever may have been the case in the past when God was construed more anthropomorphically, the concept of God has become, since at least the Middle Ages, *problematic*, and the less anthropomorphic it has become the more problematic it has become.[3] Our perplexities are such concerning the concept of God that it is anything but clear that an utterance such as "God created man in his image and likeness" could be either true or false or reasonably be believed to be either true or false. The problematicity is at least conceptual. We do not understand what we are supposed to be asserting or denying when we assert or deny the existence of God. We do not understand what we are referring to when we speak of God. Many of the allegedly descriptive terms deployed in defining "God" are as elusive with respect to their denotation as "God." *Simple* believers, agnostics and atheists alike, do not face the logically prior question about the very legitimacy of the

18

concept of God. The various conceptions extant in developed religions (religions which have ceased to be utterly anthropomorphic) are so problematic—or at least that is my claim—that it is anything but clear that we have a coherent concept of God such that that concept could have application.[4]

Contemporary atheists attuned to modernity, or for that matter postmodernity, and tolerably knowledgeable about philosophy and science will not be simple atheists, and their counterparts will not be simple agnostics or simple believers. The central issue should not be whether it is true or probably true, or false or probably false, that God exists, or not yet determinable which. The central issue should be whether a religiously adequate concept of God is sufficiently coherent such that the central strands of religious belief can make legitimate truth-claims at all or, put differently, whether talk of God makes sense. (Or, to put it more accurately, though more pedantically, does it make the kind of sense that it must make for religious beliefs to be viable?) It is my contention that it does not.

This position is best understood as a form of atheism, though it is an atheism under a broader and more adequate construal than the traditional atheism of the simple atheist. On my construal, to be an atheist is to be someone who rejects belief in God for at least one of the following reasons (the specific reason will depend on how God is being conceived): (1) if an anthropomorphic God is what is at issue, the atheist rejects belief in God because it is false or probably false that there is such a God; (2) if what is at issue is a non-anthropomorphic God (the God of the major strands of Judaism, Christianity, and Islam), then the atheist rejects belief in God because, depending exactly on how such a God is conceptualized, the very concept of God is illegitimate because the concept of such a God is either cognitively meaningless, unintelligible, contradictory, incomprehensible or incoherent; (3) the atheist rejects belief in God (here we speak of the God portrayed by some modern or contemporary theologians or philosophers) because the concept of God in question is such that it merely masks an atheistic substance, e.g., "God" is just another name for love or a symbolic term for moral ideals. So, depending on

19

how God is conceptualized, atheists reject God for different reasons, but given the evolution of our religious belief systems, it is the range of conceptualization covered by (2) that requires the most serious attention, and it is that cluster of conceptions which raises the issue of the coherence and hence the legitimacy of belief in God.[5]

Why should it be thought that non-anthropomorphic concepts of God, where they do not simply disguise an atheistic substance, are incoherent? "God," on these employments, is some sort of referring expression and so it is vital to ask about its referent. To whom or what does "God" refer? Is it a proper name, an abbreviated definite description, a distinctive descriptive predicate, or what? How could we come to be acquainted with, or otherwise come to know, what "God" stands for or characterizes? How do we—or do we—identify or indicate God? What are we talking about when we speak of God? *What* or *who* is this God we pray to, love, make sense of our lives in terms of, and the like? When we think seriously about these related questions, we will come to sense, or at least we should come to sense, how problematic our concept of God is.

Suppose we say, not implausibly, that "God" is an abbreviation for a definite description and we take Swinburne's orthodox definition of God, given above, as the spelling out of a definite description which will enable us to understand what our God-talk is about. However, if we are puzzled about what "God" refers to, we will also be puzzled about what "a person without a body" refers to, about what it is "to be the creator and sustainer of the universe," or "to be present everywhere" and (a) still be detectable and (b), be transcendent to the universe. And, to add insult to injury, how can something which is detectable be transcendent to the universe? Perhaps sense can be teased out of such notions or given to them, but as they stand, they are just as problematic, or at the very least almost as problematic, as "God." It is certainly not unreasonable to wonder if these conceptions make any coherent sense and to wonder how it could be at all possible to identify the referents of such terms. It is very natural in such a context to come to wonder whether they can be more than empty phrases which for some people in some environments have great emotive

20

force. Yet it is also the case that God is supposed to be the Ultimate Mystery, an at least partly incomprehensible ultimate reality. We are not to expect conceptions of God to be clear; a certain amount of incomprehensibility just goes with the mysterious sort of something that we believe in when we believe in God. While it is true that we do not have to be unclear ourselves to portray unclarity, still a conceptualization of God that did not make it evident that we are talking about something which is in a way incomprehensible would not be a faithful portrayal of God. The person who demands certitude in religious domains just does not understand what religious risk is.

What centrally is at issue between sophisticated believers, atheists, and agnostics is whether the incomprehensibility of God is sufficiently constrained such that we can, in certain circumstances, have some inkling that our mysterious conceptions actually answer to a reality that would also be religiously appropriate (e.g., is not like the reality Feuerbach's God refers to), or whether the incomprehensibility is so total that the concept of God is illegitimate because incoherent, or whether we are not in a position to know which it is or even to have good reasons for believing that it is one or the other, and thus, if we would keep our integrity, we must remain agnostics.[6]

Whichever way we go here, we are treating the concept of God as problematic and regarding the logically prior question of the legitimacy of the very concept of God as the central question to be dealt with before we go on, if indeed after the examination of this prior question there will be any reason to go on, to consider whether or not we can in some way prove the existence of God, given evidence for His existence, or consider whether we must assume God exists to make sense of our own existence.

I have attempted in *God, Scepticism and Modernity*, as I did in *Philosophy and Atheism* as well, to come to grips with that prior question, and in doing so I argue for the truth of atheism, namely in this context for the truth of the claim that non-anthropomorphic conceptions of God are so problematic as to be incoherent, though I am also concerned to show, against the fideist, that we need not make a desperate Pascalian wager and, against all appearances of incoherence, try to affirm the exis-

21

tence of God so as to keep nihilism at bay and in so doing give sense to our tangled lives and make sense of a commitment to morality. This is also a central theme of my *Ethics Without God.*

Summary

Let me now show in skeletal form some of the lines of reflection and argument that led me to what for some no doubt is a repugnant conclusion. Jews, Christians, and Moslems must believe that God is not only a bodiless person, a conception whose intelligibility is far from clear, but as well, this extraordinary person that God is said to be is also said to be an *infinite individual* who is everywhere and yet is also utterly transcendent to the universe while still standing to creatures in the world in personal relations of caring and loving. Here we have a string of words that, if we will think literally about what they are trying to say, do not fit together so as to make sense. An individual cannot at one and the same time both be utterly transcendent to the world and be an individual in the world standing in personal relations of caring and loving. To so try to conceptualize things is like saying that an individual is both utterly transcendent to the world and not transcendent to the world. "Infinite individual" is also nonsense. If something is an individual it is discrete and limited, and if that individual is also a person, as God is said to be, that person is only identifiable through having a body, but, even if that latter claim were not true, an individual, as a discrete being, distinguishable from others and distinct from others, can hardly be infinite and to boot be everywhere. If God is everywhere, if there is no place where God is not, then God cannot be an individual, even an extraordinary individual, for as an individual, or for that matter as a person, whatever we are referring to must be a discrete and distinct reality. It cannot, if we are talking about an individual, be an infinite or omnipresent reality. (To say the terms are not to be taken literally takes us back to difficulties like those in the doctrine of analogical predication I discussed in Chapter 14 of *God, Scepticism and Modernity.*) Again, the religious believer is in effect saying that a given reality has both property p and property not-p. Moreover, even if we can somehow make sense of "infinite person" or "infinite individual," we do not have any

22

understanding of what it would be like for something to be transcendent to the universe, the universe not being a name for a great big discrete thing but rather a label for all the distinct finite things and processes there are. But nothing could be transcendent to *all* the finite things and processes that there are, or at the very least we have no understanding of what this would be like. This becomes absurdly manifest when we come to see, as Axel Hägerström argued early in this century, that "finite thing" is a pleonasm.[7] We must, if we are struggling to see the world rightly in the teeth of centuries of religious talk, force ourselves to think literally.

If it is said, as no doubt it will be, that I am being too woodenly literal here, that I fail to see that these terms are being used in some metaphorical, symbolic or analogical way, it should be responded in turn that if this is so then we must still be able, at least in principle, to say in non-metaphorical, non-symbolic and non-analogical terms what they are metaphors of, symbols of and analogies to.[8] For these terms to function successfully in their non-literal ways, it must be at least in principle possible to do that. Non-literal meaning is parasitic on literal meaning. But then to be confident we have said anything coherent here, we must cash in the analogies, the symbolic expressions, and the metaphors, and state in literal terms what is being claimed without having reduced God-talk to: (a) something with an atheistic substance; or (b) to the sort of anthropomorphic talk where what is being claimed to be the case is not only plainly false, as in Zeus-talk, but is, as well, little more than a superstition; or (c) to using expressions in the reduction or the paraphrase which are either incoherent in ways similar to the ways exhibited above or are referring expressions where we have no way at all of knowing how either directly or indirectly to identify their referents. If the claim is to be able to identify a referent indirectly, then there can be, on pain of depriving "indirectly" of a non-vacuous contrast, be no *logical or conceptual* ban on being able to identify the referent directly as well. Yet "God" is not the sort of term, in its non-anthropomorphic employments, whose referent can even in principle be detected directly. Anything that could be seen or in any way directly observed or noted or encountered—and thus anything that could be directly experienced—would not be the God of what Judaism, Christianity and Islam have long ago become. A directly observable God is an idol. There can be no literal standing or being in the presence of God.

This is a short way with dissent, a way that might not unreasonably prompt the response that perhaps some theologian or philosopher of religion might be able to give a construal of these problematic conceptions which would reveal that after all they could sustain a reading that would exhibit their legitimacy. Moreover, it would be a construal that would not claim their legitimacy at the expense of either, on the one hand, reducing them to anthropomorphic concepts whose matching truth-claims would be intelligible enough but plainly false, as in claims about Zeus's goings on, or on the other, reducing them to such utterly secularized concepts (as in the work of Braithwaite, Hare, Dilman and Phillips) that they cannot succeed in being used to say anything that an atheist need deny. Indeed it would be dogmatic a priorism to deny that something like that may be possible.

What can be done is first to state what the problem is, as I have here. This comes to showing why God-talk is so problematic as to be at least arguably incoherent. That done, one should then proceed, as I have done in *God, Scepticism and Modernity,* and in a series of other books and articles as well, to consider *seriatim* the best attempts going to give a religiously appropriate and coherent reading to such notions.[9] If my arguments and arguments by others similarly motivated have been sound and the general challenge is sound, and if it can also be shown, as I and others have argued, that we do not need religious belief to make sense of our lives or to make sense of morality, then, if such arguments get repeated with similar results, it will become increasingly unlikely that the key concepts of Judaism, Christianity, and Islam are legitimate concepts capable of sustaining truth-claims. If something like that obtains, then the burden of proof clearly shifts to the believer to give us good reasons for believing that his very arcane and at least seemingly problematic claims make coherent sense.

The general situation vis-à-vis religion that I tried to portray is the following: now it is evident to at least most people who

24

carefully investigate these matters that no one has been able to give a sound ontological proof or disproof of the existence of God; no cosmological or design-type arguments have been shown to be sound and no other attempts to infer the existence of God from either evident or not-so-evident empirical facts have worked.[10] In addition, it has become fairly evident to most philosophically literate people that it very much looks like it is the case, to put the matter cautiously, that the very idea (where we are being literal) of seeing God or directly knowing or encountering God is incoherent. Moreover, even if we assume coherence here, there seems at least to be no reason to believe that anyone has actually seen, directly known—as in knowledge by *acquaintance*—or actually encountered God. Given all these things, the prospects for a renewal of natural theology are, to put it minimally, very bleak indeed.

If arguments such as mine about the incoherence of God-talk are sound, we, of course, have a good *explanation* of the breakdown of the various projects for constructing a natural theology. If these concepts are really incoherent, we could hardly have valid, let alone sound, arguments for the existence of God, for valid arguments require intelligible premises, and if God-talk is incoherent it can hardly provide us with intelligible premises. However, even if my arguments are unsound or at least inconclusive, and such talk, or at least some of it, is not incoherent, philosophers such as J.L. Mackie, principally in his masterful *The Miracle of Theism,* assuming, mistakenly I believe, the coherence of God-talk, reveal the inadequacy of the whole range of the best attempts, in one way or another, to establish the existence of God, or show that religious belief is a plausible option for a philosophically and scientifically educated person in the twentieth century.

This throws the believer back on the rather desperate expedients of various forms of fideism. However, it is a necessary condition for the viability of religious belief erected on such deeply skeptical foundations that it show either, on the one hand, that the moral life is undermined, or at least our moral expectations are deeply damaged, if we abandon religious belief or, on the other hand, that without religious commitments we cannot make sense of our lives, or at least that our lives without a belief in God will be impoverished. But nothing like this has been established and, as I argue in *Philosophy and Atheism* (Chapter 9), in *Ethics Without God,* and in *God and the Grounding of Morality,* such claims most certainly appear to be false. There can be plenty of intact purposes *in* life, including coherent gestalts of such purposes, even if there is no purpose *to* life. Treating people as ends, seeing ourselves as comrades in a common kingdom of ends, working to alleviate the awful burden of human suffering, and struggling for a more extensive and equitable satisfaction of human needs are ideals which remain intact whether or not there is or isn't a God or the hope of human immortality. Morality and a sense of ourselves as living meaningful lives need not totter if there is no God or no belief in God.

Hart's Criticims
I turn now to a detailed examination of some criticisms of my account.[11] Hendrik Hart, whose views I shall consider first, thinks that I take reason to be a kind of God and that my atheism is itself a religious affirmation. His discussion has the interesting strategy of trying to show that I have hoisted myself by my own petard, that the line of argument I take against belief in God can with perfect propriety be directed against what Hart takes to be my faith in reason. He does not seek to show that any of my specific arguments directed against the coherency, truth or the moral requiredness of religious belief are mistaken. Rather, he says that we all have our faiths, what in effect are our creedal systems, atheism as much as Judaism or Christianity. What we will regard as justified belief, or as what is morally required of us, or as what would constitute a meaningful life, is determined by what Hart regards as our distinctive creedal perspectives.[12] These creedal "perspectives" are different and not infrequently incommensurable; it is rationalistic idolatry to think that there is, or even could be, some Archimedean point in virtue of which we can assess these various perspectives and ascertain which, if any, is "the true perspective."

I am not, perhaps not totally surprisingly, convinced of the soundness of Hart's arguments or even that they have their target properly in focus, but before I turn to that I want first to observe that *if* Hart's criticisms of me are well taken, and if these criticisms rest on his general perspective in the way he thinks they do, this in turn would in effect provide a devastating critique of Christianity, Islam and Judaism and indeed of all the historical religious belief systems. These belief systems all make claims to having "the ultimate truth." Hinduism, at least theoretically, is more hospitable to other religions than is Christianity, but even Hinduism lays claim to Ultimate Truth and Christianity proudly proclaims that Christ is *the* Truth and *the* Way. There is no historicist relativism of perspectives in the view-points and self-images of the historic religions. If our situation were what Hart takes it to be (something, he believes, my rationalism blinds me from acknowledging) the very self-images of the historic religions would be undermined, and skepticism over religion, if not atheism, would be firmly triumphant. No person, if Hart is correct, if she understood what she was saying and could be non-self-deceptive and non-evasive, could make any affirmation of Ultimate Truth. Her severe historicist perspectivism would constitute an unsaying of what she is saying.

What is to be accepted, given Hart's way of viewing things, is entirely dependent on one's perspective and no one perspective with any objectivity (perhaps even with any coherency) can justifiably be said to be better than any other perspective.[13] Even assuming we can make sense of this, assuming self-referential paradoxes could be somehow overcome, and further assuming this historicist relativistic perspectivism could in some coherent sense be said to be true, this perspectivism would be the death knell of Judaism, Christianity and Islam, at least in anything like the forms we have come to know them. In fine, Hart's account has the key defects that I have sought in various places and in some detail, and I hope with a certain nuance, to pin on Wittgensteinian fideism.[14]

However, are Hart's criticisms sound? He takes me to be avowing and committing myself to what he calls a *rationalistic* atheism. And taking—he says—religion, any religion you like, to involve a belief in a transcendent spiritual being, I fail to see, suffering as I do from a kind of ethnocentrism about religion, my own commitment to reason or humanity to be itself religious and I do not recognize how I turn reason or humanity into divinities. This rationalistic atheism is for me, Hart claims, an ultimate position and as such, he claims, a religious position.

Since this is so, on *his* view of my view, Hart, as we have seen, claims that many of my objections to religion are also applicable to other ultimate positions including my own. In my very commitment to reason, I deceive myself into seeing my position as rational rather than creedal. My very rationalism excludes the very possibility of religious truth and it is a rationalism that I treat as being as unproblematic as a dogmatist such as Alvin Plantinga treats Christian belief to be.

Hart has not got my characterization of religion right. I make it clear in *Philosophy and Atheism* and elsewhere that a religion need not involve a belief in God, or several gods, or several spiritual beings. In *Philosophy and Atheism* I write: "We should beware of essentialist definitions of 'religion.' Theravada Buddhism, a religion of spiritual liberation, has no God or object of worship and devotion."[15] I go on to point out that while *nirvana* is a very different concept than God, it is like the concept of God in not being a naturalistic concept. But, notwithstanding that it does not refer to a transcendent spiritual being, Theravada Buddhism is just as much a religious belief system as Christianity. The above remarks were from the oldest essay in *Philosophy and Atheism* (1962) and this has been my account all along and it is not an account I have deviated from.

My commitment to reason, if it comes to that, does not, whatever else it may involve, involve any appeal to spiritual realities or to transcendental conceptions; it is thoroughly naturalistic, and thus, unlike the lesser vehicle, or so at least I would maintain, it is not a religious appeal. But this, admittedly, does not get to the heart of Hart's claim here about my rationalism, and presumably any rationalism, being implicitly religious. I shall return to this issue toward the end of my response to Hart.

I have never thought of myself as a rationalist or of my atheism as being rationalistic. Certainly I am not a rationalist in the sense in which Spinoza and Leibnitz are rationalists and Locke and Hume are not, or in the sense in which McTaggert and Blanshard are rationalists and Russell and Ayer are not or, in the domain of moral and social philosophy, in the sense in which Sidgwick and Gewirth are rationalists and Rawls and MacIntyre are not. I have never thought that there were any substantive self-evident propositions, clear to the light of reason, or that there were any synthetic a priori truths or that our belief systems, even when they were "true systems," even approximated a system of tightly knit internal relations. I am not wildly interested in ascribing -isms to myself, for they tend to be in one way or another misleading, but in the broad sense in which both Dewey and Quine are pragmatists I think of myself as a pragmatist and I think of that pragmatism in such a way that it involves the acceptance of (broadly conceived) both empiricism and realism. (Here again I think my views are like those of Dewey and Quine.) Beyond that, abandoning the attempt to articulate general philosophical frameworks for social theory, I have also come in recent years to think of myself as an analytical Marxian. I also, of course, take it that one can quite consistently be both an analyticial Marxian and a pragmatist. I doubt if there is anything interesting which counts as philosophical knowledge but I do think that we can, perhaps in a reasonably systematic way, gain an understanding of how society works and what our options are in the contemporary world. But, since my salad days, I have always rejected the doctrines characteristic of rationalism and there is, at least as far as I can see, nothing in my account of religion which commits me to such a doctrine.[16]

However, I think that Hart and I may be at cross purposes here. Hart uses "rationalism" in a very broad sense in which all the philosophers listed above, the empiricists as well as the rationalists, would be regarded as rationalists. For him the contrast between rationalists and nonrationalists would, I believe, be between Pascal, Hamann, Nietzsche, Kierkegaard, and Foucault on the nonrationalist side and Hume, Mill, Marx, Dewey, and Habermas on the rationalist side. Let me see if I can tease out what this broader sense of "rationalist" comes to and with that see whether, and if so in what sense, my atheism is rationalist and whether, and if so in what sense, I make a religion of reason.

29

How does Hart conceive of rationalism and of rationalist atheism? (Presumably because of Nietzsche, Foucault and perhaps Feuerbach, "rationalist atheism" is not pleonastic.) What, according to him, does my commitment to reason come to? Well, it comes to rejecting the supernatural and transcendent and accepting instead the authority of reason. But what is it to accept the authority of reason? Well, it comes to rejecting, as being incoherent or in some other ways illegitimate, any appeal to a "reality transcending what we empirically comprehend." It comes to (a) rejecting any claim to have access to a realm of truth or an order of facts which are even in principle empirically inaccessible and (b) to rejecting any claim to such a "non-empirical realm of fact" as being conceptually incoherent. There is and can be no gnostic knowledge. (It seems to me, by the way, that *in this sense* both Nietzsche and Foucault, and most certainly Feuerbach, are also rationalists.)

Hart adds other things to his characterization of what he takes to be my rationalism which I would dispute (particularly his strange talk about "self-grounding") but, if to accept the authority of reason is just to accept the above, I would happily plead guilty to accepting the authority of reason and thus *in that sense* to being a rationalist, *provided I am allowed to give a certain non-eccentric but still determinate reading to rejecting any apoeal to a reality transcending what we can empirically comprehend.*[17] I would want to construe this after the fashion of the logical empiricists as being constrained by what it is *logically* possible empirically to detect and comprehend and not just as to what in fact we can observe or otherwise empirically detect, or as to what it is technically possible to observe or otherwise detect.[18] Without such a construal, we would be taken to be rejecting the belief that there really are, or even can be, photons or neutrinos since they in fact cannot be observed, and such a denial of their reality I take, and have always taken, to be *a reductio.*[19] But I am not rejecting such de facto unobservables. What I am rejecting is any conception of there being any fact of the matter, any objects, relations or processes, that are not, even in principle, empirically accessible. I am rejecting any *logical* ban on their being observed. In that way for me, as for Axel Hägerström, all facts are empirical facts: "empirical facts" is pleonastic.[20]

Now, as not a few think, that may be too narrow a construal of "a fact of the matter" and of how we are to construe being able to determine what that is. Even if I am mistaken here, or if we cannot in any even reasonably decisive way determine whether or not I am mistaken, this doesn't turn such a belief on my part into a dogma or anything even remotely like a creedal statement. Whether it does or not depends entirely on how I hold it. If I hold it, as I in fact do, fallibilistically ready to abandon it in the face of rational considerations directed against it, then it cannot be a dogma with me. It may be a mistaken belief but it is not a dogma.

In speaking of "rational considerations directed against it" I have in mind such things as (1) claims that there are too many things we all, even on reflection, take to be facts which cannot be accommodated by that conception of the facts; and (2) various arguments against my conception, including alternative proposals about how to characterize the situation. If, after careful consideration, the alternatives are seen to have greater probity, I would, of course, then abandon my conception. I may very well not be able ahead of time to say what I would have to come to be convinced of to abandon the belief. After all it is a rather fundamental belief for me. But if I am open to discussion, argument and further inquiry concerning it and related beliefs, and if, in a fallibilistic spirit, I am prepared, depending on the force of the better argument in extended discourses about the matter, to abandon the belief on the basis of that further inquiry, argument, evidence and the like, then, given that is the way I hold the belief, it cannot be a dogma or a creedal matter for me.[21] But that is exactly how I hold the belief, and there is nothing in my *Philosophy and Atheism* or in *God, Scepticism and Modernity* that gives to understand the contrary.

In so proceeding, I am presumably still appealing to the authority of reason. But there seems to me nothing wrong with that and nothing in the slightest religious about it. That is just how reasonable people, rationalists or nonrationalists, religious believers or nonreligious believers, should hold their beliefs. So there is nothing in the very idea of accepting the authority of reason which requires that there can be no appeal to facts which are not empirical facts. In that way there is nothing a prioristic about my approach. It is all a matter of what, *appealing in this way* to the authority of reason and carefully reasoning and investigating, we discover or conclude. And this means that I am indeed committed to sticking with what ultimately has the force of the more adequate deliberation when we human beings dispassionately and honestly deliberate together under conditions of openness and non-domination. If to be so committed is to be a rationalist then I gladly confess to being a rationalist, but that is a low-redefinition of a "rationalist." Instead, it just partially specifies what it is like to be a reasonable person who is not affected with hubris and is open to the voices and the views of others.

Hart might respond that right here in the spirit of modernity I have at a very deep level begged the question with the knight of faith. In fixing belief, I have, in the sense gestured at above, used the authority of reason. By contrast, in the domain of faith and morals at least, the knight of faith will use instead, in fixing belief, Divine Revelation. I cannot, relevantly and without begging the question, use reason to judge Divine Revelation and we cannot, relevantly and without begging the question, use Divine Revelation to judge reason. He has his perspective and I have mine. There is the perspective of rationalism and the perspective of faith, and there is no neutral or mutually acceptable perspective or method that can be appealed to decide which has primacy when they conflict or at least appear to conflict. In this way my appeal to the authority of reason is like the appeal to a dogma and, given the determination and passion with which I appeal to it, it is, the claim goes, like a religious appeal.

I do not agree that we are caught in such irreconcilable conflicts such that we just have to leap as knights of faith. We are not caught in such incommensurables.[22] If there really were such a thing as Divine Revelation then we, of course, could use it to judge reason.[23] Knowing what human beings are and what God is, who are we to set our judgments against God's? That would be the height of irrationality and senseless rebellion. If reason seems to require *p* but Revelation—a *genuine* revelation and not merely a *putative* revelation—requires *not-p*, then it cannot be the case that reason really requires *p*. Rather, we

32

must have somewhere made a mistake in our reasoning in concluding that reason requires *p*. If there is Divine Revelation it surely can rule reason.

However, I said "*If* there is Divine Revelation." Whether we are persons of faith or what Hart calls rationalists, the facts are just there that, whether we like them or not, we can hardly miss if we know anything at all and do not avert our gaze. What I am principally referring to is the fact that anthropologically speaking and considering all the religions there are, there are simply thousands of *putative* Divine Revelations. Some may, in effect, say the same thing but most do not and not a few say what appear at least to be radically conflicting things. Where they say different things, as they at least frequently and indeed perhaps always do, at most one could be true, i.e., be more than a *putative* Divine Revelation, be instead a *genuine* Divine Revelation. Faced with that plethora of *putative* Divine Revelations often requiring radically different things, we cannot, barring a fideistic turn I will consider in a moment, reasonably (sensibly), just arbitrarily, accept one of these putative revelations. In the Middle Ages we perhaps could have just plunked for one, for the range of choice was linked to a lesser awareness of what, given all humanity, the range of choice actually is, but by now we have lost our innocence: we just know too much to be able, without being irrational, to so plunk, *if*, Barth-like, all we are relying on is some putative Divine Revelation.

Hart has structured things in such a way that between his rationalist and his person of faith the choices are stark. But this is unrealistic and unjustified. I can show this best if I proceed indirectly. If the person uses the resources of the philosophy of religion, of natural theology, of an appeal to religious experience or an appeal to morality either to justify his choice of one putative revelation rather than another or as devices for limiting the range of his choice, then he would in effect be appealing to the authority of reason and siding with what Hart called the rationalist. He must, to avoid "rationalism," take his putative revelation neat without any elaboration or defense beyond an explication of what revelation is and what that revelation is in particular. He cannot, without going beyond an appeal to revelation, say why his appeal is to a genuine revelation and the others are only appeals to putative revelations. But standing where we are now, knowing what we know, he cannot sensibly or reasonably just so take his putative revelation neat. There are just too many candidate revelations around to make such an appeal at all reasonable for anyone who is the least bit informed. Social anthropology has firmly blocked that revelationist route.

Hart might come back by remarking that by invoking concepts of reasonability and sensibility here, I have again rationalistically begged the question. But I think not. In speaking of what is reasonable and sensible I have not invoked any special conception of rationality from a rationalist or any other philosophical or scientific theory of rationality (assuming there is such an animal). I am appealing here, quite unexceptionably, to our ordinary and, if you will, somewhat loose use of "reasonable" and "sensible," captured in part in our dictionaries and employed, by believers and nonbelievers alike, in our stream of life.[24] The sense of "reasonable" and "sensible" is as much a property of the believer as the skeptic, including the atheist. I am inviting the person of faith to consider whether or not it would be reasonable for us moderns—after all the contemporary, educated religious believer is also a modern—to appeal in such a single-minded way to what he takes to be Divine Revelation, given that our actual circumstances include most crucially the fact that there are multitudes of often conflicting candidate revelations. This, in effect, by a kind of method of challenge, is an invitation to believers, here particularly fideistic believers, to deliberate with secularists in a dispassionate manner about whether that is so.

A believer might think such an appeal to his putative divine revelation to be perfectly reasonable even in the circumstances I described. If so then we, using what certainly at least appears to be our common concept of reasonability, can in turn deliberate about that. Sometimes in certain practical and particularly pressing and unnerving contexts we run out of time or patience and we then must just act one way or another, sticking, so to speak, to our guns. But theoretically speaking there is no point where we just run out of anything that can possibly be said and we must just say: my spade is turned; or, here stand I, I can

34

do no other.[25] We can in theory at least always step back and bracket for a time what we are at cross purposes about and search for a common ground from which we can deliberate and continue the dispute in a way such that, we at least can *hope*, will eventually break the deadlock. There is no a priori reason to believe we will invariably find such a common ground but there is plenty of empirical justification for thinking we will, if we are resolute enough in searching, particularly in a common culture, for shared beliefs from which we can deliberate. Wittgenstein was profoundly misleading when he said that justification must come to an end or it wouldn't be justification.[26] In a way that is so, but in the way at which I have just gestured it is not. Proof, of course, requires premises, but we can, using other premises, always challenge the premises used in the proof and, even if we get back to the rules of formation and transformation (if indeed there is anything like that in natural languages) we can always, in theory at least, challenge those rules and forge new rules and the like. This can, if there is any need for it, go on indefinitely, though, for those obsessed with Cartesian doubt, it can, as Peirce pressed home, also go on idly and pointlessly. (Philosophers have a real penchant for going on pointlessly.)[27] There is, however, no set place where we just must face each other with irreconcilable perspectives, like alternative geometries, where there is nothing more we can possibly say. This foundationalist picture is profoundly mistaken. The probing anti-foundationalist arguments of Dewey, Quine, Rorty and Davidson should have enabled us to set that old philosophical picture aside.

I mentioned a moment ago a turn the fideist could reasonably take to avoid this conclusion. It is a turn in effect powerfully taken in the past by Pascal, Hamann, Kierkegaard, and Dostoevsky (at least through some of his characters). Put without their powerful elaborations, the argument in kernel form comes to this: faced, without a belief in God, with the bleakness of life, the pressure of a Godless nihilism, the senselessness of life and the undermining of any kind of tolerable moral life, it is better to opt, however arbitrarily, however absurdly, for the claims of the putative revelation of Christianity than to live with such a black hole, to live in such a condition of utter hopelessness. With Christianity, or at least a belief in God, there is hope; with a purely secular view of the world there is none. So the reasonable person who cares about her life and the lives of others will opt for Christianity or some such religion even though she knows there is no rational warrant at all for accepting that belief system. She requires it to make sense of life—so life will not be just one damn thing after another until we die and rot—even though the leap of faith is cognitively speaking utterly arbitrary. For a caring person being reasonable requires such arbitrariness.

Leaving aside the very real question of why Christianity rather than one of the other historic faiths, it seems to me that this fideistic turn would have a very considerable force indeed if we really needed a belief in God to make sense of our lives or to justify the claims of morality. But it just is not the case that we have that need for belief in God, or so at least I have extensively argued.[28] Perhaps these arguments are defective and, beyond that not terribly surprising possibility, perhaps it is even true that such a secular humanist case, better put, cannot be sustained. But Hart, at least, does nothing to counter these arguments or to show that they rest on rationalistic excesses or unjustified assumptions. These arguments challenge the uncritical fideist assumption that we cannot have morality or an adequate sense of self without belief in God. Indeed that fideist assumption is not only challenged; it is also argued in some detail that key fideist beliefs deployed in support of that assumption are false. My argument here has not been countered and, unless and until it is, that fideistic turn will not have exposed an irrational or even an arbitrary or creedal core in what Hart takes to be my rationalism.

Hart says things about what he takes to be my view or theory of rationality which I find very puzzling. Indeed I hardly recognize them as my views and I fear that there we are so speaking past each other that I hardly know where to start. (That does not mean that there is no place to start, it just means that it is hard to find a common ground on which to begin the discussion.)

I recognize, and indeed stress, that rationality is a very complicated concept subject to persuasive definition and ideological deformation. It is perhaps what has been called an essentially contested concept.[29] I do not try to develop a ramified theory of rationality but try to stay as close to common sense as I can, and I remain resolutely eclectic between instrumental and non-instrumental conceptions of rationality. (I do not make the rather typical analytical assumption that instrumental rationality is the only rationality there is.)[30] Hart thinks I make a god of reason and then treat reason wantonly, using it so broadly that it becomes simply a term of approval for anything I take to be good. Indeed he believes I use "rational" like many others use "good." "Reason, reasonable, and rational," he tells us, seem, on my usage, "to acquire the meaning of terms of approval for whatever is dear to Western people."[31] Like a good rationalist, I identify rationality, Hart would have it, with whatever I take to be deeply desirable and I "acknowledge the deepest meaning of all meaning to be rational meaning."[32]

I do nothing of the kind. (Or could it be that in some way I do not see the mote in my own eye?) For starters, I do not even understand what "rational meaning" means. Is it supposed to be contrasted with "irrational meaning?" But what is that? Words have meaning—that is, they have a use in a language—and this use, per se, is neither rational nor irrational. What I do, building on our public use of the terms, is try to say what rational beliefs are, what rational principles are, and what it would be like to be a fully rational person, stressing that this latter conception is a heuristic ideal and that this characterization of rationality, as indeed any good characterization, has a certain indeterminacy but certainly not such an indeterminacy that the term "rational" simply becomes a general term of approbation. Rational beliefs, I say unexceptionably, perhaps even platitudinously, "are typically beliefs that can withstand the scrutiny of people who are critical of their beliefs: that is to say, they are beliefs typically held open to refutation or modification by experience and/or by reflective examination."[33] They are beliefs which those holding them will hold in such a way that they will not brush aside an examination of their assumptions, implications and relations to other beliefs. Moreover, they are beliefs which their holders, knowing what, under

37

the social circumstances they can be expected to know, will, relative to that knowledge, have good grounds for believing are free of inconsistencies, contradictions, or incoherences.[34] I also specify a number of rational principles of action, only some of which I will advert to here.[35]

To act rationally is, *ceteris paribus*, to take the most efficient and effective means to achieve one's ends. Moreover, the ends which help form or are at least in accordance with a dispassionate and informed point of view, and which a person values higher than her other ends, are the ends to which, *ceteris paribus*, she should give priority. The *ceteris paribus* clauses are not just decorative here, for life is sufficiently complex that exceptional circumstances will sometimes arise when a rational belief will not have those features, or when acting rationally will not come to acting in accordance with those rational principles of action. At what point this occurs will inescapably be a matter of reflective judgment.[36] There is no Benthamite or other formula which will relieve us from the making of those judgments. If we reflect carefully on this and if we are reasonably rational we will recognize that such indeterminacy is in fact not to be lamented. The principles mentioned above are a good subset of the principles of rationality and, like prima facie duties, they *always usually* hold. It is, that is, always the case that these principles, where applicable, usually hold in a way fully analogous to the way that for everyone all of the time it is the case that promises, *generally* speaking, are to be kept.

Fully rational people will, keeping firmly in mind the *ceteris paribus* clauses, have, under the above description, rational beliefs and rational principles of action. In addition, fully rational people will be enlightened and emancipated human beings. They will have achieved a firm sense of self-identity and adult autonomy (an autonomy which is compatible with a firm appreciation of human interdependence), will have a good understanding of human needs and will be liberated from the various illusions that fetter humankind.[37] No one is, of course, a fully rational human being. It is plainly a heuristic ideal, and rationality does, equally plainly, admit of degrees. But it is an ideal that can be approximated and it is plainly a desirable thing that it be so approximated.

The various criteria for rational belief, rational principles of action and for being a fully rational person are in various ways indeterminate and context- dependent. However, it does not follow from this that they are vague or opaque, or just ideological slogans. Even "enlightenment" and "emancipation" cannot mean just anything. They are not mere hurrah words. Moreover, *pace* Hart, my usage of "rationality" is not a usage such that I can just use it as a general term of approbation or so that it becomes equivalent to whatever I would refer to as being good. Furthermore, again *pace* Hart, it is not something scientistic applying only to scientists and philosophers and not to poets or theologians or—perish the thought—to plain folks who are none of these things. Rational beliefs and rational principles of action are things that anyone can have. Whether we have them or not depends on how we behave. Being fully rational is, of course, very demanding indeed and, at least as things stand, few will even approximate it. But it is not a scientistic conception which can be approximated only by scientists and analytical philosophers. It is also not something which, Hart to the contrary notwithstanding, is self-grounding. Indeed I am not even sure that I know what that means but, to the extent that I have some inkling, there is nothing "self-grounded" about my conception of rationality or my alleged rationalism.[38]

I have given a conceptualization of rationality that I hope, while being in accordance with our common concept of rationality, extends it in certain ways and makes it more determinate. To have a concept of rationality, or of anything else, it is necessary for there to be a term with a determinate use in a language (e.g., Dutch, French, English, German, Swahili). "Rationality" has a use in English. Building on that use, I tried to go some way in articulating what *we* take that rationality to be. Whether I have succeeded or not depends on whether my account squares with our public use of "rationality" and whether people on reflection will conclude that the extensions I have made help capture our sense—our public sense—of what rationality and reasonableness should come to. We want to know whether it matches people's considered judgments in wide reflective equilibrium about what rationality and reasonableness come to.

Have I, in effect, made reason into a kind of Divinity? I have treated being fully rational as a very desirable thing indeed, but I have plainly not made reason the sole good thing or the "ultimately good thing" and, indeed, to do so would surely be absurd. I think having a good time, experiencing love, being a caring considerate person, having something one very much wants to accomplish and sticking with the struggle to accomplish it and (among other things) committing oneself to the moral point of view are all good things. But while I think reason *permits* these things I do not claim reason *requires* them. I have argued long and strenuously against moralists such as Kurt Baier, Alan Gewirth and David Gauthier, that rationality does not require morality, that in certain circumstances it is quite possible that a rational person could be a man of good morals without being a morally good man, i.e., a person could be rational, perhaps even through-and-through rational, without being a person of principle.[39] I have argued that if we are not caring persons we are going to fail as persons in very significant ways though that failure need not be a failure in rationality. (Person, as Rawls argues, is a moral category.)[40] I have even acknowledged, in discussing Pascal and Kierkegaard, that if it were the case that life would be meaningless without belief in God this would constitute a good reason for believing in God.[41] This is hardly the view of someone who thinks reason is the sole good, the sole intrinsic good, the ultimate good, or who treats reason as a god.

Hart believes that because I take rationality to be ultimate it must be for me a divinity. Moreover, he goes on to argue that "it is questionable whether an ultimately rational point of view can be rationally grounded without begging the question of its own grounding."[42] Because of these things, it is possible, he believes, to see my position as a religious position because "what makes a position religious is that it *ultimately* judges everything from that position, while never questioning that position without begging the question."[43]

There are, I believe, both multiple confusions here and unwitting misrepresentations only some of which I will canvas. Why call a position religious simply because it ultimately judges everything from that position while never questioning that position without begging the question? Would it not be more appropriate to call such a position ideological or, alternatively, metaphysical or just more descriptively a comprehensively question-begging position? Perhaps all religions have that characteristic, but that fact, if it is a fact, does not justify the claim that what is perhaps a necessary condition is also sufficient condition for something being a religion or even being religious. A materialist metaphysic or Freudian psychology may have that feature as well but it would be, to put it mildly, misleading to regard these holistic theories as religions or as being religious. Hobbes and Freud are not charismatic creators of new religions. The most that could justifiably be maintained is that such holistic theories have one of the features characteristic of a religion.

Failing to consider the criticism I made of Paul Tillich for taking what *might* be another necessary condition—being ultimately concerned or being ultimate—to be a sufficient condition for a view's being a religious view, Hart himself makes a very similar mistake to that of Tillich.[44] Consider the matter this way. I am not sure that I know what it means to take rationality as ultimate, but, even assuming that a plausible reading can be given to that and even if I do somehow unwittingly take rationality to be ultimate, that in itself does not at all make a commitment to rationality a religious commitment or make reason a god. I do not believe that I do take rationality to be ultimate but even if I did there would not be such a linkage as Hart alleges with being religious. To maintain that if you take something to be ultimate you must believe in God is a form of attempted conversion by stipulative redefinition.

There are a number of belief systems that, prior to any attempt at a definition, we antecedently clearly recognize to be religious, namely the historic religions, East and West, and cosmological belief systems like those of the Dinka or the Neur. *Sometimes* with primitive societies, though not with the Dinka or Neur, we are going to be unsure whether what we have is simply a set of magical practices or whether it is as well a religion. In defining "religion" we want to see if we can catch features which are common to and distinctive of those practices and belief systems paradigmatically and commonly regarded as religions.

41

This may not be easy to do. For a Westerner, for example, believing in God, or the gods, or in spiritual beings, is as natural a thing to fasten on as capturing what it is for a belief system to be religious, but it will not quite do as a characterization of religion for, as I mentioned earlier, it rules out—and this is a *reductio*—Theravada Buddhism as a religion since Theravada Buddhism does not commit its adherents to any belief in God at all but instead to a social structure sustaining practices aimed at spiritual liberation.[45] Theravada Buddhism has no concept of God or of worship, but it does have another non-naturalistic transcendental concept, namely *nirvana*. It is an alleged spiritual state in which those who are enlightened in a certain way achieve liberation from the endless series of rebirths of a life that is full of suffering. The goal of Buddhism, as much as that of Islam, is a spiritual one, namely, in Buddhism's case, to attain nirvana, a spiritual liberation.

In this way, all religions, besides committing their faithful to some form of ultimate concern or to some form of ultimacy, also have some concept of the sacred or some concept of spiritual reality. These last two features are features which atheism, rationalistic or otherwise, does not have. Only by playing with words, by giving "low-redefinitions" of terms like "sacred" or "spiritual reality," can it be made even to seem otherwise.[46] It is like, in trying to define an MD, calling anyone who can perform first aid a doctor. Ultimate views may or may not be religious. Ultimacy may be a necessary condition for being religious but it is surely not a sufficient condition. However, that the belief system have a belief in spiritual realities or the sacred is clearly a less problematic candidate for a necessary condition for being religious or being a religion. Metaphysical views and perhaps other worldviews are indeed good candidates for ultimate views. But not all of them involve a belief in spiritual realities or the sacred. Moreover, "a religious world-view" is not a redundancy and a "nonreligious worldview" is not, as we use language, a contradiction. The same thing can be said for a metaphysical view. Plainly there are worldviews and mytaphysical systems that do not involve any belief in God or the gods or engage in any positing of spiritual realities or sacred realities.

42

Hart, in order to characterize my views as religious, departs radically from how we speak and think in characterizing what makes something a religion, but he has given us no good reason at all for following him in his stipulative departure. And while, in what he thinks is a too intellectualistic way, I do stress that religions are belief systems, I do not say or give to understand that they are *only* belief systems. Religion has very much to do with the *attitude* we take to life and with how we live or at least try to live. But I do not deny that or even underplay it. I am only concerned to assert in this context, what is obvious anyway, namely that religions are necessarily also belief systems. Hart ignores this side of things. To be justified in calling my atheism a religious view, he has to give us a justification for such a radical departure from how we think and speak. And that, to repeat, he has not done.

Szabados's Criticisms

I turn now to Professor Béla Szabados's criticisms.[47] Strong, tendentious philosophical claims require, to have any reasonable force, strong arguments. My claim that belief in God is in our time irrational for a scientifically and philosophically sophisticated person is just such a strong and, to put it minimally, contentious claim. Indeed it is a claim to which not a few would take exception and some, no doubt, will find it offensive. Szabados does well to focus critical attention on that claim, for, if it is to be persuasive, it must be very well supported indeed. I do not know whether I have done anything more than make a start at providing that support, if such support can in fact be sustained. It surely would, to understate it, not be unreasonable to be wary of that claim. But, that to the contrary notwithstanding, it does seem to me, everything considered, the correct claim to make, so I will stick by my guns and, facing Szabados's objections, continue to argue, though with a full sense of my fallibility here, that such belief is irrational.

However, I should here first make a disclaimer, for if my views here are misunderstood, as they might be by a careless reader or, more easily and more understandably, by someone who simply hears them, they could rightly be dismissed with contempt. I am not claiming that all or even most Jews, Christians or Moslems are irrational. That is just too grossly *parti pris* and too absurd to even be worth considering. Indeed, it would be a silly form of hubris as if I were claiming I am more rational than Professor Hart or claiming that such paradigm Christian philosophers as John Hick, William Alston, Terence Penelhum or Hugo Meynell are irrational or less rational than I am. Anyone who knows them—and they are tokens of a familiar type—knows that such a claim is absurd. Béla Szabados does not, of course, think for a moment that I believe anything like that, but my plainly contentious claim might be confused with that absurd claim. So I make the disclaimer and append an explanation.

What I am claiming instead is that, if my analysis of the concept of God is on the whole well-taken and non-arcane, belief in God is irrational for a philosophically sophisticated and scientifically knowledgeable person in our cultural space, standing were we stand now in the Twentieth Century. I am *not* saying the religious believer is irrational—he may or may not be, just as the atheist may or may not be irrational; what I am saying is that, if the believer is a Twentieth Century person, with a good scientific and philosophical education, his or her belief in God is irrational if what I say about God is so. It is the *belief* for such a person and not the *person* himself that I am claiming is irrational. And there is no hubris or exaggeration in that claim, though the claim may well be false or unproven (as Szabados believes) or perhaps even incoherent.

To claim that reasonable people can have some irrational beliefs should be little more than a common place. Indeed, if our criteria for a reasonable person are so strong that, if a person is properly said to be rational it could not be the case that he had any irrational beliefs, then the class of rational people would most probably be empty. Freud gives a partial explanation why, but, Freud or no Freud, it is as evident as can be that manifestly reasonable people not infrequently have a few irrational beliefs. My suit is not to convict the Christian of irrationality but to show that a key frame-work belief of his is an irrational belief for him to hold if my analysis of the concept of God is non-arcane and near to the mark, and if he lives now in a society such as ours and has been educated in the way I have

44

specified.

I will concede to Szabados, and acknowledge the importance in the context of my argument of making this very point,
that the believer need not hold his belief in an irrational
manner. What I will stand pat on is the claim that, if my
arguments about the incoherence of non-anthropomorphic
God-talk are sound and non-arcane then for a believer who
could reasonably be expected to understand them, it would be
irrational for her to believe in God. The crucial thing is not the
propriety of my charge about irrationality but the soundness of
my arguments about the incoherence of the concept of God.
Moreover, I am not absurdly maintaining that believers' rationality or lack thereof in so believing depends on their having
studied my views. Views bearing a family resemblance to mine
are firmly fixed in the social space of our intellectual culture
and are, as I see it, but a consistent drawing out of the implications of a current of thought which has been growing and
developing from its inception in Enlightenment thought, including its response to the Counter-Enlightenment. Even
Richard Rorty, a philosopher deeply influenced by the Counter-
Enlightenment and by historicist modes of thought and fundamentally opposed to empiricist programmes like those of
Hume, Hägerström, Russell or Ayer, states unequivocally in his
Philosophy and the Mirror of Nature that "the preservation of the
values of the Enlightenment is our best hope," and that "the
positivists were absolutely right in thinking it imperative to
extirpate metaphysics when 'metaphysics' means the attempt
to give knowledge of what science cannot know."[48]

Szabados, like Hart, is perplexed and deeply skeptical
about my account of rationality and its use in assessing religions
as forms of life. He thinks, as does Hart, that I have not come
within a country mile of showing that belief in God is irrational
for critically educated people situated as we are now. Why and
how does Szabados think I fail here? Unlike Hart he finds my
account of rationality attractive, but he finds the application to
which I put it in criticizing religion problematic, and he
maintains that I do not recognize how problematic the concept
of rationality is. Still, it is not that but my alleged failure
properly to apply my own criteria of rationality to religion on

45

which he fastens.

The principles of rational belief and rational action I adumbrate are, on my conception of things, universal and "we can use them to appraise institutions, practices and forms of life...."[49] Judaism, Christianity and Islam are such forms of life and they are so appraised by me. My argument has been that when we appraise them in such terms they have little rational warrant.

I agree with Szabados, or rather he agrees with me, for I stressed just that point in *Philosophy and Atheism,* that the notions of rationality and irrationality are not pellucid or unproblematic and, given that, we should not throw caution to the winds in making sweeping claims about the irrationality of religious belief.[50] But, as he, in effect, also acknowledges with his remarks about my responses to anticipated objections, qualifications and the like, I am not so incautious. What he needs to do, to show that the problematicity of our concept of rationality is damaging to my case, is to show: (a) that my account of rationality is seriously defective or (what itself is a distinctive way of being defective) that it is ethnocentric in being (as Hart believes) just our modernizing Western account of rationality: and (b) that because of these inadequacies what I say about the irrationality of religious belief is skewed.[51] (It could be the case that (a) is true without it being the case that (b) is true.) But he claims none of these things and in fact makes no specific criticisms of my account of rationality.

What he actually does is something else and that something else, *if well taken,* would be a legitimate criticism of my account. He seeks to show that at least some religious believers and some religious beliefs can satisfy my various criteria of rationality, and that belief in God is among those beliefs. That is to say, given my own criteria of rationality, there is nothing irrational about the believers and the beliefs in the way I contend. And that claim, I admit, if true, would without doubt be damaging, indeed devastating, to my case. Given, Szabados argues, what I take rationality to be, there is no good reason for believing a reflective, religiously interested, scientifically aware and philosophically astute believer must be behaving irrationally in believing in God, or that this belief of his must be

46

irrational.

The religious person's belief need not be internally inconsistent and he may be sensitive to relevant evidence, attend to it, recognize where it points and face its implications. Szabados believes that I, in effect, deny this, for in making my claims about the irrationality of religious belief, I just assume, Szabados further believes, that religious language is incoherent and that a rational believer must acknowledge this if he is philosophically sophisticated and attends to the argument. I do indeed largely assume that such religious beliefs are incoherent in the two essays in my *Philosophy and Atheism* Szabados discusses, which are, it is important to note in this context, the last two essays in that book, but in earlier essays in that volume, namely "Does God Exist?", "Reason and Commitment" and, most centrally, "In Defense of Atheism," as well as in *Contemporary Critiques of Religion, An Introduction to the Philosophy of Religion* and in *Skepticism,* I do not assume but argue in some detail that central strands of the religious discourse of the developed religions of the West are incoherent. And in the essays reprinted in *God, Scepticism and Modernity,* I return repeatedly to that issue from a number of quite different angles. Perhaps my arguments are unsound or in some way question-begging or even themselves incoherent, but I do not just *assume* that religious talk and belief (including belief in God) are incoherent. Indeed, I stress, like Szabados, that religious discourse does *seem* to make sense, that religious people do not typically go around making *plainly* contradictory remarks, and that we do in a way understand some plain God-talk whatever may be the case for some kinds of theological talk (e.g., some of the talk of Tillich or Bultmann). But, to repeat, I argue in detail that central stands of God-talk—God-talk that claims, as Ninian Smart puts it, "the transcendent reference point"—make cosmological claims which, when we inspect them carefully, turn out *not* to make sense in the very specific sense in which they *purport* to make sense, for they actually fail to make anything that we on inspection would recognize to be a truth-claim while still purporting to make grand cosmological claims and while being taken by their adherents to be somehow making such claims.[52]

Some of my central arguments for this do indeed depend on a demarcated and very moderate and nuanced verificationism, but others do not, and the ones that do not are very prominent in a, perhaps *the*, central essay in *Philosophy and Atheism,* "In Defense of Atheism," in my book *Skepticism,* and in the first chapter of *God, Scepticism and Modernity.* Szabados does not even advert to these arguments, let alone refute them or even deflect them. Moreover, *pace* Szabados, not all forms of incoherence are contradictions or inconsistencies. "Procrastination drinks melancholy," "Alienation eludes being," "Being unfolds itself into utter transcendency" or "Being itself is the ground of being and meaning" do not say anything sufficiently clear to clearly count as being either contradictory or non-contradictory, yet they are surely good candidates for incoherences. I maintain that central strands of plain God-talk in our religious discourses are, though in a less evident way, similarly incoherent. I try, particularly in the first chapter of *God, Scepticism and Modernity* and again in *Philosophy and Atheism* and elsewhere, to exhibit specific ways in which certain very determinate strands of God-talk are incoherent, or at least have all the appearances of incoherence. Szabados no more than Hart has shown that appearances are deceiving here.

Some religious-talk may encourage paradox, and *perhaps* in some contexts rightly so, but sensible religious people, as Szabados well says, do not "revel in or encourage contradictions as such."[53] But, *pace* Szabados, I never argued or even suggested that they do. I argued instead that, in spite of what often is a firm determination on the part of their users to make sense, close inspection of central strands of, say, Christian religious discourse reveal incoherences that appear at least to be inescapable, to be part, as they used to say, of the very logic of religious discourse. Again, neither Szabados nor Hart does anything to show that I am mistaken here.

Szabados, like Hart, would in turn obliquely respond by saying that he does not see how it is possible, without begging the question, impartially to resolve issues concerning whether non-anthropomorphic God-talk is coherent, or whether it is irrational to believe in God. There is, he claims, no impartial non-question-begging stance available to us here. I agree that burden of proof arguments are difficult to establish and that in fundamental philosophical disputes, if they are really pushed hard, it is difficult to avoid begging questions or assuming, often unwittingly, a problematic stance about the burden of proof. (I said it was difficult but I did not say it was impossible.)

With this in mind, let us try to see if I have begged the question with religious believers or at least whether Szabados has given us good reason for believing I have. In attempting to show how I have begged the question Szabados seeks to show how a thoughtful philosophically and scientifically educated believer might continue to believe in God without lapsing into irrational belief. Such believers, he argues, might acknowledge that attempts to prove or establish the existence of God have all failed. In doing so they have on my own conception of rationality taken a rational stance; they, as Szabados puts it, "have not ignored criticisms or objections but took them to heart."[54] Moreover, the unbeliever, as I stressed, cannot give an a priori proof that no proof of God's existence is possible. Of course, if the very concept of God is incoherent, then no proof of God's existence is possible but Szabados could perfectly rightly respond that arguments for incoherence also require premises and these premises could always be challenged—they are not all necessary truths—just as the premises used in that challenge could always in turn be challenged themselves and so on and on we can go without there being any a priori terminating point.

Because of these considerations and because of similar remarks about my rational principles of action, Szabados claims that fundamental arguments used in disputes between people like myself and reflective believers are question-begging. But if this is our criterion for stances being question-begging then all or at least almost all arguments are, and unavoidably so, question-begging, for, as I have just remarked, arguments require premises and premises can always be challenged. Even alleged claims to self-evidence and certainty, assuming (which is indeed to assume a lot) they are substantive enough to support anything, can be challenged, and even if we get back to the rules of formation and transformation they in turn can always be challenged. There is no safe Cartesian harbour here.

In *that strong sense*, as Gilbert Ryle argued, there can be no proofs in philosophy or indeed anywhere else.[55] And it should be noted in this context, and with respect to the above, that there is nothing unusual in that respect about the dispute I have set up between the kind of atheist I am and the reflective believer. *In the sense Szabados gestures at,* the arguments made in the attempted resolution of any dispute, or at least almost any dispute, will be question-begging, indeed they *can* hardly be anything else, and if that is so, then that is a *reductio* of Szabados's argument in effect depriving "question-begging argument" of a non-vacuous (significant) contrast and thus rendering it a claim without any force. One tell-tale evidence for that is that, on such a way of contending that arguments are question-begging there is no need at all to examine the specific argument to maintain it is question-begging. The tides of metaphysical illusion are running high here.

Szabados rightly sees that for me the heart of the matter, in the dispute between belief and unbelief, is over belief in God. After all, if I thought it made sense to say that God exists, that God has a certain nature and that, in addition, it is reasonable to believe that He really does exist, I would not think that there was any moral alternative to obeying his will. (That does not entail that anyone should accept a morality of Divine Commands.) But, since I reject those fundamental framework-beliefs, these other issues do not even come up for me.

Szabados, however, has not got my picture of what faith is right. Since I believe that belief in God is in most circumstances irrational for us (where "us" ranges over contemporary intellectuals in Western countries), I also believe that faith is in most circumstances irrational for us.[56] Szabados is right about that. But he is thoroughly off the mark about why I think faith is irrational and about what I think the knight of faith is like. The person who has faith in a Zeus-like God may be as Szabados characterizes the person of faith, and some of the more Neanderthal Christians may be such believers. But the reflective knight of faith—and certainly there are many such people—of developed forms of Christianity (mainstream Catholicism or Protestantism) is not someone who obstinately insists on believing something for which we do not now have adequate evidence or grounds, pig headedly being certain of something

50

that is really at best uncertain. (Recall here Kierkegaard's ironical parodies of Hegelianism. And do not confuse Pascal with Plantinga.) But that is not my picture of faith at all, though I agree that there is a kind of idolatrous belief that does have that kind of faith, treating God, as Kierkegaard quipped, as if he were some kind of great green bird. But this is an uninteresting, religiously insignificant religiosity which is little better than mere superstition. My picture of the knight of faith, and thus of faith, is that of a person with a full sense of the objective uncertainty of the object of worship, committing himself to what he acknowledges to be an incomprehensible ultimate mystery who in some sense is said to be, and thought by him to be, a person who is also an utterly spiritual being, who is as well an omnipotent, perfectly good, infinite individual who transcends the world, is beyond the bounds of space and time, and who still is encountered in a caring, saving relationship by the believer who, seeking salvation, will turn to him with purity of heart. The knight of faith is perfectly aware that such a conception is deeply problematic. His faith comes in trusting that this alleged utterly mysterious reality is indeed a reality, in trusting this alleged reality and in trusting that he and others can have sufficient understanding of this Incomprehensible Other to make faith possible, for, after all, we could not, no matter how much we might want to, have faith in anything of which we have no understanding at all.[57]

If God is utterly and totally incomprehensible, we cannot have faith in God, for then we will have no understanding of *what* it is we are being asked to trust, or of *whom* or *what* we are to take on trust. "Having faith" presupposes some minimal belief *that*, just as "belief in" presupposes "belief that." And belief *that* in turn implies some understanding of what it is we are supposed to believe to be the case.[58] We can only believe something to be the case if we can understand to some extent at least what it is we are to believe is the case. But if God is said to be *utterly* incomprehensible, we cannot have faith in such an incomprehensible God for then we will have no understanding of what it is we are being asked to trust or of whom or what we are to take on trust. It would be like being asked to trust Urdink when we have no understanding of what "Urdink" means or

51

refers to. We will not even know, if God is utterly incomprehensible, if the object of our discourse is a who or a what. It is, rather, a something we understand, not a what.

Szabados confuses my picture of faith with that of someone like Sidney Hook where the picture of religious faith comes to be something very like a picture of believers as stubborn people trusting that a system of rather wild speculative hypotheses might, after all, turn out to be true.[59] Faith is not (*pace* Hook) a matter of trustingly waiting for the evidence to come in. Recall Tillich's scornful remarks about not being interested in waiting around for a letter from the postman so that we could finally verify, or at least confirm, that God does really exist, or perhaps disconfirm it and abandon Christianity. (Kierkegaard's ironical remarks here are also important.) The believer cannot specify what would verify God's existence so that he could, either pig headedly (to use Szabados's phrase) or otherwise, believe in something for which he did not yet have adequate grounds, like someone might pig headedly believe that Santa might after all come down the chimney even though no reliable person has ever observed him doing it or seen him flying about in the sky on his sled. This is the great bird phenomenon that Kierkegaard rightly mocked.

The knight of faith of mainline Judaism, Christianity and Islam has no idea of how to identify his non-anthropomorphic God. He does not know what it would be like to specify the referent of "God," except intra-linguistically using terms whose referents are equally opaque, such as "infinite individual" or "omnipotent reality beyond the bounds of space and time."[60] The knight of faith, with fear and trembling, trusts that these opaque notions have just enough sense to make the religious life possible without requiring utterly irrational beliefs. (I do not speak here of the knight of faith who would voluntarily crucify his intellect.)[61]

My argument has been that when we clearly see what talk of God commits us to, we will come to see that such talk is incoherent. Zeus-talk, by contrast, is mere superstition, but a person need not be superstitious to believe in the God of Maimonides, Aquinas, Luther and Hamann. Such traditional God-talk is deep incoherence—deep because it reflects what something would have to be to be an adequate object of unqualified worship—but, deep or not, it is incoherence all the same.[62]

Szabados's central puzzlement about my views, to return again to the beginning, is about my account of rationality and its use in assessing religion as a form of life. I have maintained that for *us*, educated in the way we have been educated, belief in God is irrational. (Remember the restriction of "us" to critically educated people in modern industrial societies.) A belief is irrational on my account if the person holding it, on the one hand, either knows or, standing where he stands, can reasonably be expected to know that the belief is either inconsistent, unintelligible, incoherent or false. Or, on the other hand, the person has very good grounds for believing that that belief is either inconsistent, unintelligible, incoherent or false or that it is reasonable to expect, whether he has them or not, that someone standing where he stands would have readily available to him such grounds. If the arguments I have made about the incoherence of non-anthropomorphic God-talk are non-arcane and sound or even very close to being on the mark, and if the truth-claims made by anthropomorphic God-talk are either patently false or are of such a low order of probability as to not even be creditable, as I have also argued, then, if these things are really so, for us (assuming we are philosophically and scientifically literate) belief in God is irrational on the quite unexceptional criteria of rationality I have adumbrated, criteria Hart admits square with our common sense conceptions of rationality.

Such a startling claim is, of course, a complicated hypothetical. It rests centrally on the claim that such God-talk is incoherent, that anthropomorphic God-talk results in false or very probably false truth-claims and that my account of rationality is approximately correct. None of these things may be true, though neither Szabados nor Hart even attempted to do anything to show that any of these central things in my account are mistaken. They simply dance around them. It is also the case that my arguments and claims here, true or false or incoherent, are not arcane. They can readily be grasped by anyone standing where we stand. If this is so and my arguments are sound or nearly so, then it is irrational for us to believe in God. (Remember the limitations of what the "us" ranges over.)

I am not saying (*pace* Szabados) that if one is a competent philosopher one must or even will assent to these claims. That would be stupid arrogance on my part. Rather I am arguing for, as specified and qualified, the incoherence of God-talk and then claiming that, *if* these arguments are near to their mark and non-arcane, it is irrational for someone, in a good position to know that, to believe in God. The voice of philosophy, if it is at all functioning according to its vocation, is not the voice of freely proclaiming thunderous truths or (for that matter) thunderous untruths or incoherences. It is rather that of *argument* or *reflective deliberation* (sometimes more of the one and sometimes more of the other) set in a *narrative* (in the ideal case a comprehensive narrative) aspiring to some approximation to a comprehensive truth, or a comprehensive cluster of truths, which, if such is ever to be had, will be had in forms of reflective intersubjective communication approximating the conditions Habermas characterizes for undistorted discourse.

NOTES

[1]Kai Nielsen, *Philosophy and Atheism* (Buffalo, New York: Prometheus Books, 1985). See also my *Contemporary Critiques of Religions* (New York: Herder and Herder, 1971); *Skepticism* (New York: St. Martin's Press, 1973); and *An Introduction to the Philosophy of Religion* (London: The Macmillan Press, 1982).

[2]Richard Swinburne, *The Coherence of Theism* (Oxford, England: The Clarendon Press, 1977), p. 110.

[3]In the lengthy exchange between John Skorupski and Robin Hortin these issues are brilliantly probed. Robin Horton, "A Definition of Religion and Its Uses," *The Journal of the Royal Anthropological Institute of Great Britain and Ireland*, Vol. XC, pp. 201-26; Robin Horton, "African Traditional Thought and Western Science" *Africa* 37 (1967). pp. 131-171; John Skorupski, "Science and Traditional Religious Thought I and II," *Philosophy of the Social Sciences* 3 (1973), pp. 209-230; Robin Hortin, "Paradox and Explanation: A Reply to Mr. Skorupski I" *Philosophy of the Social Sciences* 3 (1973), pp. 289-312; Robin Hortin, "Levy-Bruhl, Durkheim and the Scientific Revolution," *Modes of Thought*, eds. R. Horton and R. Finnegan (London: Faber and Faber, 1973). pp. 249-305; John Skorupski, "Comment on Professor Horton's 'Paradox and Explanation,'" *Philosophy of the Social Sciences* 5.1 (1975): 63-70; and John Skorupski, *Symbol and Theory* (London: Cambridge University Press, 1976).

[4]Antony Flew, "The Burden of Proof," *Knowing Religiously*, ed. Leroy S. Rouner (Notre Dame, IN: University of Notre Dame Press, 1985) 105-106, 112-14.

[5]See the references to John Skorupski in note 3.

[6]This is the kind of agnosticism Ronald Hepburn defends. See his "Agnosticism" *The Encyclopedia of Philosophy*, ed. Paul Edwards, vol. 1 (New York: The Macmillan Co., 1967), pp. 56-59. See also my *Philosophy and Atheism*, 55-75.

[7]Axel Hägerström, *Philosophy and Religion*, trans. Robert T. Sandin (London: George Allen and Unwin Ltd., 1964), 175-305.

[8]Paul Henle, ed., *Language, Thought and Culture* (Ann Arbor: The University of Michigan Press, 1958) 173-95.

[9]See the references given in note 1 of this chapter.

[10]This has been powerfully argued by J.L. Mackie, *The Miracle of Theism* (Oxford: Clarendon Press, 1982); Wallace Matson, *The Existence of God* (Ithaca, NY: Cornell University Press, 1965); Ronald Hepburn, *Christianity and Paradox* (London: Watts, 1958); Michael Scriven, *Primary Philosophy* (New York: McGraw Hill Co., 1966); and by various authors in the collection edited by Peter Angeles, *Critiques of God* (Buffalo, NY: Prometheus Press, 1976).

[11]Hendrik Hart, "Kai Nielsen's *Philosophy and Atheism*" and Bela Szabados, "Religion and Irrationality" both in the symposium on my *Philosophy and Atheism* at the Canadian Philosophical Association

Philosophy and Atheism at the Canadian Philosophical Association Meetings, Winnipeg, Manitoba 29 May 1986. The present chapter is a developed version of my response at that symposium. Hart's paper in a somewhat revised form has been published in *Philosophy and Theology* I.4 (1987): 334-46. Further modified, it is the opening chapter of the present volume.

[12]Hart takes it to be typical of creedal beliefs "both that they make the impression of being self-referentially incoherent from a rational-conceptual point of view and that they are held with great conviction." Creedal beliefs for him become religious beliefs "when their authority is ultimate and spiritual, when their role in life is destiny directing" (v.5). There seem to me to be a number of errors here. Most centrally in making all beliefs which are destiny directing and ultimate into religious and spiritual beliefs, we confuse what could plausibly be maintained as a *necessary* condition for something being religious with a *sufficient* condition. That bit of conceptual legerdemain has the effect of making materialist and naturalistic worldviews into religious worldviews by stipulative redefinition. It is also at best misleading to speak of something appearing incoherent from a rational conceptual point of view with the implied suggestion that from some other point of view it could be coherent or at least appear coherent. What is involved here can be brought out by showing something of what is wrong with Hart's remarks about my alleged rationalism. Hart maintains that my "ultimate position" is my rationalism and this he construes as the belief—a belief he ascribes to me—that "truth can only be truth empirically accessible to reason and whatever is not thus rational is not true" (v.6). I would not talk that way or conceptualize things in that way. On a straightforward reading, it is false to say that that which is not thus rational is not true. That many poor people play the lotteries is true, that couples often fight over trivial things is also true; neither is rational. For something to be true it need not be rational; we need not understand why it occurs or have ascertained a rationale for it for it to be true. Thus in this straightforward way truth need not be accessible to reason. However, if something really is unintelligible or self-contradictory it cannot be true. There can be no married bachelors and if "Mulroney sleeps faster than Turner" is incoherent it cannot be true. It is, if it is incoherent, incoherent *sans phrase*. Moreover, it isn't from a point of view (rational or otherwise) the case that "Mulroney is Prime Ministry of Canada" corresponds to the facts. It just corresponds to the facts period. Sometimes talking about something being true or false or coherent or incoherent from a perspective is itself incoherent.

[13]Hart, in a very unconvincing way, reminiscent of Peter Winch and D.Z. Phillips, denies that he is a relativist (v.10). He correctly avers, mistakenly thinking it enough to rid him of the charge that he is a relativist, that the fact that we "all have faith does not mean everybody's

faith is equally good. " However, if all claims are what they are because of the perspective they are taken from, if there are radically different perspectives, and if no one can make any non-perspectival claims, (e.g., the atheist has his perspective, the Christian hers, the Hindu his and the Dinka hers), and there can be no Archimedean point, as Hart accepts, in virtue of which we can coherently argue that one of these perspectives is more adequate than another, then we are caught in a relativism. But this is exactly the position Hart is in. In fighting off rationalism he has saddled himself with relativism.

[14]I have criticized Wittgensteinian fideism in a variety of forms and in a variety of ways and in a number of places: in chapters 6 through 11 of my *God, Scepticism and Modernity*, in chapters 3, 4 and 5 of my *An Introduction to the Philosophy of Religion*, in chapter 5 of my *Contemporary Critiques of Religion*, in chapter 2 of my *Skepticism* and in chapter 10 of my *Philosophy and Atheism.*

[15]Kai Nielsen, *Philosophy and Atheism* 125.

[16]I have developed my more recent metaphilosophical views in the following articles: "Challenging Analytic Philosophy," *Free Inquiry* 4.4 (1984); "Rorty and the Self-Image of Philosophy," *International Studies in Philosophy* 18 (1986):19-28; "How to be Sceptical about Philosophy," *Philosophy* 61.235 (1986): 83-93; "Scientism, Pragmatism and the Fate of Philosophy," *Inquiry* 29.3 (1986): 277-304; "Can there be any Progress in Philosophy?" *Metaphilosophy* 18.1 (1987) 1-30; "Searching for an Emancipatory Perspective: Wide Reflective Equilibrium and the Hermeneutical Circle," *Anti-Foundationalism and Practical Reasoning*, ed. Evan Simpson (Edmonton: Academia Press, 1987); and "Reflective Equilibrium and the Transformation of Philosophy," *Metaphilosophy*, 20.3-4 (1989) 235-246.

[17]In claiming that rationality is self-grounding Hart acknowledges that his talk is strange. What he means in saying that rationality is self-grounding is that "when one believes that we ought only to believe what we have good grounds to believe, we have problems with the good grounds for this belief itself" (v.12). But, as I make evident in my text, I do not for one moment think we either have, or need to have, good grounds for believing everything we believe or even should believe. Rather, as is particularly evident in chapter 9 of *God, Scepticism and Modernity*, but is made evident elsewhere in my writings as well, I believe that it is, reasonably and humanly speaking, perfectly inescapable that we will have many beliefs for which we do not have grounds. As I have put it again and again, we reasonably believe things for which we do not have a reason. Hart just unjustifiably imputes a rationalism to me in which I trust reason for its own sake as ground and not on grounds. I do not even remotely hold, and indeed do not even properly understand, the belief that rationality is our only ground for believing.

[18]Derek Parfit, in discussing personal identity, has recently shown

57

the importance of that old positivist distinction without at all accepting positivism. Derek Parfit, *Reasons and Persons*   (Oxford: Clarendon Press, 1984) 199-252.

[19]This is a point that Hugo Meynell repeatedly misses in his criticisms of me and in his criticisms of verificationists. See Hugo Meynell, "Aspects of the Philosophy of Kai Nielsen," *Dialogue* XXV.1 (1986): 83-92. One general problem I have with Meynell's generous criticisms of me is with his belief that if we can spell out reasons for which a belief or set of beliefs is to be accepted we thereby commit ourselves to foundationalism. This seems to me plainly false. Dewey and Quine are paradigmatic anti-foundationalists, but they also, though fallibilists, are not skeptics and do not have problems about the very possibility of the justifying of beliefs and sets of beliefs. But I proceed in the same way. Meynell commends my appealing to considered judgments in wide reflective equilibrium as a promising method for showing how moral beliefs can be justified, but this method, taken from Quine and Goodman, is with its coherentism (*pace* Meynell) just the opposite of a foundationalist approach.   See Meynell, 91-92 footnote 20.

[20]Axel Hägerström, *op.cit.*, 224-59.

[21]Here, in general methodology, I follow Jürgen Habermas.

[22]I extensively argue against such incommensurability claims in my "Scientism, Pragmatism and the Fate of Philosophy," 277-304.

[23]Kai Nielsen, *Philosophy and Atheism*, 145-57.

[24]*Ibid.*, 189-210. Kai Nielsen, "Principles of Rationality," *Philosophical Papers* III.2 (1974): 55-89; and Kai Nielsen, "The Embeddedness of Conceptual Relativism," *Dialogos* XI.29-30 (1977): 85-111.

[25]Isaac Levi, "Escape from Boredom: Edification According to Rorty," *Canadian Journal of Philosophy* XI.4 (1981): 589-602 and Kai Nielsen, "Scientism, Pragmatism and the Fate of Philosophy," 277-304.

[26]I followed him here too closely in my "On the Rationality of Groundless Believing." See chapter 9 of *God, Scepticism and Modernity*. For the necessary correction see *Philosophy and Atheism*, 221-24 and my "Scientism, Pragmatism and the Fate of Philosophy," 277-304.

[27]Hart tells us (v.7) that the religion of the Enlightenment is the belief that "rational grounding is the final authority in the grounding of our beliefs." He thinks of me and of Richard Rorty, and no doubt of many other modernists as well, as adherents to this faith. I have in the body of this chapter argued that that claim is false as far as it is a claim about religion. But what about rational authority being the final authority in the grounding of our beliefs? Even here there is a lot of sorting out to be done. In chapter 9 of *God, Scepticism and Modernity* I argued, following Wittgenstein and Malcolm, that we have many groundless beliefs, indeed many more than we typically realize, and that there is nothing unreasonable about that. If, even after a diligent

search, I cannot find my watch I do not entertain, even as a possible wild hypothesis, that it might have just vanished into thin air. That is not something I would even think about at all or take as a possibility. That such things cannot happen may be for me a groundless belief. But it does not follow from that that it is an unreasonable belief. There are many things, I have repeatedly argued, we reasonably believe that we do not believe for a reason. What is more dicey is to claim that such a belief *could not possibly be rationally warranted* (come to be grounded) and that I could know that and still coherently claim that I know that unwarranted belief to be true or that I could reasonably assume its truth or acceptability. See Ernest Nagel, *Logic Without Metaphysics* (Glencoe, IL: The Free Press, 1956) 143-52. I should also remark here that *pace* Hart, I do not claim anything to be the "only and final truth" or regard my own position as unproblematic. These things would not fit in with my pragmatist fallibilism or with my coherentist methodology of appealing to considered judgments in *wide* reflective equilibrium. See chapter 2 of my *Equality and Liberty* (Totowa, NJ: Rowman and Allanheld, 1985). My version of what is rational is, of course, like every other person's—just one version. Hart asks: why accept it if it excludes religious faith as irrational? Well, if it is to be accepted as more than just my idiosyncratic version, it must be seen to square with how we use "rational," "reasonable," "rationality" and the like and with what reflective people, who are informed about these things, would accept after dispassionate and probing deliberation. It must, that is, meet Habermas's conditions for undistorted discourse. I throw it out as a hypothesis to be so tested. Surely it will need to be refined, and whether it has the force I believe it to have depends, if you will, on whether such ideas get a "democratic acceptance," though here the electorate must have proper qualifications. (*If* that is elitism, make the most of it.) They must be aware, on all sides of the issue, what is at issue. It is what people would agree to under conditions of undistorted discourse that is vital. It is never a matter of simply tallying up the numbers.

[28]See my *God and the Grounding of Morality* (Ottawa, ON: The University of Ottawa Press, forthcoming 1991), my *Ethics Without God* (Buffalo, NY: Prometheus Books, 1973), my *Reason and Practice* (New York: Harper and Row, 1971), chapter 22 and my *Philosophy and Atheism* (Buffalo, NY: Prometheus Books, 1985) chapter 9.

[29]Kai Nielsen, "On Rationality and Essentially Contested Concepts," *Communication & Cognition* 16.3 (1983): 269-81; my "True Needs, Rationality and Emancipation," *Human Needs and Politics*, ed. R. Fitzgerald (Sidney, Australia: Pergamons' Publishers, 1977); and my "Is there an Emancipatory Rationality?" *Critica* VIII.24 (1976). In the context of talking about an emancipatory rationality, Hart's remarks about what he takes to be my views of rationality and my utopian emancipatory hopes should have a brief comment. Utopian

hopes (*pace* Hart, v.8) need not at all be beliefs "whose scope transcends the empirical world." One utopian hope I have is the hope for a classless and genderless society. Whether such a hope will ever be realized or indeed can be realized is unclear, but we can say in perfectly empirical terms what it would be like for such a society to come into existence. Such a conception has what the logical empiricists used to call empirical meaning. It is not, like God, something which transcends the empirical world and does not admit of a purely empirical description. Moreover (again *pace* Hart), having utopian hopes does not show that my "belief in reason is not ultimately grounded in reason but rather in hope" (v.8). I hope that certain things I judge to be desirable will come to obtain. But what I hope for is constrained by what I think is possible, and there reason does come in. But I do not tie my utopian hopes to what I take the most likely outcome to be. And what I take to be the most likely is not determined by what I most hope for. What is most *firmly* in accordance with reason may not be what is to be hoped for. It may very well be more likely than not that we will blow ourselves up in the next fifty years, but that surely is not the object of our utopian hopes.

[30]Here I think Jürgen Habermas's work has been very significant indeed. See particularly his *Theorie des kommunikativen Handelns*, I & II (Frankfurt am Main, West Germany: Suhrkamp Verlag, 1981).

[31]Hart, *op. cit.* Note, particularly, what he says about this on v.4 and v.9.

[32]*Ibid.* v.4.

[33]Kai Nielsen, *Philosophy and Atheism* 192.

[34]*Ibid.*

[35]*Ibid.*, 192-95. See also my "Principles of Rationality," 55-89 and my "The Embeddedness of Conceptual Relativism," 85-111.

[36]Kai Nielsen, *Philosophy and Atheism* 189-209.

[37]Kai Nielsen, "Reason and Sentiment: Skeptical Remarks about Reason and the 'Foundations of Morality,'" *Rationality Today*, ed. Theodore F. Geraets (Ottawa, ON: University of Ottawa Press, 1979) 249-279. See also my "Distrusting Reason," *Ethics* 86.4 (1975) and the references in note 29.

[38]Hart, *op. cit.*, v.12 and my remarks in my endnotes 17, 26 and 29.

[39]Kai Nielsen, "Against Ethical Rationalism," *Gewirth's Ethical Rationalism*, ed. E. Regis (Chicago: University of Chicago Press, 1984); my "Must the Immoralist Act Contrary to Reason?" *Morality, Reason and Truth*, eds. David Copp and David Zimmerman (Totowa, NJ: Rowman and Allanheld, 1985) 212-27; my "Reason and Sentiment" and my "Why Should I be Moral Revisited," *American Philosophical Quarterly* 21.1 (1984): 81-92. Several of these essays have been reprinted in my *Why Be Moral?* (Buffalo, NY: Prometheus Press, 1989).

[40]John Rawls, "Justice as Fairness: Political not Metaphysical," *Philosophy and Public Affairs* 14.3 (1985).

[41]Kai Nielsen, "Linguistic Philosophy and 'The Meaning of Life,'" *The Meaning of Life*, ed. E.D. Klemke (New York: Oxford University Press, 1981). pp. 177-203 and my "Religious Perplexity and Faith," *Crane Review* VIII.1 (Fall, 1965).

[42]Hart, *op.cit.* v.7.

[43]*Ibid.* v.7.

[44]Kai Nielsen, "Is God So Powerful that He Doesn't Even Have to Exist?" *Religious Experience and Truth*, ed. Sidney Hook (New York: New York University Press, 1961) 270-281.

[45]Ninian Smart, *A Dialogue of Religions* (London: SCM Press, 1960) and Ninian Smart, *Reasons and Faiths* (London: Routledge and Kegan Paul, 1958).

[46]On "low-redefinition" see Paul Edwards, *The Logic of Moral Discourse* (Glencoe, IL: The Free Press, 1955). This is also usefully related to what Charles Stevenson says about persuasive definitions. Charles Stevenson, *Ethics and Language* (New Haven: Yale University Press, 1944) 206-226.

[47]Bela Szabados, "Religion and Irrationality." I should also re-mark (again *pace* Hart) that there is nothing in my utopian hopes that is spiritual and transcendent. Of course, if through low-redefinitions, carrying us far from Christian orthodoxy, we simply mean, in talking about the spiritual and the transcendent, that which has to do with our future and our destiny, then I can, of course, be said to be concerned with the spiritual and the transcendent. All atheists by such a playing with words can be led gently to religious belief. But this, as Sidney Hook would put it, violates the ethics of words. When God is said to be transcendent and when God is said to be a spirit, what Christian orthodoxy or even near orthodoxy is trying to say is that God is beyond the world and God is not a material entity, a strange thing among things in the world, but is an infinite, non-spatial individual beyond the bounds of space and time. God is not even the world itself viewed in a certain way. To give the implicit low-redefinitions Hart gives is to take us back to either the errors of the reductionism of Braithwaite and Hare discussed in chapter 13 of *God, Scepticism and Modernity*, or to the errors of the more elusive reductionism of Phillips and Dilman discussed in chapters 6 through 11 of that same volume.

[48]Richard Rorty, *Philosophy and the Mirror of Nature* (Princeton, NJ: Princeton University Press, 1979) 335-6, 384.

[49]Szabados, *op.cit.*

[50]Kai Nielsen, *Philosophy and Atheism*, 189-210.

[51]Clearly this is what Hart thinks but, as I have argued in earlier sections of this chapter, it is not something that he has been able to show.

[52]Ninian Smart, "On Knowing What is Uncertain" *Knowing Religiously*, ed. L.S. Rouner (Notre Dame, IN: University of Notre Dame Press, 1985) 86.

[53]Szabados, *op.cit.*

[54]*Ibid.*

[55]Gilbert Ryle, *Collected Papers*, Vol. II (London: Hutchinson and Co., 1971) 153-169, 194-211. See also F. Waismann, *How I See Philosophy* (London: Macmillan, 1968) 1-38.

[56]Hart is exercised about what "us" refers to or my "we" (v.8-9,14). He thinks my views here are elitist, showing scant respect for ordinary people. But just the reverse is the case. I do not say that many ordinary people believe irrationally in believing in God, or that intellectuals at other times and other places are irrational in believing in God. What we can rationally believe is in large measure a matter of what we are in a position to come to know, and that is in considerable measure a matter of time and circumstance, and good or bad fortune. Those of us who are relatively lucky can rightly say "And there by the grace of God go we."

[57]Kai Nielsen, "Can Faith Validate God-Talk?" *Theology Today* (July, 1963). See also my "Faith and Authority," *The Southern Journal of Philosophy* 3 (Winter 1965) and my "Religious Perplexity and Faith," *Crane Review* VIII.1 (1965).

[58]Norman Malcolm tries to get around that but he fails. Norman Malcolm, "Is it a Religious Belief that 'God Exists'?" *Faith and Philosophers*, ed. John Hick (New York: St. Martin's Press, 1964) 103-109. See my critique of Malcolm in my "On Believing that God Exists," *Southern Journal of Philosophy* (September 1967).

[59]See the exchange (which among other things catches generational differences between contemporary secularists) between Sidney Hook and myself. Sidney Hook, *The Quest for Being* (New York: St. Martin's Press, 1961) Parts 2 and 3 and the appendix; Kai Nielsen, "Religion and Naturalistic Humanism: Some Remarks on Hook's Critique of Religion" *Sidney Hook and the Contemporary World*, ed. Paul Kurtz (New York: John Day Co., 1968) 257-79; Kai Nielsen, "Secularism and Theology: Remarks on a Form of Naturalistic Humanism," *The Southern Journal of Philosophy* XIII (Spring 1975):109-26; Sidney Hook, "For an Open-Minded Naturalism," *The Southern Journal of Philosophy* XIII (Spring 1975):127-36; Kai Nielsen, *Philosophy and Atheism* 9-28.

[60]Kai Nielsen, *An Introduction to the Philosoohy of Religion* 1-42 and Kai Nielsen, *Philosophy and Atheism* 9-31. See also Kai Nielsen, "On Speaking of God" *Analytical Philosophy of Religion in Canada*, ed. Mostafa Faghfoury (Ottawa, ON: University of Ottawa Press, 1982) 75-96.

[61]Kai Nielsen, "Religious Perplexity and Faith," *The Crane Review* VIII.1 (1965).

[62]See chapters 2 and 3 of *God, Scepticism and Modernity*.

3. CAN NIELSEN ESCAPE BOTH GOD AND RORTY?
Hendrik Hart

Introduction

Since the publication of *Philosophy and Atheism* (1) and his 1984 presidential address to the Canadian Philosophical Association (2), Nielsen has been unfolding his struggles with the contemporary state of philosophy in much greater depth. Many recent papers deal with this metaphilosophical concern (v. ch. 2, endnote 16). He emerges as a philosopher who continues to subscribe to a classic statement of what philosophy is: the rational-critical assessment of how, generally speaking, things hang together seen in as coherent and comprehensive a conceptual pattern as we can manage. Philosophy constructs a comprehensively coherent conception of the most general structure of reality, though not as a mere abstraction. To be worth doing, philosophy needs to be contextualized by and focussed on human problems and to find its validity in contributing to solving these (2:8,10; 4:91; 7:1,3,7; 11:155). Nielsen is concerned that something be done about "the genuine and serious conflict of competing social practices" (7:5). He complains about "too many different ways of life, points of view, universes of discourse, conflicting ideologies, to possibly just naively accept the doing of the thing done in our society" (7:10).

In his own version of philosophy thus conceived, however, Nielsen seems to stay well within the parameters of the rationalism I examined earlier. He still seems reluctant to let go of the cultural privilege of reason. "We want, if such a thing is possible, a moral and social theory that can produce a critique of culture, a critique of society, and a critique of ideology" (2:8). All the conflicts may at bottom be unnecessary, because consensus is possible if we all search for wide reflective equilibrium (11:159-160). "There can be no genuine solutions to the problems of

63

men if we do not have such universal rational standards of criticism and validation" (7:9). I continue to worry that Nielsen may underestimate our conflicts by too simply suggesting that our problems can be solved if we choose his rationalism from among the competing views.

I will argue again that in his assessment of philosophy, Nielsen is still not as viable an atheist as he wants to be (v. ch. 2). My assumption here is that Richard Rorty's atheism is more consistent. For Rorty norms that will universally justify our present practices are traces of religion. Perhaps not religion as Nielsen would define it, but this notwithstanding in a sense that communicates well in our postmodern situation (7:10). Nielsen yearns for universal justification of our practices (7:5,11/12; 11:146). And he sees it brought about by reason in a way that makes him, as he recognizes, a religious or ideological rationalist in Rorty's view (7:25). Nielsen has argued in response to my earlier analysis of his views that I am mistaken to see him as a rationalist (v. ch. 2). He also denies his position is religious. Perhaps he is right. It is not always easy to understand one another on complex issues. But I am not convinced yet. So I will try again.

Rorty, Reason, and Relativity

Richard Rorty rejects belief in God and along with it anything we may characterize as God's-eye-views: apriori concepts, ahistorical ideas, permanent neutral frameworks, reason as a divine judge of culture, or ideologies. Nielsen admires Rorty's antifoundationalism (2:6-7). But just as he does not believe we need to forego morality without God (26:13), so he also does not believe we have to become relativists, where relativism is his construal of Rorty's position (7:22-24). His moves between 1984 and 1986 have stopped short, in spite of much appreciation, of embracing Rorty in every respect. Relativity yes, relativism no.

Nielsen's problem, which I share, is serious and genuine. He finds it repugnant, given our interest in the human condition, to say that our most cherished beliefs about justice and morality are tribal only. In that case there is no rational-moral basis for rejecting Afrikaner apartheid (7:24-25). Nielsen does not want to reject apartheid just for himself. He wants to say that Afrikaners ought to reject it. He wants more rational-moral authority than Rorty's tribal recommendations of American liberals. Liberal views of justice may work well for them, but Nielsen thinks moral relativism is less benign than Rorty portrays (7:24).

Rorty, of course, denies that he is a relativist. His morals, values, norms, principles, or whatever we may wish to call them are those of the Enlightenment (1:333). His emancipatory commitment shortcircuits relativism (2:165-166). He claims only that, outside of his commitment, no emancipation-independent, no emancipation-transcending foundation objectively grounds his commitment. The emancipatory commitment of the Enlightenment, though believed to be the only game in town by Enlightenment believers, is itself a tribal commitment in Rorty's view.

I agree that, on his views, Rorty has no choice. Without a God or God's-eye views we have to go with whatever we're going with. Obviously, outside of what we're going with, there is for us nothing else worthwhile going. If a someone accepts that outside of this or that belief E there just is nothing else going, such a belief E would make that person a non-relativist in her own eyes. It is clear to me that a demand for an objective norm to justify this belief E, or for an Archimedean point outside of this belief E seems like a leftover of religion, a stubborn piece of divine shrapnel once God has been blown apart. Whether we should call such behavior religious seems less important than our placing it within that universe of discourse.

Perhaps we want to say more than: outside of the Enlightenment no hope; or outside of a rational critique no valid critique (7:24-25). Then we need grounds for what we are saying outside of what we are saying. Rorty claims there are no such outside grounds. Beyond proclaiming reason and living by your rational commitment, there is no other ground. Those who make this proclamation are a tribe of sorts. But they are not relativists. They just believe other tribes are wrong: no truth, objectivity, universality, or norms unless they are rational. But Nielsen wants more. He wants to detribalize a commitment to rational criticism. He wants an impartial, supertribal point of view (7:11,12).

It seems to me that there is no going with Rorty and at the same time retaining an objectivity that can justify us outside of our commitments. You either go with the Rortean relativity which from your own point of view is far from relativistic, or you go back to God—or religious substitutes. It is conceivable that this positing of a dilemma depends on choices belonging to a paradigm which is no longer applicable to a postmodern situation. But it seems hard to deny that if you are committed to reason and you believe you can accept all of Rorty except the relativism, you are not just a rationalist, but an ideological one. Especially because talk about relativism may well be a rationalist narrative about a world without a permanent neutral framework. For it seems clear to me that seen *from within* such a framework, relativism is an apt name for a world without the framework.

There is a genuine problem in judging new proposals by standards belonging to old solutions. Is all talk about real universality necessarily realistic or rationalistic? Is a non-parochial tribe the same thing as a person prejudiced to believe that critical minds have no prejudices? Is social critical theory scientism by another name? Science seems to deliver what for all practical purposes seem like universal goods in the world of numbers and molecules, when we reduce that world to certain of its sides for the sake of human control. But even in that limited world the reductionisms are beginning to reveal their darker sides. It certainly seems much more risky to use achievements of science as models for treating human problems. If we do, that seems to betray a faith in theory for which the warrant is thin. But in the postmodern situation we are only now beginning to rethink these old problems. For now we will have to do with a mix of new and old categories. My worry about Nielsen is that he self-deceptively believes his reason is an emperor clothed with justification that goes beyond the specific justification of specified beliefs under given conditions at some time and place.

Nielsen's Rationalism
Since Nielsen has explicitly rejected my claim that he is a

rationalist (v. ch. 2, endnotes 12, 13, 17, 27, 29), I will state what I mean by his rationalism and how I think he espouses it. I will distinguish between his *stated* views on the matter and his *operant* views. In his stated views he unfolds arguments against ascriptions of rationalism to his position. I will not deal with these here, in part because I do not believe they are convincing, but even more because in this paper I am especially interested in his operant views. How do reason and rationality, or terms such as reasoned and reasonable, actually function in his work? Rorty disclaims relativism, but Nielsen tries to show that functionally speaking he is a relativist (7:19-26). Nielsen disclaims rationalism. Is it similarly possible that he nevertheless operates like a rationalist?

For the purposes of this paper I will simply say that someone is a rationalist whose loyalty to the emancipatory interest of the Enlightenment is crucially pinned to the rational grounding of our hopes for the future, to the rational justification of norms we employ to be moral, to the rational determination of what will solve our present problems. Such a person will typically move toward better morals, improved politics, a happier society, or a more just economy via moral theory, political theory, critical social theory, or economic theory. If rationalism is too strong a characterization of this position then I'm also willing to call it intellectualism.

Nielsen may *claim* that rationality here is just one crucial ingredient. But I challenge him to show *evidence* for this in his recent papers in metaphilosophy. These do not show how, functionally speaking, reason is but a relative and partial ingredient here. In these papers Nielsen is no proponent of anything universal, objective, grounded, or justified unless rationally so. When I say that truth is rational for Nielsen I do not mean to suggest that he claims something strange like: whatever is the case is rational (v. ch. 2, endnote 12). What I mean is that for him truth is primarily a matter of rational-conceptual determination of what is the case, though what is the case might well be outrageously irrational.

Despite explicit denials about doing philosophy in the grand old imperialistic style "as cultural overseer" (7:13), Nielsen plainly talks about critical theory "as a successor to philosophy"

67

(7:18) in the bad sense in which Rorty talks about it, namely the guardian of culture: "It could criticize culture, provide a rationale for criticizing culture and help us render some tolerably objective judgments about which social practices ought to endure, which should be reconstructed and which should be abandoned" (7:18).

How is that not being a cultural overseer? God would be quite satisfied with such honors. In the paper I am quoting here critical theory is nothing but the universal, disciplined, critical, normative deployment of reason in the formation of rational arguments and rational theories. Nielsen is talking about "the core Enlightenment notion of a rational criticism of existing institutions..." (7:18).

Objectivity, grounding, and justification are notions of rationality. For Nielsen the expression "rational justification" is even a pleonasm (7:7). In agreement with Habermas, it is "rational consensus" or "rational criticism" that emerges as the "Archimedean point" which will deliver us from relativism and ideology (7:9, 18, though see 11:151 for denial of an Archimedean point). If our practices of justification are themselves to be justified, we will need to look to reason (7:12). The wide reflective equilibrium on which Nielsen depends so heavily is, once again, the sound, shared, and systematic use of reason (11). It is the "best rationalized" theories we go for, (11:152) and "reasonable" hopes and understandings (11:154). It is "rational consensus" we are looking for and if our "only constraints" are those of "careful deliberation" and "better argument" we will get there (11:158).

Nielsen may deny that if he believes these things this makes him a rationalist. He may not mean by rationalist what I mean by it. But all I will mean by a rationalist—or more weakly, an intellectualist—is a person who believes the things I just showed Nielsen to be believing. And, as I noted earlier, Nielsen knows that Rorty also would call him a rationalist for these reasons, and an ideological or religious one at that (7:9/10, 25). But the name rationalist is not first of all what is at stake here. The real issue is whether Nielsen believes what I ascribe to him here.

68

Nielsen's Justification of Rationalism

Let me now try to show what Nielsen's rationalism comes to. One of his strategies is to describe the qualities of his critical theory (CT) or wide reflective equilibrium (WRE) that would qualify them for all the awards he wants to bestow upon them, but without showing how anything could in fact have all those qualities. How, for example, do you combine an Archimedean point to escape "a very relativistic context-dependent social criticism" (7:9) with fallibilism (11:150/51)? How do you combine universal standards (7:9) with rejection of ahistorical norms? How do you escape relativism when you are dedicated to given times and places (11:150)? Again, this may be taking new problems within the horns of old dilemmas. But it is Nielsen who claims that relativism needs to be headed off with universal standards of justification. When you are dedicated to given times and places, have you not foreclosed on universality? And if the latter, are you then not committed to relativism by your own reckoning?

Just to claim that you want WRE to have these qualities does not in fact bestow them on anything real. I'd imagine that Nielsen would insist that his own accounts are reasoned, conceptually coherent, and empirical. He thinks he has given reasons to believe that difficulties in WRE can be overcome (7:19). But again, merely stating that rejection of foundationalism or supertemporal positions does not preclude good answers to hard questions (7:5,18), is not the same as giving a reasoned account which shows coherently and empirically that such answers go beyond our presently available relative resources (7:11/12).

What makes Nielsen content to admit that genuinely practical, empirical problems may in fact prevent us from achieving WRE, so long as there is no conceptual incoherence in his views? (7:8,13, 11:157). That seems to me to be rationalism pure and simple: if something is thinkable—read: conceptually imaginable—it must be possible. Why does Nielsen not go into greater detail in the many places in which he himself displays insecurity about his views, to investigate the basis for his doubts? He frequently refers to the possibility that his proposals are utopian or illusory (2:8-10, 4:93, 7:7, 19, 24/25, 27, 11:155).

But he does not investigate his reasons for these worries. Are the tensions he notes not real tensions?

If we carefully note what Nielsen means by empirical there are equally worrisome implications. When he calls his proposals empirical, what is he referring to (11:160)? When he claims to have given reasons for thinking that his program needs to be taken seriously, what is he talking about (7:19)? These claims are, as far as I can see, purely conceptual. They are thought experiments at best and possibly just intellectual phantasies. What Nielsen wants "will have" such and such characteristics (11:156). But how in reality? He himself sees his reality as counterfactual with regard to his proposals (11:158). So what reality, what actual and achievable practice is he talking about when he mentions that by 2035 we will know whether he was right or not (7:19)?

Does Nielsen's notion of empirical include what may never be realizable? By empirical he seems to mean no more than the positivist notion that our concepts must refer to what is conceivably observable. Empirical means that we can describe what something would be like if it were to be realized (v. ch. 2, note 29). But in fact—that is: empirically—there may be insuperable obstacles in the way of its ever being realized. That, of course, would make unicorns empirical. If WRE or CT are like unicorns, fixing the hope of humanity on them becomes little more attractive than Rorty's relativism (7:27).

But WRE and CT not only have troublesome conceptual and empirical problems attached to them. Their worst problem is that no attempt is made to show that they can do what they are designed to do, namely overcome relativism. As far as I can see Nielsen fails, perhaps does not even attempt, to show how when you stress the complete relativity, fallibility, and historicity of WRE and CT these are nevertheless not relativistic entities. When and if they are achievable, they still remain tied to a "given" tribe at a "particular" moment in history (7:5,24; 11:150,152). And how does that differ from what Rorty claims? Just to say over and over again that your morality is rational, or that your theory is critical, or that your point of departure is in consensus does not miraculously overcome relativism. It can do that for you only if you have a hidden assumption that reason is in fact immune to relativism. But on what grounds do we hold that?

If Nielsen were doing nothing more than making research proposals along the lines of: "if we were to do x, y, and z we might possibly find that the results will encourage us to p, q, and r," his recommendations about CT and WRE would be much easier to entertain. But he is not doing that. He is asserting the firm expectations of the hopeful. His language would in some quarters be called overly optimistic. In other quarters it would be recognized as the secular analogue of faith language.

There is no firmer attachment to Enlightenment emancipation in Nielsen than there is in Rorty. Rorty is just a little more empirical and realistic in claiming that attachment to the Enlightenment, though it may justify all we hope for and dream about, can itself not be justified by appealing to some independent agency (1:389 ff). Rorty would simply say that those who are working on WRE (a version of Rorty's conversation of mankind rationally carried on?) are a tribe in their own right. In recommending the Enlightenment to another tribe, there is not a Kantian non-tribal tribunal (xi/xii) which, following the laws of Reason, will independently justify WRE. Nielsen is far from having given grounds that justify us fixing our hopes on WRE non-relativistically. All he has shown is that following certain techniques may at some time, in some place, given certain conditions, lead to considerable agreement in some tribe, for example our Euro-American philosophy departments. How much real hope that would give modern global society is a matter of considerable controversy and very little evidence. It certainly would do little for the African National Congress.

Ideology and Conversation
Where, in fact, do Rorty's conversation of mankind and Nielsen's "absolutely free and unlimited discussion" differ (11:158)? In my view Rorty, though himself appearing like a conservative member of the liberal establishment politically, is willing to let more people into the conversation than Nielsen is. Rorty creates the impression that his discussion is quite open (1:384/85). Nielsen creates the elitist impression that he must limit the conversation to enlightened discourse (11:157-159). A partici-

pant in Nielsen's open discussion "must have proper qualifications" (v. ch. 2, endnote 27). Those qualifications, no doubt,
include being philosophically-scientifically sophisticated, as
Nielsen does not tire of saying (1:23, 40, 41, 100, 126, 146, 151,
164, 184/5, 189, 195, 201-203, 219, 224/5). Nevertheless, the
two are less far apart than Nielsen makes out. What both are
deeply interested in is community, agreement, overcoming the
incommensurability. Both are also agreed that the role of
reason in reaching agreement is crucial.

So what's the difference? We may say Rorty's hope is in
continued conversation and Nielsen's in a WRE. Both limit
constraints to openness in their processes (Nielsen, 4:22; Rorty,
2:165). Given some flexibility we may say that both focus on a
critical rational process intended to achieve agreement
(Rorty1:318; 2:166). For Rorty the conversation is critically
dependent on rationality (1:389). For Nielsen WRE is a method
of unifying diverse positions (11:144). Depending on the
measure of agreement achieved, both could refer to the common framework that is the outcome of their processes as
universal and objective. Both would want the agreement to be
temporary and value oriented. Science as the paradigm of free
and open discussion is a favorite of both Rorty and Nielsen.

But there remains a critical difference. Nielsen holds out
hopes of universality and objectivity that are somehow more
universal and more objective than hopes fully dependent on
our own relative, fallible, timed subjectivity. Though he explicitly rejects independent, outside, apriori, permanent positions,
the sort of objectivity and universality he talks about can differ
from Rorty's only in not being fully human, historical, here and
now, social. I know very well that Nielsen denies this. But I do
not see him replacing what he rejects in Rorty with anything
that is substantially different. Except that he, unlike Rorty,
claims that Rorty's position is relativist and demands that we
escape the relativism of the position. But the ingredients are,
unless I've missed something crucial, Rorty's ingredients with
different labels.

For someone not already committed to Nielsen's position
I can see no other end to a critical investigation of his position
than the following conclusion. Nielsen, like Rorty, refuses to

admit that his position is relativistic. He rejects all the marks of relativism. But for their opposite numbers he has no room. What this comes to is that Nielsen has a Rortean relativism about which he deceives himself and on the basis of which he refers to other positions as ideological (11:157/58). Rorty simply says: I am going for reason as the best Enlightenment hope for emancipation and I know that outside of this hope and my experience of living by it, I have nothing to offer other tribes. Nielsen hopes and dreams on the sure foundations of what he takes to be universal rational criteria, though he calls them historical. And universality has traditionally been equated with time-transcending realities. Has Nielsen offered us a description of an impractical method for achieving exceptionally widely shared moral consensus? Can the justified objectivity he wants become grounded in temporary generalizations? And he makes no attempt to justify his attachment to the Enlightenment or to show that we have real reason to hope for emancipation. He acts both as though there is no need for such justification and as though these things are in fact already justified (11:151,157-160). In that, too, he is different from Rorty.

I am not discrediting dreams and hopes here. Neither do I want to undermine our quest for norms that transcend tribal interests. To the contrary, all I want to say is that between Nielsen's WRE and the best possible end of Rorty's continuing conversation the only difference I see is that Nielsen thinks he can make up the balance in fifty years, while Rorty is more pessimistic. On the other hand, Nielsen will admit to all hope being lost if the balance is negative, while Rorty is willing to continue the conversation. But both use "universal" and "objective" in highly unusual senses, which makes them relativists in the eyes of people who have more conventional meanings for these terms. Nielsen deceives himself if he believes that his use of these terms is commonly acceptable (11:159-160). And if he admits the novel usage, it is hard to see how he can escape the relativist label assigned by those whose rationalism demands the more conventional meanings.

73

Making Progress

I share Nielsen's desire for normative universality. Is there in fact any possibility for such universality? Is universality, as we traditionally refer to it, a bad debt? Is it a category of Reason in which more is claimed than we can claim for ordinary rational generalizations? Can we somehow get beyond the merely subjective, the here and now, transcending our tribe, and so on and so on, to demand that all people always and everywhere be just, to posit that all human beings everywhere may realistically hope to be happy and so on and so on? On what is such universality grounded? We all want to overcome hurtful differences in a way that is not arbitrary, incommensurable, or relativistic. But why settle on reason to do the job? What is the legitimate role of votes, hard choices, tolerance, authority, differences in priorities, religion, commitments, and perspectives? Why do these not function in Nielsen's discussions?

I agree we must not reject the claims of reason too quickly here. I agree science is a term which designates a world in which reason, understood as the domain of valid argument concerning empirical reality, functions optimally. In science reason's potential for agreement and impartiality have been sought out, practiced, researched, critically reflected upon, and widely shared. That world of science gives us warrant to claim that reason often justifies agreement and consensus. But a rational person's knowing for a fact that Brian Mulroney is Canada's present prime minister and perhaps knowing this independently of some perspective or commitment is hardly a monumental enough indication, as Nielsen seems to think, that it is reasonable in our society to build hopes for moral and social consensus on reason (v. ch. 2, endnote 12). Such hope is the optimism of an Enlightenment ideology or a core belief of the religion called scientism.

If in conversations toward community we want to be truly enlightened as well as truly postmodern, I would think WRE can have no privileged position. Nor do we have grounds to believe WRE will lead to universally shared hopes and dreams. WRE can be little more than a historicized foundationalism, naturalized rationalism, or relativized intellectualism. When Nielsen rejects my view that his position is religious because he

74

thinks I assume definitions of religion that make believers of us all (v. ch. 2, endnote 12), I can only think of his definitions of reality that either make Enlightenment rationalists of us all, or exclude us from the company of modern people. I do not believe Nielsen sufficiently honors the combination of rational agreement with incommensurable perspective. Rather than pitting commensurability against incommensurability it is more likely that we will make progress with a combination of the two when our shared beliefs are embedded in divisions among communities. It is the often incommensurable perspectives which can make our position so unrelativistic to ourselves that not only does it seem that nothing else is going, but also that all reasonable people must believe in hidden variants of our position. On these matters we differ and we do so incommensurably, while on others we agree. But most of our significant beliefs share aspects both of incommensurability and agreement.

Good evidence for incommensurability here is Nielsen's strategy of declaring it a pseudo reality, so incommensurability is no problem. The rest of us just simply refuse to go away. The moment he wants to introduce WRE or CT and its promises as the only way out of incommensurability, we have incommensurable differences. For Nielsen to say: if only we would all share WRE and CT, the incommensurability problem would go away and there would be rational consensus, is the same as for a religious person to say: if only all people believed in God and practiced Christianity according to the Bible all hate would go away and there would be real love. None of us will get away with this just yet.

What we can do is to work hard at sharing commensurable universals through reason, contextualized by incommensurable perspectives. I think all humans want the same: joy, health, meaning. The test will be whether living out of our perspective we actually achieve this in the communities guided by these perspectives, in ways that will recommend themselves to others. And besides argument we will also have to make room for hard decisions, votes, authority, and others. The record of Christianity is not without serious blemish here. But the legacy of Reason has not fared much better.

People do in fact pin their hopes on many incommensurable grounds (11:159). All behave non-relativistically about their perspective. Rorty does too. Nielsen's position is an intellectualist position at best, which he thinks is non-relativist. And in the best tradition of rationalism, he also thinks it is universal, non-prejudiced, neutral, objective. But I think he is mistaken. Demanding that for the sake of solving the problems of humanity we all come in one (his) camp is proselitizing. For the time being we will have to survive with the multiplicity of perspectives. And that's our peculiarly modern predicament. We are too dangerously divided. Reason is a good instrument for reaching agreement in beliefs of a certain kind. But life is more than reaching agreement about such beliefs. If rational agreement were to function, important as it may be, as one ingredient next to others without playing any superjudge role in culture, its contributions may be positively welcomed. But viewed as setting universal standards for all judgment this instrument turns rationality into ideology.

Rorty's game in this arena is to recommend conversation and to admit he can't see any other outcome than others joining him if they want happiness. But since he claims God is dead he radically recognizes this amounts to having no substitute of any kind in reason, objectivity, universal normativity, WRE, or CT. I don't see how Nielsen has avoided Rorty's conclusion. Indeed, does Nielsen truly think that the answer to Afrikaner apartheid is our WRE, which we will tell blacks they should wait for till 2035? Or will we get farther with Rorty's conversation? Participants might urge that this should take the form of negotiation (as a form of talk), or of disinvestment (as a form of argument). As conversation this seems meaningful, as WRE it would make little sense. [Fortunately we can now be thankful that this closing paragraph has become somewhat "academic," because Mandela is free and the conversation with de Klerk has begun.]

4. INCOMMENSURABILITY AND OBJECTIVITY: REASONABLENESS WITHOUT GOD OR GOD-SUBSTITUTES
Kai Nielsen

Introduction

I respond here to Hendrik Hart's Second Critique "Can Nielsen Escape Both God and Rorty?" I have argued elsewhere against the relativist side of Rorty.[1] This—or so I shall argue—is a Rorty I can escape without (*pace* Hart) making a God of reason or engaging in any other mystification. But, as I shall also argue here, Rorty's views have developed in such a way that there is a later Rorty, a Davidsonian, wide-reflective equilibrium, non-relativist Rorty, I have no wish or need to escape from, for on philosophical, though not on political, fundamentals there are close affinities between our views.[2] Only my espousal of a form of critical theory distances us, though even here there are resources in Rorty that could pull him in that direction.[3] (They could but haven't. Perhaps Rorty is too literary a figure to take the social sciences seriously.)

As for God, there is no possibility of escaping or not escaping something which, in its religiously appropriate forms, is incoherent. If my arguments (for example) in my *Skepticism* and in my *God, Skepticism and Modernity* are near to the mark, the Judeo-Christian-Islamic concept of God is incoherent and not as believers believe a profound, nearly incomprehensible Ultimate Mystery. It is surely understandable that believers in their deepest sincerity should take God to be the Incomprehensible Mystery essential to their lives. But that is not the way things are. There not only is not, but there could not be, a non-anthropomorphic God, and only a non-anthropomorphic God would be an adequate object of worship and reverence.

However, this claim about incoherence is not my task here. I simply state above what I have argued in detail elsewhere. But such a statement does clear the air. My task is (1) assessing Hart's specific arguments in his Second Critique and (2)

77

establishing that talk of "incommensurable perspectives" or "incommensurable frameworks" and the like with the resultant conceptual relativism rests on a mistake. I do the former in II-VIII and the latter in IX-XI. The belief that there are deep relativities between which we just must choose, if we are to make sense of our lives, is itself a conceptual confusion answering to nothing.[4]

The God of Reason
Many of the issues discussed in our first exchange return like the repressed in this our second exchange. I shall, however, try to avoid going over well- trodden ground. I shall set out here a new cluster of considerations. Hart persists in claiming that I make a God of reason, that a set of supposedly objective universal norms serves me as a substitute for God and that, my disclaimers to the contrary notwithstanding, I am a rationalist. Hart, however, attempts here to specify more clearly the sense in which I am a rationalist than he did in his earlier essay. I will return to a consideration of that specification in a later section of this paper.

Toward the end of his paper Hart remarks: "Nielsen hopes and dreams of the sure foundations of what he takes to be universal criteria, though he [Nielsen] calls them historical" (v. 73).[5] There are, of course, as I recognize, a myriad of competing views. But if we would but choose to utilize, and then utilize intelligently and persistently, the method of wide reflective equilibrium, we would have a way of reasonably adjudicating between these conflicting views. But this, Hart would have it, is simply to opt for or choose my rationalism. My critical theory seeks, in what Hart takes to be an unrealistic and unjustifiably but implicitly foundationalist way, to provide something of the basis of a universal justification of social practices. We could, that is, if the theory were sound, come to know which of these practices are worthy of our allegiance and which are not, which ones we would reflectively, non-evasively and informedly accept and which not. Such judgments are, of course, difficult and demanding and there is room aplenty for double-mindedness here. Still, a worked out critical theory would yield some tentative judgments here. To use such criteria is not to make a

God of reason. It is not at all to commit yourself to rationalism in any plausible sense. Moreover, there need be no traces of religion in so proceeding, though it *may* reflect an unjustified optimism. (Recall, however, that I am fond of quoting Antonio Gramsci about the pessimism of the intellect and the optimism of the will.)

I have tried in various of my essays to explicate and defend a critical theory of society which utilizes wide reflective equilibrium (WRE).[6] It seeks to give us an objective (informedly intersubjective) justification of certain practices. It seeks to make such assessments in the way referred to in the previous paragraph. Philosophy, for me, should *transform* itself into critical theory. This, Hart claims, is plainly rationalism, for the justification of practices, on his account of my account, is "brought about by reason" (v. 64); it is in effect, he claims, a rationalism which "still seems reluctant to let go of the cultural privilege of reason" (v. 63).

However, to claim these things about my account is just plain false. WRE, which is integral to my critical theory, is a justificatory method which inescapably appeals to considered judgments and traditions.[7] What is reasonable and justifiable is always determined with reference to them. We could not get a purchase on "what reason requires or permits" except by reference to considered judgments and traditions. We, in turn, can and should be critical about them, seeking to get these considered judgments, standardly rooted in certain traditions, into a consistent or coherent whole in which they must also square with what we reasonably believe about the world, including what we reasonably believe about ourselves. But this is not rationalism gone wild or even rationalism at all, where reason is culturally privileged or where things are brought about by reason (whatever that means). There is no appeal to a God's-eye-view, or a view from nowhere, or a permanent neutral framework, or to robustly substantive ahistorical moral principles.

However, because we cannot justifiably claim such a God's-eye-view perspective it does not follow that the very notion of a rational moral authority becomes a Holmes-less Watson. But it would not on my account be a rationalistically conceived moral

authority and it would not be a moral authority that would try
to operate within "the limits of reason alone." Instead it would
operate by appealing to those considered judgments, standardly given in a tradition, which are in wide reflective equilibrium. Again, this is not a rationalism or a cultural privileging of
reason or indeed a cultural privileging of tradition either.
There is no appeal to an Archimedean point which gives us
such a God's-eye-view of things or a postulate of pure practical
reason (whatever that is). Such talk is just metaphysical slush.
Defenders of the Enlightenment have sometimes made such
extravagant and incoherent appeals, but it is certainly not
something that the basically empiricist and naturalistic temper
of the Enlightenment tradition requires.

Hart contrasts what he takes to be my rationalism with
Richard Rorty's operant but denied relativism. (The claim is
that while Rorty doesn't think he is a relativist he actually is.)
Rorty is willing to settle for the tribal commitments of a liberal
Enlightenment culture as just those commitments, while I, less
realistically, according to Hart, seek a more universal justification of a more impartial, supertribal point of view. Rorty,
particularly in some of the essays reprinted in his *Consequences
of Pragmatism,* does—his disclaimers to the contrary notwithstanding—articulate a form of relativism. But Rorty, who does
not provide a sitting target, in two late but extremely important
essays, defends in one a form of WRE, following John Rawls
and, in the other, following Donald Davidson, develops a
disquotational account of truth that (among other things)
rejects as incoherent incommensurability theses which talk of
alternative incommensurable frameworks.[8] This development
of Rorty's account makes his account and my own in fundamentals very similar. They are both non-relativist accounts, including non-relativist accounts that reject the incommensurability
theses of conceptual relativism.

The use of WRE affords the possibility of attaining a
modest impartiality without anything like a claim to an
Archimedean point or a God's-eye-point of view or some
cultural privileging of reason. It yields a recognizable form of
objectivity and impartiality without rationalism. We start with
our commitments and return to them, but there is no concep-

80

tual imprisonment within the system or cluster of our commitments; and we have a way of critically inspecting and, in some instances, coming to reject, things we have been committed to, though there is no way of all at once rejecting the whole system of commitments. But we can, without being the creature of our commitments, repair the ship at sea (to use a by now overworked metaphor). There is here a perfectly mundane basis for claiming an impartiality that takes us beyond tribalism. But this is an impartiality that has nothing to do with God or any religious substitute at all. Hart's criticisms here are off the mark.

Operant Rationalism

Hart is aware from our previous exchange that I reject, and give reasons for rejecting, the claim that I am a rationalist. Instead of confronting these responses and showing why they are mistaken, if they are, he seeks to distinguish between my *stated* views and my *operant* views and to claim that when my *operant* views are taken into consideration they reveal that functionally speaking, in spite of my self-image, I am a rationalist, making a God of reason. If you look at what I do, that is, you will see that I operate like a rationalist.

What is involved in such a claim? First, Hart gives a stipulative characterization of rationalism. A rationalist, on his eccentric and stipulative reading, is someone who (a) has an emancipatory interest in the Enlightenment but (b) this interest somehow finds its rationale in "the rational justification of norms we employ to be moral" (v. 67) and (c) this rational justification, in good Deweyian fashion, is conceived as something which, as part of a good critical theory, will guide our practices toward a better future. Hart alternatively calls this view intellectualism. It is in this sense that he claims I am a rationalist.

This is a sense of "rationalism" that is distant from the tradition of rationalism, for it is a view shared by empiricists and pragmatists as well as rationalists traditionally conceived. In this weak sense I am tolerably content to be called a rationalist though (a) so labelling the position confuses things and (b) "rationalism" so conceived, as my above arguments for WRE

81

show, does not stand free of particular contexts, considered judgments and traditions and thus need not make a God of reason.

Hart remarks, "Outside of rational critique there is no valid critique" (v. 65). He takes this to be rationalist ideology; but in reality it is but a trivial grammatical remark like "Emerald things are green" which simply reminds us of the meaning of "critique." "Rational *critique*" is pleonastic but critiquing something is not the only ground for rejecting something. Its not answering to human interests, its failing to meet needs, its being something you do not like, its not squaring with our considered judgments, its not being part of our tradition are others. Some rationalists, in Hart's broad sense of "rationalist," including paradigmatically myself, do appeal to all these considerations in accepting and rejecting beliefs and practices and many, including myself, do not have a lexical ordering for the weighting of these considerations. The evidence for this—to respond directly to Hart's challenge to show that I so view things—is in the characterization I give of WRE in those papers.[9] There these various elements are plainly displayed.

Hart, trying to show that *operantly* I am really a rationalist, in some stronger way than his characterization of "rationalism" allows, claims that in WRE reason is not "a relative and partial ingredient" (v. 67). It is rather the sole ingredient. He claims that on my account nothing is "universal, objective, grounded or justified unless rationally so" (v. 67). This remark is either trivial or false. It is trivial as "rational critique" is trivial if we simply, *for whatever the justification or ground is,* use the word "rationally" to characterize it so that "rationally grounded" or "rationally justified" is pleonastic. I think this goes with the natural lay of the language: the logic of the language so to say. It is false, however, if taken to be a claim that being rational is the final court of appeal or the only universal element that can be appealed to in justificatory quests. There are, as David Braybrooke has well argued, universal needs that are vitally relevant to our determination of the good life.[10]That we need food, water, rest, relaxation are just facts about us. They are neither rational nor irrational and its being true that these are facts about us is again something that is neither rational nor irrational. The sentence "Whatever is the case is rational" is plainly false. It is the case that I just sneezed, but that is not rational; yet it is not, for all of that, irrational either. Truth for me, accepting as I do a basically Davidsonian disquotational account, is certainly not a *rational-conceptual* determination of what is the case. Not even the determination or ascertainment of what is true is always "a rational-conceptual determination of what is the case" (v. 67). It is true that I left my brief case in my office, that there was a frost last night, that frustrated people tend to respond with aggression, that politics is typically a dirty business and that love is rare, but none of these propositions are propositions whose truth is determined by rational-conceptual means, though the last two truth-claims could profit from some preliminary conceptual elucidation.

Rorty rejects, and I reject as well, *philosophy* as a distinctive disciplinary matrix that could function as a culture overseer.[11] I have argued, as has Rorty, that philosophy cannot sustain that role. But critical theory is not philosophy but philosophy's *successor*. It has elements of philosophy in its conceptual elucidatory side but it is also an *empirical* social theory and a *normative* social theory where some of its source of normativity is considered judgments and traditions. Here, without standing free of culture, it provides a critique of culture, that is, of our social practices and moral beliefs and ideological conceptions in the way WRE specifies. However, critical theory in large measure is an empirical endeavour. This empirical interpretive-explanatory theory does not make even a tacit appeal to God or Reason. Hart just reads traditionalist conceptions into my account where as a matter of fact it sets its face against such epistemological and metaphysical traditions as thoroughly as do Wittgenstein or Rorty.

Rational Consensus
I also make it clear that I am not claiming that we will actually get unconstrained discourse, free of ideology and any widespread rational consensus. I only claim, against a currently fashionable, rather uncritical cultural pessimism, sometimes religiously based, that the very idea of a rational consensus or an undistorted discourse which would yield a perspicuous

representation of a good life for human beings, is not an incoherency. It can, and should, serve at least as a heuristic ideal for reflective moral agents. But again this does not make one a believer in the sovereignty of reason (whatever that means). One might, while keeping the above ideal as a heuristic ideal, continue, as Freud did, to believe that dark, irrational forces play a very fundamental role in shaping our destinies.

In some earlier writings, uncritically following Rawls's metaphor, I mistakenly talked about an Archimedean point. My later and more extended writings on WRE do not appeal to such a conception. But I do combine there an appeal to universal norms with fallibilism, a stress on context and, where they have much in the way of substance, a rejection of ahistorical norms. There these matters are stated in a careful and nuanced way. Here I can only be brief and rather crude. Universality comes in by my appeal to moral truisms: vague, general propositions at least some of which are at least putatively universal. I have in mind propositions such as: promises should be kept, truth should be told, suffering avoided, torturing is wrong, pleasure is good, meeting needs is desirable, and the like. These things, culturally speaking, are *de facto* universal and, left vague and indeterminate like that, there is no clearly even *intelligible* reason, let alone a *justified* reason, to reject them or their claim to universality. So we can say they are *de jure* universal as well. Any putative ethical theory which said we should reject them or be skeptical of them would be less plausible than the truisms themselves. But being vague truistic generalities they do not get us very far in ethics. It is, for example, plain enough that we need a practice of promise keeping. But what form should it take? It is not *even* plausible to claim that promises are *never* to be broken or lies are *never* to be told. But just what contours should the practices of promising and truth telling have? When we move beyond truisms to rather more substantively demanding moral norms we do not get something which is ahistorical and noncontextual. Fallibilism is the name of the game here and we do not get things which are self-evident or not historically determinate. But that does not yield relativism. That we cannot overleap history for such substantive judgments, if this is true, does not mean that there

84

is no way of correcting moral views and moral practices from inside: repairing the ship at sea. WRE is a representation—I believe a perspicuous one—of how this works.

WRE and Utopia

I have not said, or given to understand, that WRE has been instantiated somewhere, let alone that my own substantive normative views have been successfully put in WRE. It would be a remarkable bit of hubris on my part to claim that. Such an instantiation, of course, is what ideally I seek to achieve and the degree of justification of my substantive moral views (views such as I argue for in my *Liberty and Equality*) depends on the extent I have gotten my beliefs in WRE. That is a bit of a dark saying, so I should give some further specification.

I seek, in the first instance, to develop an ethical theory which when worked out will be in WRE. This would, if I succeed, be a clear and rationally justified representation of what a good life would be for human beings. (This, of course, includes a moral life.) This is something (though not the whole thing) that we as critical theorists could possibly do. That is the kind of instantiation I seek to achieve as a theorist. But the most fundamental underlying reason for doing this, its purely intellectual interest aside, is in the hope that such an intellectual construction, after repeated testing and adjustments in social interaction in the lives of ordinary human beings, would find, though surely in some modified form, an instantiation in our social structures. But here we are beyond theory and in the domain of political and social action and struggle. Here we do not need, and certainly should not have, philosopher-kings or critical theory-kings.

WRE is a picture of justification. To the extent we have our moral views in such an equilibrium, to that extent, if the method is correct, we can be confident they are justified. But I have made no claim about how well my specific substantive moral accounts—say my justification of revolution or my arguments against paternalism—have gotten themselves into WRE. And I have not made any claims concerning how far the extant moralities in our societies have tended to even approximate anything that would look like being in wide reflective equilib-

85

rium. Their even being in such an approximation is not bloody likely in a world of television evangelists and political leaders of the likes of Bush, Mulroney, Reagan, Kohl and Thatcher. Given the fact that I believe that the extant moralities of class societies are in fact moral *ideologies*, I would also *not* believe (if I were at all concerned with being consistent) that there is anything like a good approximation of WRE in our culturally reigning moralities, including, of course, Christian morality. (For a critique of the latter see my *Ethics Without God*.) My claim is that WRE is conceptually imaginable and thus in some possible world at least it could be instantiated. In this very weak and uninteresting way WRE is possible.

What I find baffling (to put it minimally) is Hart's claim that I have made no attempt to overcome relativism (v. 70). I have from my earliest writings struggled in various ways with the problem, or better the problems, of relativism.[12] I have tried repeatedly to show that relativism is more of a problem than most philosophers are inclined to acknowledge. But I have also tried to show that there are good reasons to think that relativism is mistaken. (1) I have tried to do this by attempting to show that there are good reasons, objectively good reasons, in ethics, and what they are.[13] (2) I have tried to show that we have a methodology available to us, namely WRE, which gives us a way, working from inside, with a sometimes culturally diverse cluster of considered judgments, to a reflective and informed consensus about which of these considered judgments to stick with after such a reflective winnowing. (3) Having characterized and defended that method, I have used it to articulate in my *Liberty and Equality* and again in my *Marxism and the Moral Point of View* an account of justice which is argued to be superior to the other reigning accounts. Perhaps my arguments here are bad arguments but, good or bad, they certainly are arguments against relativism. (4) I have also carefully characterized types of relativism seeking out difficulties in their formulation and critically inspected their various rationales.[14] I have also distinguished these various forms of relativism from things, frequently confused with relativism, but which are not forms of relativism, namely contextualism and historicism.[15] These latter two things, I have argued, yield in morality a reasonable form and extent of objectivity even in the absence of "eternally true moral principles" or "universal moral norms." (5) I have also argued and shown how the noting of factual considerations, including factual considerations about human nature, social structure and the function of morality in society, can be of help in assessing diverse moral codes and claims.[16] So it is completely off the mark to say, as Hart does, that I have made no attempt to show that relativism can be overcome and how it can.

WRE and CT (Critical Theory), of course, have their origins in a particular cultural context. (Indeed, everything does.) But that their *origin* is there does not mean at all that their *rationale* or *justification* is so limited. I have tried to show how someone, whether out of the Enlightenment tradition or not, could use that method to correct and rationalize her moral judgments to see if they form a coherent and consistent set squaring with everything relevant we know or reasonably believe.

WRE and Morality

Hart also in effect asks how probable it is that any actual morality will ever instantiate WRE or even approximate it. What reason, if any, have I for thinking that the actual morality of our society will ever be in such an equilibrium or even (somewhat more realistically) in anything like an approximation to it? Am I not simply engaging in a thought experiment which is also expressive of wishful thinking? Have we any reason at all to believe that anything like this is on the historical agenda? Isn't to think so, given the ideological distortion around and the amount of superstition and irrationality in our extant moralities, pure fantasy?

I was not, in articulating WRE, doing social history or social description or trying to predict rather specific ways in which our societies will change. I was not trying to say what our societies would look like in the next several years or so, though I did make one incautious throwaway remark about what might be the case fifty years down the road. But the theoretical force of my remarks are (among other things) to show that a society with the developed productive forces that we have and the

87

technical mastery of the world that is ours could have such and such a morality (a morality of a certain reasonably determinate type) and that it could develop a rational method for assessing moral claims, alternative moral theories and extant moralities. I try to show, abstractly considered, how our actual morality could correct itself by WRE and get into reflective equilibrium and that doing so, if it were to occur, would be a very good thing. Whether it will or not, I do not attempt to say, though I do argue (consider here my defense of historical materialism, something Hart completely ignores) that our society actually has the material resources and intellectual resources for it to be the case, if they were reasonably developed over a period of time, that it could come to have a morality in some reasonable approximation to WRE. But what is even more vital to see is that we have a conceptual model here for assessing moralities or moral theories that makes no appeal to any foundationalist conceptions, classical or modest, or to synthetic *a priori* moral principles or anything like that. Yet it, as well as more rationalistic methods (Sidgwick's for example), is used to try to defeat relativism and subjectivism in ethical theory.

WRE and Elitism
Hart contrasts my appeal to unconstrained discourse with Rorty's appeal to the conversation of mankind and finds my account more constraining and elitist than Rorty's. But this is like comparing apples and oranges: the respective conceptions play different roles in our accounts. I try to show what conditions should be met to gain discourse which is as distortion-free as possible. I say that if the discourses were philosophically and scientifically sophisticated they would, *ceteris paribus,* be in a better position to engage in such discourse. This is not to make the antidemocratic and elitist political judgment that only such persons should be listened to, have a say in society, have full rights, be participants in social argumentation and the like. I make it plain enough that I am utterly opposed to all such elitist and reactionary demands. What I am saying is quite a different thing, namely that for an agent who wants to throw off the shackles of ideology and see the world as clearly as possible, scientific *and* philosophical sophistication are very important.

With only one, or even more so with neither, one is very likely to go astray: to be led down the garden path by ideology. We, in any event, are all very ideology prone, but ignorance here makes us even more at risk. Ideology is a very pervasive thing in our lives.

WRE and Rorty's conversation of mankind are on different logical levels. WRE is a particular move *within* that conversation and when we ask for a justification for WRE itself it would in some considerable measure at least be done by engaging in such Rortyian conversation. (For a justification of any matter, hard scientific experiments, mathematical calculations and formal logical calculations aside, we have to rely finally on such a conversation. It is our highest meta-language so to speak.) How much objectivity will be or can be achieved here will depend on how the conversation goes or can go. (Here theory and practice interact.) If it goes in a Habermasian or Rawlsian direction there will be the hope of attaining some reasonable objectivity. If, instead, it goes in a Derridian direction there will be very little hope for showing that our discourses can come to have much in the way of objectivity. If my arguments for historical materialism, for WRE and concerning undistorted discourse are near to the mark, we can hope in optimal circumstances for a not inconsiderable measure of objectivity in the discussion of human affairs. I do not (*pace* Hart) shut others out of arguments for it but set them forth for all and sundry to study and assess.

Proselytizing

Hart sees me as in a self-deceived way unwittingly doing a bit of proselytizing. He takes me to be demanding that people adopt an Enlightenment perspective as adumberated by critical theory. But I am not *demanding* anything. I characterize my version of critical theory and set forth its rationale and respond to criticisms and queries about it. Like any other intellectual construction, I set it afoot in the intellectual world to see what, if anything, will be made of it in the varied and diverse conversations of humankind. This is just the opposite of a proselytizing set of demands thrust on people. Rather, following the vocation of an intellectual, I set forth a cluster of considerations for the reflective consideration of people; they are considerations for them to take or leave as their reflective judgments move them.

Universality and Incommensurability

There are differences between people, differences between ways of life and systems of morality that may be non-benign or at least have different momentous consequences. There have been not a few who have thought that some of the most significant differences here rest on incommensurabilities that cannot even in principle be reasoned out. That is, the belief is, we cannot reason through to a sound judgment about who is right and who is wrong in such matters. It isn't, the claim goes, that reason is wanton here but that it is simply helpless. (This, or course, does not mean that it is helpless in all contexts.)

Hart too hopes that we are not just faced at crucial junctures in life with arbitrary incommensurable differences. He shares my wish for a normative universality but, as we have seen, he thinks I pursue the search in too rationalistic a way. Hart strangely wants to honor what he calls "the combination of rational agreement with incommensruable perspective" (v. 54). It is unclear what he has in mind here but it is clear that he thinks that in the divisions which actually divide us in our "postmodern situation" we have irreducible elements of incommensurability along with agreement (v. 48/49, 54/55). But, he also clearly thinks, that the rational agreements that we have or can achieve will not be sufficient to overcome these elements of incommensurability. Where we have genuine incommensurability we have untranslatability and we thus have differences which of their very nature cannot be argued out or deliberated out. Indeed, since untranslatability is involved, they cannot be both mutually identified and compared. Hart thinks that I mistakenly reject this whole conception of incommensurability as a pseudo-problem. In effect, he appears to be using what I reject.

His way of facing what he takes to be the problem of incommensurability is to come to see how we can share "commensurable universals through reason, contextualized by incommensurable perspectives" (v. 55). All of us, he would have

90

it, pin our "hopes on many incommensurable grounds" (v. 55). We all behave, but by way of self-deception, non-relativistically about our own incommensurable perspective. But, all the same, there is no way to establish the non-relativistic position of such perspectives. We, he seems at least to be giving us to understand, just have this multiplicity of incommensurable perspectives with no way of establishing one or another as "the true perspective" or even as a more adequate perspective, though we all *feel* ethnocentrically our own perspective to be the most adequate. All we can do is take one or another perspective on trust and make or keep it as our own. We subscribe to it but we do not, and cannot, know it to be true. We cannot even, in an appropriately objective sense, have a justified belief that it is true. This is our modern predicament. Reason cannot be king here; it cannot be the arbiter of such fundamental perspectives; we only have stark Kierkegaardian arbitrary choice and commitment.

I want now to argue that we need not face such stark existential predicaments where human reflection and deliberation are helpless or, more modestly, that, if finally at the end of the day we do just have to choose, it is not because, as Hart claims (and here he is not alone), that we just have these incommensurable perspectives from which, when push comes to shove, we must just choose. (When we interject "finally" it becomes, of course, very unclear what we are saying. There may be no "finally" anymore than there is "a *last* word.") I want to argue that the very idea of incommensurable perspectives and its cousin, conceptual relativism, with its incommensurable conceptual schemes, is incoherent. I shall do this, borrowing a leaf from Donald Davidson, simply by straightforward analytical arguments, along with the making of a few utterly unproblematic empirical assumptions. I shall not appeal in so arguing to such possibly problematic conceptions as WRE and Critical Theory. If my arguments are sound, Hart's problem about incommensurable perspectives is simply a non-starter.

Incommensurability and Translation
Claims about indeterminacy of reference have sometimes occasioned forms of relativism or of idealism that should be

91

looked at with a not inconsiderable amount of skepticism. Given Putnam-type arguments about word-world connections, some have thought (though not Putnam himself) that we should conclude that truth is relative to a scheme of thought. People, and particularly different peoples, the account goes, have various visions and versions of the world. Indeed the world, on such accounts, is such a noumenal object that perhaps we have (if that makes sense) just versions *sans phrase*. But this plainly is an implicit *reductio*. That there are sticks, stones and bits of earth around is not something that is mind-dependent or depends for its being the case on the adoption of a conceptual scheme or framework or the like. These realities are not a matter of our devising, though just how we classify them is. (One can see here the slippery slope to the noumenal world.) That there are, will be or could be, cognizers capable of conceptualizing and cognizing such phenomena has no bearing on its being true that there are sticks, stones and bits of earth around. (They are just there to be discovered.) It is plainly more reasonable to believe this than to believe *any* philosophical claim, no matter how carefully argued, that would deny it. If a philosophical claim (to adapt G.E. Moore) is incompatible with its truth, then the philosophical claim should be rejected or at least revised until it is compatible with its truth. Whatever we may want to say about metaphysical realism, this common sense realism is perfectly firm and quite unproblematic.[17] If a skepticism or a relativism purporting to counter this is pushed to such an extreme as to try to deny this, it thereby begins to reveal its absurdity.

While these Moore-like moves rid us of idealism and global skepticism, they will not suffice to rid us of more local skepticisms or of all forms of relativism. (It may very well not be desirable to be rid of all such skepticisms or relativisms. Religious skepticism is only the most obvious case.) If, facing more modest and less global forms of skepticism, we do not accept foundationalism of even a modest sort, are we thereby caught in a form of relativism? I do not think that it is obvious that we are. Here we can perhaps take a page or two from Donald Davidson.[18] Perhaps we can soundly reject relativism (at least in its non-benign forms) without being foundationalists of any sort. Davidson famously has denied that it even makes sense to speak of alternative realities or perspectives, each with their own truths untranslatable into another way of thinking. The literal meaning of sentences is given by their truth-conditions. To know the truth-conditions of a sentence, an utterance, thought or thought-event is to know the conditions under which it would be true or false. The sentence "The eraser is on the table" is true if and only if the eraser is on the table. But in doing this we do not compare that sentence or any other sentence with the eraser being on the table. Rather Davidson, like Quine, is much more holistic. Our sentences are part of a web of sentences whose truth-conditions depend on one another.

How does this bear on the rejection of the claim that truth is relative to a scheme of thought and to the related claim that there are some others (perhaps in a different culture) who have a different version of the world with alien concepts that can have no place in our lives but which are still no worse for all of that but which, being untranslatable into our scheme of things, are incommensurable with our views? (Indeed "incommensurability," if it has any tolerably clear meaning at all, just comes to "untranslatability.")

Davidson responds that there is no good reason for accepting claims of incommensurability or untranslatability either complete or partial. We come to understand the languages of others, including people from very different cultures, with very different languages, in basically the same way we come to understand our own language, namely by systematically coming to understand the truth-conditions of the sentences in the language in question. To understand the language of another is to follow a systematic method for generating the truth-conditions of her declarative sentences. If I am a field linguist and I profess to understand the language of another society, I match their sentences with our truth-conditions. I understand the German sentence *Schnee ist weiss* if I know it is true if and only if snow is white. What I am doing here, acting as a field linguist, is to propose in our language an account of truth for their language by proposing a systematic set of hypotheses, of which this hypothesis is simply one, concerning the truth-conditions

93

of various sentences in their language.

That sounds commonsensical and straightforward enough but how can we be confident, say if the people we are studying are Azande or Doubuans, that they do not have a scheme of thought *wholly* alien from our own, a scheme untranslatable into our own language? Davidson asserts, again famously and at least initially surprisingly, that we cannot attribute a *wholly* alien scheme of thought to an *articulate* people.

This claim of Davidson's is a remarkable claim in any event and indeed if true a very important one. Is it just a sophisticated form of footstamping on Davidson's part? And, if not, what are his arguments here, and are they sound? Or can sound arguments be teased out of the core of what he says?

For starters, though important starters, as different as people are in various culturally specific ways, it is perfectly evident that there is at a certain level of abstraction a common human nature.[19] All peoples have beliefs and desires and have a language which they use. Given all this—things which are evident as evident can be—we are perfectly justified in attributing to other people in other tribes a massive number of mundane beliefs and concerns which run together with ours. They (that is all statistically normal people in all societies), like us, see the rain coming and hear the wind and feel the rain on them and the sun warming their skin. They too believe they need water to drink, food to eat, that they require upon occasion rest, need upon occasion to defecate, that they will have young and that the young for a time need to be cared for to survive (even the IK believed that), that there is such a thing as its getting dark and its getting light and on and on. We can so list beliefs (commonplace beliefs) in massive numbers and in an indefinitely extended number of ways.

That these beliefs are true, that these things are so, is as plain as anything can be. If we know anything at all we know these things and that we do not know anything at all, to put it minimally, is vastly less evident than that we know these things. (Here we have Moore again.) Moreover, we not only know that all people have these beliefs, we know these beliefs are true or (if that is too strong) at least we know it is more reasonable to believe that they are true than to believe *any* philosophical

94

theory or account or any other kind of theory that would deny that we can know these things to be true or (if that is also too strong) that would deny that we are justified in believing them to be true. (Here G.E. Moore—though some say he was only copying Locke—made, or at least should have made, a permanent difference to philosophy. If we take Moore seriously— think carefully through what he says and then take it to heart— we cannot go on doing things in the old way.[20] We will either stop doing philosophy altogether, something Wittgenstein would approve of, or philosophy will be radically transformed.)

If we do not assume such Davidsonian things about other tribes with radically different languages (as well as tribes nearer to home, including our own) we could not even understand what it is for them to have a language for us to try to interpret or understand, for if we did not make such assumptions we could not match their utterances with our truth-conditions. For the literal meaning of an utterance is given by its truth-conditions. Thus, if I walk up to a high mountain stream with a person from an alien culture whose language I do not understand and I see him put his foot in the stream and then, as he quickly pulls it out, I hear him utter a set of sounds I can reasonably conclude (though surely not with any great confidence) that he is saying in making those noises something like "The water is cold." He may, of course, not be; he might have been saying instead "I don't like its feel," "It feels funny," "It tingles," "Shit!" or any of a rather limited range of things. In the light of other things he utters and other things he does I could correct my original hypothesis (if I am systematic and persistent enough) until I can be reasonably confident that I have a correct translation. (Remember fallibilism is the name of the game.) Our sentences, as I have remarked, following Davidson and Quine, are part of a web of sentences whose truth-conditions depend one on another. The identifying of truth-conditions doesn't simply go one by one. But my initial hypothesis about what he would be saying in such a circumstance is very likely right and we can correct it or refine it by utilizing the coherentist method of reflective equilibrium. (This could, very well, include abandoning my original hypothesis for another one.)

95

It is, of course, *logically* possible that his utterance could have meant "God speaks to me" or even something more plainly nonsensical such as "Water speaks harshly" or any of a considerable number of odd things (sensible or otherwise). (We see here, once again, of what little interest *mere* logical possibilities are. This should chasten us about the demand for proofs.)

However, if the field linguist gives such an exotic reading to all or even most of his informant's utterances, given our common situation in the world and our common human nature (having beliefs, desires, intentions, needs and interests), we have the best of reasons for thinking the field linguist has mistranslated at least most of the utterances. (Natives *sometimes* say exotic things but then sometimes so do we as well, for example, talk of God; but these are very much the exception.) It makes no sense, to repeat Davidson again, to attribute a *wholly alien* scheme of thought to an *articulate* people. If we tried to we could not even identify it as "a scheme of thought" or as "a language;" we can have no understanding of it (if such it be) such that we could say coherently that it is alien, if all the utterances or even the great mass of the utterances, were "translated" in ways that made no sense to us or did not run together with a not inconsiderable portion of the great mass of our commonplace beliefs. (*Perhaps* that is overstated but then a more moderate replacement will do. We should not look for an algorithm here.)

To have an understanding between different cultures we must have such bridgehead beliefs and they must be reasonably extensive.[21] And (their theories to the contrary notwithstanding), as a matter of fact, as even Edward Sapir and Benjamin Lee Whorf believed, there is cross-cultural understanding and there are, at least as a matter of fact, no untranslatable languages and thus, popular intellectual culture to the contrary notwithstanding, there is at least no global incommensurability either.

What makes us go wrong here and fly in the face of common sense and our actual human and anthropological practice of cross-cultural understanding is adherence to a deeply beguiling and deeply culturally embedded (at least in intellectual circles) basically Kantian conception, a conception that has its hold on both Alvin Goldman and Hilary Putnam, as well as on Nelson

Goodman, namely what Davidson calls the dogma of scheme and reality.[22] As part of an ancient philosophical tradition, it sets mind, thoughts, thought-events, words, utterances, cognizers and reactors (somehow magically) apart from the world—as if they were not part of the world—and then worries about how to get them with their conceptual schemes back together again with the world. The tides of metaphysics are running high again. The picture which is beguiling us, a picture Davidson thinks, correctly I believe, is incoherent, is basically the idea that there is a given unconceptualized reality and then there are various human schemes for perspicuously presenting (displaying) this reality by carving it up or categorizing it in different ways. What tempts us to think it makes sense to go in this way—that indeed we must go in this way—is a comparison with literal (actual) maps with their different ways of mapping the earth. We have stereographic maps and Mercator maps, etc. These projections do give us contrasting ways of mapping the earth. But there is nothing untoward here or conceptually problematic, for we simply have different methods for mapping an *independently identifiable earth.* But in the wide ranging Kantian picture of scheme and reality (scheme and content) there is, as the account stresses, no way of independently identifying "the reality." There is no possibility of standing outside one or another of these conceptual schemes and identifying the reality we are talking about. Unlike maps these putative conceptual schemes are utterly ubiquitous. We are, the narrative has it, in a kind of linguacentric predicament. This is not at all the case with the literal mapping of the earth. There we have independent access to both the map and earth but this is not and cannot be the case with scheme and reality. Once this is seen and firmly taken to heart we should recognize that there is nothing to the scheme and reality conception and the picture should no longer entrap us. (Here we need Wittgensteinian therapy, not a new metaphysics.)

Freed from this beguiling philosophical picture, we simply work, in the way I have described with our own language, with the languages of other cultures by ascertaining as best we can the truth-conditions of their sentences in a systematic way, taking those sentences as a part of a web of sentences whose truth-conditions depend on one another. We make hypotheses in our language about sentences in the alien language. We do not try to get below the level of truth-conditions for sentences to how individual words refer. Reference *may* be inscrutable. The problem posed by Putnam about the relativity or at least the indeterminateness of reference that bedevils all forms of foundationalism is not a problem here. We do not have with such a Davidsonian approach a building block method where we are trying to show for individual sentences (some of which are supposed to express basic propositions) how the basic individual sentences correspond to the world: the world just being something which contains fact-like entities, there like trees to be discovered. The kind of objectivity we achieve is not achieved in this foundationalist way or is not of a foundationalist sort. Rather, the objectivity comes to a way of seeing how the sentences of a natural language hang together as part of a web of belief whose truth-conditions are in a parallel way mutually dependent. In understanding someone from an alien culture or another person from our own culture or even in understanding ourselves, we, by our own lights—the only lights, as Hacking well puts it, we can have—arrange the beliefs, desires and utterances of others (from our own tribe or from another) into as coherent a bundle as we can get.[23] (This does not mean, however, that over time "our lights" cannot change; but at a given time, and necessarily and trivially, our lights are what they are and not another thing.)

When it is another language of an alien belief-system that is in question, we have good reason to believe we have correctly interpreted it when we have got the sentences, desires and beliefs into a coherent set. Where it is our own belief or our own belief-system, we are justified in believing the belief or belief-system to be true to the extent that we have shown it is maximally coherent. (Justification is clearly something that admits of degrees.) We are *not* in so speaking saying truth is coherence or is what is maximally coherent; "The eraser is on the table" is true if and only if the eraser is on the table, "The pencil is yellow" is true if and only if the pencil is yellow and so on. (This is one of the virtues of the disquotational theory.) But to so regard things need not come to believing that truth is a property of any kind and it need not assume *any analysis of truth at all.* It could very well take "truth" as primitive. But we *are* saying that it is coherence and perhaps something else *as well,* say experience embedded in a web of belief, that *justifies* an ascription of truth to a belief, utterance, thought or sentence. But we need not try to state or search for any set of foundational beliefs or basic propositions which must be true in a correspondence sense (weak or otherwise) and on which all other beliefs must be based if they are to be justified beliefs.[24]

Global and Local Relativism

This may all be so and yet it may not have solved problems about local skepticisms or relativisms. For such Davidsonian moves may very well block *global* skepticism without appeal to foundationalist epistemology or perhaps to any epistemology at all, but not block, or evidently block, more *local* skepticisms or *local* relativisms. Let me explain. Someone might say about such mundane, utterly commonplace, bridgehead beliefs that it is true that we must assume such cross-cultural general agreement, if cross-cultural communication is to be possible. (And remember crosscultural communication does in fact extensively occur.) But we cannot reasonably assume such consensus about scientific beliefs, political beliefs, some moral beliefs, beliefs about religion and a host of really crucial beliefs. The fit between the bridgehead beliefs and the more exotic beliefs is not so tight that with these bridgehead beliefs we must have a given set of religious or irreligious beliefs or other exotica.

Now it should be no difficulty for the underlying rationale (as distinct from the letter) of Davidson's account if there is divergence, intraculturally and sometimes interculturally as well, in the more exotic beliefs; or if (*if* indeed there is) nontranslatability of some of the theoretical concepts of some societies, such as the concepts mass or fields of force, extant in the scientific community of our society. In that case we have partially distinct conceptual systems, but not the "different worlds" that give the scheme/content dualism metaphysical bite. Davidson does not say all beliefs are unproblematic, only the great mass of commonplace beliefs, and then not all of them. Azande belief in witchcraft and North American belief in God

99

are, to understate it, pretty strange and pretty problematic, and they are only some of the more obvious examples of a plethora of strange beliefs that circulate in the various tribes of the world (including, of course, our own). We should beware (to understate it) of principles of charity here which seek an interpretation of "Matter is infinite evil and mind is infinite goodness" (to paraphrase Mary Baker Eddy) or even of (to use something presently in wider currency) "God created the heavens and the earth" or "History has an end" which makes such sentences come out true. Between foreign beliefs and our own we may rightly assume that in commonplace matters they come out pretty much the same as ours or so close to being the same as to make no difference and that these beliefs are generally true. But about a host of speculative and ideological matters there is, as Hacking puts it, "difference aplenty."[25]

It may be, as Davidson believes, that in every natural language we can find structures of first order logic that we can use in the proofs of Tarskian T-sentences so that every language (everything that is to be counted as a language?) will have an underlying logic identical to our own.[26] But, even so, do we have a translation manual that will get us and others to the more *recherche* beliefs in our language or any language so that we could assess whether they are sensible or nonsensical or (once that is settled) true or false? We can perhaps develop a theory here as a *horizontal* extension of an account of truth for structures of first-order logic. This extended theory will perhaps have sufficient structure to give us rulings on the more *recherche* beliefs or at least some of them. A Davidsonian hope (though I do not know if it is Davidson's himself) is that, given the immense agreement about mundane matters that actually obtains (that is agreement about what is true and false here), once there is translatability of simple sentences in which this agreement obtains, "then the recursive generation of truth-conditions for more complex sentences will enforce such a uniform method of translation that the spectres of incommensurability and indeterminacy will vanish in the dawn of a thoroughly worked out theory of truth."[27] This is an interesting and not implausible speculative (though empirically disciplined) possibility, but it is hardly luddite to be skeptical of such a grand holism, given the

100

multiplicity and complexity of social practices and their related language-games and the at least seemingly very different styles of reasoning that not infrequently go with them.[28] In such situations it appears at least to be the case that we have rather more localized social epistemic authorities, though appearances here *may* be deceiving.

Incommensurability and Perspectives
The above may, in effect, provide some sense for Hart's dark but suggestive saying that what we need is "the combination of rational agreement with incommensurable perspective" (v. 75). (Why, by the way, do we need it?) That is to say—giving Hart's claim a reading—within a culture, and between cultures as well, the great mass of beliefs are commensurable, but within each culture and each sub-culture there are some *recherche* beliefs which are incommensurable at least to those outside the sub-culture or culture. A cluster of such connected beliefs forms, the claim goes, a distinctive incommensurable perspective.

What is the likelihood of this being so? Is this just, in effect, an obscurantist evasion? We do know (as an empirical fact) from anthropological research that no cultures have been so opaque to us (that is to the dominant Western culture) that we have not learned to translate their languages. If it is responded that sometimes we *really* cannot understand the sentences of another tribe, though we can match up some truth-conditions, we must beware of the deployment here of an implicit persuasive definition of "understand." If we can match up truth-conditions in the way we have specified above, we have plainly achieved some cross-cultural understanding, though perhaps we do not have all the nuance that we would desire. Nonetheless, we have the conceptual materials to build from our cruder understanding to a more sophisticated one. We have no grounds for thinking we are simply blocked here. At any given time there may be some sentences in language A (say Dinka) that we have not yet found English translations of (let us call it language B), but that is no reason for thinking these Dinka sentences are untranslatable, particularly given the extensive track record of successful translations of languages of the various tribes of the world. Incommensurability comes to untranslatability but we do not have any

101

good evidence that any sentence in any language is untranslatable. So the grounds for there being incommensurable perspectives looks at least to be pretty thin. (There is also the puzzle about how, if there were, it could ever be discovered?) Let us look at an example from within English itself that is of special interest to the argument between myself and Hart. Among English speakers we have a subgroup (perhaps rather small) who think that non-anthropomorphic God-talk (in English or any other language) is incoherent and a group (rather larger) who think it is not, though it is, they stress, talk of an Ultimate Mystery that we can only very inadequately comprehend. (We can, though a bit exaggeratedly, speak here of two sub-cultures in a common culture.) Let us see if it is plausible to claim that though there are a massive number of connected commensurable beliefs that they share, they still have very different, possibly incommensurable beliefs and perspectives in or over religion. Let us see if it is plausible to believe that these beliefs and perspectives are incommensurable. In standard Judeo-Christian discourse God is said to be eternal. Even the atheist who thinks that the concept of God is incoherent understands the following bit of syntax and bits of syntax like it. "If God is eternal then God could not have come into existence or cease to exist and the question 'Who made God?' is senseless, for anything that could be made would not be God." Such atheists and believers, as the above remarks show, do not occupy incommensurable perspectives for they both grasp at least some common part of the logic of God-talk. Now consider "God is an infinite personal and loving individual utterly transcendent to the world yet active in the world." An atheist will say that this shows, if that is a genuine bit if God-talk and if "infinite," "individual," "transcendent" and "active in the world" are used in anything like their standard uses, that the very concept of God is incoherent, for nothing can be "infinite and an individual" or "utterly transcendent to the world and still active in the world." (A being utterly transcendent to the world cannot—logically cannot—have causal effects in the world.) The believer can acknowledge that and still respond that there are metaphorical uses of God-talk or special uses which actually are the actual uses when such religious/theo-

102

logical conceptions are actually employed in religious discourses. The atheist can in turn ask what they are metaphors of and press, when that is the example, for an accounting of whether the utterance (given such metaphorical uses of God-talk) can continue to have its appropriate religious significance. (We need, if we are to take a religious perspective, to be on guard against religion being—particularly when under attack—construed simply as morality touched with emotion.) If, alternatively, the sense is said to be special, the atheist can ask for an elucidation of that and for the point of the special use. If the believer in turn can say nothing, then the question of whether "special" has any sense or point in this context comes trippingly on the tongue. At issue is whether that concept of God is really incoherent or alternatively an appropriately and unavoidably stumbling way of speaking of a partly incomprehensible Ultimate Mystery.

Whether there is or can be closure of argument here or, if so, which way the closure appropriately goes, is not for me to try to show here, though I have in detail argued about it elsewhere. But what this discussion is further evidence for is that there is no incommensurability here. Christians and atheists are not locked into incommensurable perspectives incapable of reasoning and deliberating with each other over this. It is sometimes said that they are conceptually imprisoned because the issue cannot intelligibly arise, because of incommensurability, as to which party is closer to seeing things like they are.[29] But there are no sound arguments for believing this paradoxical claim to be true. Talk about "incommensurable perspectives" or "incommensurable framework beliefs" may be an unwitting evasion for some religious thinkers who so stress incommensurability. Also an implicit ideological defense of religion rests on holding that there are incommensurable perspectives which just must be acknowledged. Moreover, on such an account, they are taken to be beliefs that once acknowledged, and even superficially dwelt on, are beliefs that will make us aware that there is a lesser scope for reason than Enlightenment rationalists recognize. My response to that is that global incommensurability is an incoherent conception and that there are no sound reasons for believing that more local incommensurabilities actually obtain.

NOTES

[1]Kai Nielsen, "Can There be Progress in Philosophy?" *Metaphilosophy* 18:1 (January 1987), 1-30 and Kai Nielsen, "Scientism, Pragmatism, and the Fate of Philosophy," *Inquiry* 29:3 (1986), 277-304.

[2]Richard Rorty, "The Priority of Democracy to Philosophy" in Merrill Petersen and Robert Vaughan (eds.), *The Virginia Statute For Religious Freedom* (Cambridge, England: Cambridge University Press, 1988), 257-282, and Richard Rorty, "Pragmatism, Davidson and Truth" in Ernest LePore (ed.), *Truth and Interpretation* (Oxford, England: Basil Blackwell, 1986) 333-355.

[3]Kai Nielsen, "Philosophy as Critical Theory," *Proceedings and Addresses of the American Philosophical Association* Supplement to Volume 61, Number 1 (September, 1987), 104-108.

[4]Kai Nielsen, "Linguistic Philosophy and 'The Meaning of Life'" in E.D. Klemke (ed), *The Meaning of Life* (New York: Oxford University Press, 1981), 177-203.

[5]Hendrik Hart, "Can Nielsen Escape Both God and Rorty?" chapter 2 in this volume. All my references to Hart in this chapter will be to chapter 2.

[6]Kai Nielsen, "Searching for an Emancipatory Perspective: Wide Reflective Equilibrium and the Hermeneutical Circle" in Evan Simpson (ed.), *Anti-Foundationalism and Practical Reasoning* (Edmonton: Academic Printing and Publishing, 1987), 143-164 and Kai Nielsen, "In Defense of Wide Reflective Equilibrium" in Douglas Odegard (ed.), *Ethics and Justification* (Edmonton: Academic Printing and Publishing, 1988), 19-37.

[7]Kai Nielsen, "Philosophy as Critical Theory" and Nielsen, "On Transforming Philosophy," *The Dalhousie Review* 67:4 (1989), 439-56. See, as well, the references in note 6.

[8]See my references in note 2.

[9]See references in notes 1, 3, 5, 7 and see as well my "On Sticking with Considered Judgments in Wide Reflective Equilibrium," *Philosophia Tidsskrift for Filosofi* 13:3/4 (1985), 316-21. The references in note 6 are probably the most central here.

[10]David Braybrooke, *Meeting Needs* (Princeton, NJ: Princeton University Press, 1987).

[11]Richard Rorty, *Consequences of Pragmatism* (Minneapolis, MN: University of Minnesota Press, 1982), "Introduction," and Nielsen, "How to be Skeptical About Philosophy," *Philosophy* 61:235 (January, 1986), 83-93, and Nielsen, "Rorty and the Selflmage of Philosophy," *International Studies in Philosophy* XVIII:1 (1986), 19-28.

[12]Some of them are reprinted in my *Why Be Moral?* (Buffalo, NY: Prometheus Press, 1989), 39-122. See also the references in note 14.

[13]Ibid.

[14]Kai Nielsen, "On the Diversity of Moral Beliefs," *Cultural Hermeneutics* 2 (1974); Kai Nielsen, "On the Doing of Moral Philosophy,"

Reason Papers 1 (Fall, 1974); and Kai Nielsen, "The Embeddedness of Conceptual Relativism," *Dialogos* (1977).
[15]Kai Nielsen, *Marxism and the Moral Point of View* (Boulder, CO: Westview Press, 1989), 6-12.
[16]Kai Nielsen, "Can there be Progress in Philosophy?", Nielsen, "Scientism, Pragmatism and the Fate of Philosophy," and Nielsen, "Philosophy as Critical Theory."
[17]G.E. Moore, *Philosophical Papers* (London: George Allen and Unwin, 1959), 32-59, 127-150, 227-251. Of Moore's many commentators, Arthur E. Murphy has best brought out the *general import* of Moore's work here. See Arthur E. Murphy, "Moore's 'Defense of Common Sense'" in P.A. Schilpp (ed.), *The Philosophy of G.E. Moore* (New York: Tudor Publishing, 1942), 301-317.
[18]Donald Davidson, *Inquiries Into Truth and Interpretation* (Oxford, England: Clarendon Press, 1984), 183-241 and his "A Coherence Theory of Truth and Knowledge" and his "Empirical Content" both in Ernest LePore (ed.), *Truth and Interpretation*, (Oxford, England: Basil Blackwell,1986), 307-332.
[19]Norman Geras, *Marx and Human Nature: A Refutation of a Legend* (London: New Left Books, 1983).
[20]See the references to Moore and Murphy in note 17.
[21]Steven Lukes, "Some Problems about Rationality" in Bryan R. Wilson (ed.), *Rationality* (Oxford: Basil Blackwell, 1970), 144-213, and "On the Social Determination of Truth" in Robin Horton and Ruth Finnegan (eds.), *Modes of Thought* (London: Faber and Faber, 1973), 230-248. Martin Hollis, "The Limits of Irrationality" and "Reason and Ritual" both in *Rationality* 214-220 and 221-239, respectively, and his "Witchcraft and Winchcraft," *Philosophy of the Social Sciences* 2 (1973), 89-103. Kai Nielsen, "Rationality and Relativism," *Philosophy of the Social Sciences* 4 (1974) and Kai Nielsen, "Rationality and Universality," *The Monist* 59:3 (July 1976), 441-54.
[22]Davidson, *Inquiries into Truth and Interpretation*, 183-198.
[23]Ian Hacking, "On the Frontier," *New York Review of Books* XXXI:20 (December 20, 1984), 54-8. For a perspicuous depiction of the varieties of objectivity, see Thomas Nagel, "The Limits of Objectivity," *The Tanner Lectures* Volume 1 (Salt Lake City, Utah: University of Utah Press, 1980), 77-139. The work of John Rawls and Norman Daniels extensively operates with this conception of objectivity. How we are not, all the same, trapped in an ethnocentrism here is brilliantly portrayed by Charles Taylor in *Philosophy and the Human Sciences*, 116-133.
[24]Richard Rorty, "Pragmatism, Davidson and Truth" in Ernest LePore (ed.), *Truth and Interpretation*, 333-355.
[25]Ian Hacking, *Why Does Language Matter to Philosophy?* (Cambridge, England: Cambridge University Press, 1975), 148.
[26]Ibid., 154.

[27]Ibid., 156.

[28]Ian Hacking, "Wittgenstein the Psychologist," *The New York Review of Books* XXIX (April 1, 1982), 42-44 and his "Styles of Scientific Reasoning" in John Rajchman and Cornell West (eds.), *Post-Analytic Philosophy* (New York: Columbia University Press, 1985), 145-164. Of course, *if*Davidson is proceeding purely *a priori*, as C.B. Martin thinks he is, then it is a metaphysical enterprise and, as Martin shows, a vulnerable one. But a Davidsonian account need not take such a high *a priori* road as it has not in my (possibly) scaled down formulation of it. But it is thereby also not metaphysical. Rorty remarks, significantly I think, "...the positivists were absolutely right in thinking it imperative to extirpate metaphysics, when 'metaphysics' means the attempt to give knowledge of what science cannot know." *Philosophy and the Mirror of Nature*, 384. (And this, note, from an opponent of scientism and from someone who regards logical positivism as, philosophically speaking, a reactionary movement.) Metaphysics (when it has a determinate sense that links it with The Tradition) wants to give us *a priori* knowledge of 'ultimate reality' or the underlying structure of the world or the basic 'categories of being.' But there is no such knowledge to be had and probably the very conception of gaining such knowledge is incoherent. The sad thing is that so very late in the day there are still philosophers around who want to be ontologically serious and do what, if it can be done at all, can only be done by science. Philosophers ought to either close up shop or turn to other things. C.B. Martin, "The New Cartesianism," *Pacific Philosophical Quarterly* 65 (1984), 236-258.

[29]For a neglected exchange that brings this out brilliantly, see the exchange between John Skorupski and Robin Horton. John Skorupski, "Science and Traditional Religious Thought I & II," *Philosophy of the Social Sciences* 3 (1973): 209-30. Robin Horton, "Paradox and Explanation: A Reply to Mr. Skorupski I," *Philosophy of the Social Sciences* 3 (1973): 231-56 and Robin Horton, "Paradox and Explanation: A Reply to Mr. Skorupski II," *Philosophy of the Social Sciences* 3 (1973): 281-312. Skorupski, "Comment on Professor Horton's 'Paradox and Explanation'," *Philosophy of the Social Sciences* 5.1 (1975): 63-70.

5. BLIND SPOTS IN NIELSEN'S FIELD OF VISION?
Hendrik Hart

A Philosopher of Vision

Although Nielsen formally launched his metaphilosophical reflection with his Presidential Address of 1984 to the Canadian Philosophical Association, it was not till he took his concerns to the American Philosophical Association in 1987 that he fully accepted Rorty's historicism and acknowledged that such historicism need not be interpreted as a relativism. From the start, however, he has linked his current discussions about the future of philosophy to his program for "considered judgments in wide reflective equilibrium" (WRE), referring to it as an "attractive consensus model of justification that will survive the death of foundationalism" (2:6). But only in his address on "Philosophy As Critical Theory" did he reveal to his colleagues in March of 1987 at the APA's Pacific Division panel on "The Future of Philosophy" in San Francisco that WRE could be worked out in a way that would shed all vestiges of realism and foundationalism. And with that move came an increase in the pace of writing on the current crisis in the philosophical tradition. Nevertheless, the devotion to reason and rationality remains so strong, and his denial of rationalism continues with such vigor, that I will attempt once again to find an entry into the Nielsen framework for my argument that even in the context of a thoroughly historicized WRE he still remains a rationalist.

It will be no surprise to students of his work that what he sees as the future of philosophy is closely allied to his own style. His version of critical philosophy as wide reflective equilibrium (WRE) is presented, justly so, as a humane, rational, comprehensive, normative, and open approach, and he recommends it for the future of the profession. Philosophy will, in Nielsen's view, have an honorable future if philosophers adopt this style.

107

I call this a visionary view of the future of philosophy. In 1984 Nielsen said that what it all would come to was "not clear" to him (2:9-10). By 1987, however, he is sure that the program is achievable (8:104). And the program, as I see it, is thoroughly rationalist. I admire the vision, I also have profound respect for the potential of the program. But I am leery that Nielsen is not aware of what to me appear as blindspots. I will focus on them in yet another attempt to understand the role of reason in Nielsen's thought. After I have made an atempt at showing what these blindspots are, I will argue that they affect the above-mentioned humane, rational, comprehensive, normative, and open dimensions of Nielsen's work.

The Enlightenment Background

Nielsen is not caught in the vicissitudes of a neutrality postulate for philosophy. He acknowledges that he represents one par-ticular tradition as well as a specific spiritual climate in which his version of that tradition is rooted. His tradition, which I just called visionary philosophy and to which he refers as the "folk conception" of philosophy (8:98), is as old as Plato and Au-gustine, and is powerfully present in moderns such as Dewey, Jaspers, and Marx, or renewed again in contemporaries like Habermas and Rorty. The spiritual climate which shapes this tradition is the Enlightenment. Thus he subscribes to a cultural commitment in which the millenia-old Western devotion to rationality surfaces in the emancipation from religion, tran-scendence, and revelation, in favor of placing the secularized hope of a naturalized humanity in reason.

A peculiar predicament of the Enlightenment, I believe, is its prejudice against prejudice. This prejudice, put differently, is its blindness to rational justification as a prejudice. Openly acknowledged prejudices can enlighten us. But the Enlightenment's denial of prejudice becomes a blindspot. I shall say no more about this except to point out that I subscribe here to Gadamer's analysis and critique (235-274). What I wish to discuss in this paper is Nielsen's awareness of the problem and his lack of success, as I see it, in finding a solution. I see it as a problem for Nielsen because, in my view, the prejudice against prejudice gives especially a philosopher of vision certain debilitating blindspots.

Nielsen acknowledges the existence of beliefs and opinions within the web of our beliefs to which we are deeply attached, of which we may not be so articulately aware, and which did not originate in critical reflection, though their influence on our positions may be strong. He speaks of them as "considered judgments" which he likens to "some 'prejudices' in Burke's sense" (8:102). They are "socialized into our marrow" (8:102). So far, Nielsen seems tolerant of prejudice. He also recognizes and rejects blindness to it. If foundationalism can be characterized by its unfounded assumptions, Nielsen rejects *its* "considered opinions" as false consciousness, because he detects an uncritical hiding from prejudice (8:92-95).

A foundationalist epistemology in the Enlightenment tradition would be one in which emancipation by rational criticism has its resources in rational certitudes, in beliefs whose simple empirical origins would make them immune to correction or whose conceptual self-evidence would make them infallible. These beliefs, the foundationalist tells us, we are rationally justified in holding as true without doubt. And whatever other beliefs we can bring forth from these eternal verities by infallible methods or can link to them by irrefutable evidence will qualify as truth. Nielsen rejects this outright. He identifies it as the current tradition in the profession. Talk about the combination of privileged foundations with privileged methods to bring about the full and true knowledge of the enlightened mind reminds Nielsen of "religious conversion" rhetoric (8:91-95). This characterization may be embarrassing, but Nielsen needs to expose it as "the deep underlying rationale of the tradition" (8:94).

Nielsen has lately begun to acknowledge "religious" traits in traditional philosophy. He has recognized it in the "quest for certainty" (17:214) as well as in "ontological commitments" (21:442). My intent in this essay is to discuss with Nielsen the possibility of such traits in the Enlightenment movement, in the entire rationality tradition (as described in Alasdair MacIntyre's *Whose Justice? Which Rationality?*), as well as in his own work. Since religion is irrational for Nielsen, it will not at first sight seem possible that the rationality tradition is religious as such. However, if the quest for certainty and ontological commitments have been constitutive for rationality in the West, the idea of religious rationality is not *apriori* ridiculous. At any rate, now that *he is using* "religious" in a sense *akin to my use* of it in the preceding pieces, attention can be focussed on whether or not Nielsen's views are religious *in that sense.*

His rejection of foundationalism, though clear and strong, is not necessarily a rejection of the prejudice against prejudice. It is possible that Nielsen has taken the matter of "prejudice" and its link to "the deep underlying rationale of the tradition" too narrowly. I will argue that some of his taboos remain closeted in WRE. Briefly, the matter is this. In the Enlightenment no belief is authorized unless its has been rationally justified. A belief judged acceptable *before* such justification is a *pre*-judgment. Someone who holds on to the validity of such beliefs has not been judicious or rational about what is acceptable. That sort of pre-enlightened darkness is what the Enlightenment calls prejudice.

. The core of the Enlightenment's program of emancipation is the rational purification of human belief. It is highly unlikely that such worthy causes as the emancipation of workers and women were at all in view in the Cartesian foundations of the Enlightenment. And in spite of Nielsen's laudable inclusion of these and other worthy causes in his quest for emancipation, there is every reason to think that the purification of belief remains the core of his emancipation as well. When Nielsen claims that counterfactual ideals of critical theory are worthy of our allegiance, he backs that up with important statements such as: "Certain attitudes are very difficult to sustain given an accurate, factual understanding of the world." And "modernity itself" in spite of being a "particular kind of culture" still "extensively wins out" in the clash of "belief systems" (10:22-23).

Nielsen's awareness in this area seems combined with undetected confusion. When he mentions "the *justifiability* question" as "the very *raison d'être* of epistemology" (8:94), it is not clear whether he rejects just the epistemological tradition, or also the preoccupation with justification. When he wonders whether the expression "rational justification" might be "pleo-

110

Blindspots in Nielsen's Field of Vision

nastic..." (8:99), it seems not only that he is committed to justification, but also to the belief that besides rational justification there is no valid justification. But that, I suggest, is a prejudice in the uncritical sense of prejudice. For such a judgment about rational justification is obviously vulnerable to all the self-referential incoherence arguments regarding foundationalism.

On closer examination Nielsen's *commitment* to rational justification appears beyond doubt. His critical theory as WRE stands or falls with it (18). He believes that rational justification is salvageable if it is purged of certainty and foundations (18:20). All that has changed, as far as I can see, is that the certainty and the foundations have become historicized. But once WRE puts them in place, they are as reliable as ever, for as long as they last. And underneath the temporarily reliable beliefs lies an everlasting source of undubitable certitude. There remains a sure foundation in "reflective ... commitments which will not be extinguished..." (8:22). Similar tensions can be found in Nielsen's on the one hand being doubtful about our ability "to speak of our human condition so monolithically" (16:410) and on the other hand not wanting to reject "the universalistic ideals of the Enlightenment" (9:388).

The tradition's "underlying rationale," I submit, is not only visible in its fundamentalist form of foundationalism, but rather in every manifestation of the Enlightenment's concept of our rational emancipation from prejudice. I see it present still in Rorty and Habermas. That we are justified only if rationally justified is a belief that cannot be rationally justified and is, therefore, in the Enlightenment's own sense, a prejudice. It is an unfounded, absolutized belief in rational autonomy. From time to time we see Nielsen worrying about this himself. "Perhaps I am too much a child of the enlightenment..." But as a true believer he comforts himself. "The above are indeed versions of enlightenment beliefs, but so what? What reasons do we have for believing that they are mistaken?" And in a very sober paragraph we see him wondering if he is "hankering" after all after a "philosophical fix" to such a degree that his usually "unextinguishable commitment" becomes a deflated: "But perhaps we humans will sometimes use our

111

collective good sense..." (16:410, 413, 415).

Someone may object that we are only talking about the rational justification of beliefs here and that no indication has been given that for Nielsen other actions or attitudes could not be otherwise justified, even if not rationally justified. Perhaps rational justification, if limited to beliefs, is not intended as ultimate or total justification. But this argument fails, because the Enlightenment sees beliefs as the sole or core content of knowledge, and truth and uses true belief as supernorm for the rest of culture. All other culture is submitted to the judgment of reason, which adds up to ultimatization, totalization, and absolutization. Nielsen in his official position rejects the tradition's "underlying intent ... to treat philosophy as foundational to the rest of culture" (17:221). There is no "strictly philosophical account that ... will enable us to make sense of our lives..." (21:447). But "the task of philosophy" remains "the pressing problems of life" (21:448). And reborn in critical theory as WRE it will chase "our reflective expectations and hopes ... in order to make sense of our lives..." (21:453).

So with respect to the recognition of prejudice, I read Nielsen's project as admitting that we start from prejudices, but saying also that we can work on them to become part of WRE and thereby to remove their prejudicial character. We may start with prejudice, we should end without it. It either disappears by being rejected as prejudice, or it becomes justified and then will be prejudice no longer. But no emnacipated person can remain stuck in prejudice. If we can filter prejudice rationally, that will domesticate it for universal acceptance in Nielsen's favorite environment, the modern world of educated people who are scientifically informed. He does not discuss the possibility that some knowledge is impossible without permanent prejudice, that is: without some prejudice impenetrable to rational criticism or rational justification. Hence he does not overtly entertain the possibility that the elimination of prejudice through WRE is itself a prejudice of a certain kind. He certainly does explore whether, just as foundationalism "hoists itself by its own petard...," (8: 92) so WRE may be pulling itself up by its own bootstraps. All the hopes that philosophy as foundationalism had are retained in every respect, because the "underlying rationale," *pace* Nielsen, is the unrelenting commitment to rational justification, the undying reflective hope. WRE is, in the final analysis, the self-legitimation of critical rationality, made possible by a fundamental prejudice in favor of critical rationality, which can itself neither be legitimated any further nor easily recognized as an uncritical prejudice. Nielsen's cautious fear that scientific method might not be self-correcting is *instantly* muffled with the (though equally cautious) hope that WRE might help us here. And there is no reflection at all on the possibility that scientific method and WRE are, *in principle*, twins (16:413/414). WRE appears to be nothing less than scientific method imported into the social sciences and via them becoming the universal standard for justifying human practices.

The difficulty in detecting the prejudice against prejudice by someone who has it, is that apparently it can only be recognized if you don't have it. From the point of view of the ultimacy of rational justification, every judgment that has not (yet) been so justified *can* only be characterized as prejudgment, as having come *before* rational judging, before legitimation or justification. If someone is committed to reason *as* supernorm, that commitment need not be treated as a judgment to be judged *by* that norm. Indeed, if it is norms that justify actions, to ask for a justification of any norm seems odd, because that is treating a norm as though it were itself such an action. But in that case acceptance of rationality as autonomous, totalizing, and ultimate norm is not the objective or justified outcome of a process of empirical theory building subject to rational justification. As Nielsen says, "...there are no firmer 'foundations' to be had over normative matters" than in WRE and its consensus (3:316). There remains an incredible optimism about transformed philosophy: "What then should philosophy, in seeking to transform itself, do?" The answers would put no traditional philosopher to shame (21:449-451). It is, ultimately, a choice, a commitment.

Acceptance of rationality *as* ultimate norm must precede any actual judgment *by* that norm. Acceptance of rationality as norm for judgment is, in that sense, an unavoidable pre-judgment acceptance. Yet the absolute, autonomous, ultimate, and totalizing character of this acceptance of rationality in the Enlightenment also makes it impossible to recognize the acceptance as a prejudice. The ultimacy of rationality makes anything a-rational in the field of ultimacy appear irrational and thus unacceptable. Nielsen's language here is in terms of *legitimacy* of belief, which will vindicate "the Enlightenment's ideal of emancipation" (10:17). Outside of those boundaries we speak of ideology and distortion. Predictably, the influence of that sort of faith has made Christian philosophers ask for centuries: is our faith reasonable? Equally predictably, that sort of "tension" as he calls it is also present in the bosom of Nielsen the Marxian (24:1).

The Enlightenment's typical quest for ultimacy is identified by Derrida as "the project of becoming God as the project constituting human-reality. Atheism," says Derrida, "changes nothing in this fundamental structure." And he aptly names the project, following Heidegger: "ontotheology" (132). The ultimization of rationality to get rid of the God's-eye view in fact raises a new god—*pace* Rorty's "without God or his doubles"—whose divine status is not recognized, not unlike the nakedness of a certain king without clothes. WRE seems dressed in provisionality, though rational consensus sits nakedly enthroned forever underneath. If this is not a classical divinity, it is in any case a functional double in the modern world.

Nielsen's Critical Theory as Wide Reflective Equilibrium
The Enlightenment prejudice can best be found in what I will call the *operant tradition* in Nielsen. This operant tradition is the position revealed in Nielsen's practices. It differs from what I call the *official tradition*, by which I mean the tradition which Nielsen rejects as foundationalist epistemology; and from what I call the *adopted position*, by which I mean the position which Nielsen openly embraces in WRE. The latter two are formulated and explicitly articulated. The former is hidden, though actively present as the Enlightenment prejudice in Nielsen's actual work. The operant tradition is a hidden leftover of the official tradition after Nielsen has rejected part of that tradition in his adopted position. An extensive analysis of these matters in this limited context is impossible. I will confine myself to

114

noting what might be called "rejection" words and "expecta-tion" words in Nielsen's 1987 text (8). I believe these add up to a rhetorical *rejection* of beliefs in the official tradition for reasons that seem equally applicable to other beliefs, embraced in the operant tradition, that are the basis for Nielsen's *hopes*.

Nielsen's essays on meta-philosophy exhibit a rhetoric of terms that signal a taboo to prejudice-wary Enlightenment believers in reason. Examples are easily found (my emphases). There is a reference to Alvin Plantinga who allows "such *tendentious* beliefs as 'God spoke to me...'" (8:92). Tarski's talk "of correspondence... is just a *mystification* ..." (8:93). Nielsen hopes we come to see "a representational model as a *myth* ..." (8:93). He asserts that the view of language "apart from the world to hook onto the world is a *weird* conception" (8:94). He appeals to "the *illusion* behind the tradition..." (8:95), and refers to the analytic tradition's "special expertise with con-cepts" as "a piece of philosophical *mythology*" (8:96). Sometimes it is even "just a *conceit*" (8:97). Nielsen is looking to be absolved from responsibility for "the taking of any epistemological or metaphysical position. We can be free of such *tendentious and arcane* matters" (8:104). "We can, in this way, reasonably avoid *existentialist high drama or Fideist plunking*" (8:104).

What these rhetorical rejections come to, I believe, is an appeal to rationally enlightened people to go for nothing except what is clear, open, grounded, argued, justified. By attaching certain negative terms to other positions these be-come automatically stereotyped—provided we first accept the appeal—as unclear, hidden, closed off, unfounded, fideist-type positions. They are, that is, stereotyped as not sufficiently rational on the assumption that everyone knows what *that*'s all about. Belief not formed within WRE is characterized as dis-torted, unemancipated ideology. Only within WRE will we be able to achieve non-relative, universal identity as human. The stakes are high indeed (see 9 and 10).

What is Nielsen after? Simply put: critical theory. And here is how he characterizes it. "Critical theory is a definite project of modernity, growing out of the Enlightenment" (8:100). What will it give us? "We can have an empirical-theoretical-cum-normative theory which can provide guidance in wrestling with the problems of life and which can help inform our understanding of who we are and who we might become" (8:104, see also 90, 98, 99). These expectations are descriptions of imaginings about what things could be like were WRE to come about. Critical theory is a *hope* expressed over and over *as* hope (See 21:453). But if a *theory*, properly a tool of understanding, becomes a culture's source of hope, we have shifted ground from reason to faith, from philosophy to religion.

Critical theory will, hopefully, and unlike the official tradition, not be or claim to be ahistorical or context independent, autonomous or absolute (8:95, 98, 101). It will not be overseer or arbiter of culture (8:95). It will not have the task of deciding between the rational and the irrational. (This has to be one of Nielsen's more mysterious claims, considering that rational justification is the aim and that the exclusion of distortions belongs to the program). In this regard Nielsen wants to "guard against ideological distortion" within critical theory (8:100). He also wants to avoid, though perhaps not every form, in any case "what is clearly some form of relativism" (8:102). But he seems to overlook the possibility that some characteristics of foundationalist positions may accrue to them *as* unavoidable characteristics of the Enlightenment prejudice. In that case, in abandoning foundationalism the "deep underlying rationale" may itself not yet have been abandoned. Rejection of foundationalism may not suffice to outrun the rational prejudice against prejudice in the Enlightenment. The *official tradition* may not have been fully excorcised in the *adopted position.* It is characteristic of Nielsen's powerful self-reflective openness that from time to time he intimates awareness of this. It is then also characteristic of the depth of his commitment here that he remains loyal to *reflective* hopes.

Nielsen does mention what the positive characteristics of WRE will be. It will be empirical (8:99), rigorous and argument-based (8:98), descriptive, explanatory, interpretive, and normative (8:99). It will "provide a comprehensive critique of culture and society and of ideology. In this way it will not only have both a descriptive-explanatory thrust and an interpretive side but a critically normative emancipatory thrust as well" (8:99). Its normativity will consist in "rational justification..."

(8:99). And though I have looked for it in Nielsen, I have not found any attempt to justify rational justification.

The hopes Nielsen has riding on this can be gleaned from the expectation words he attaches to critical theory (emphases mine). He wants to meet "our *reflective expectations* and *hopes"* (8:103). That will add up to a critical theory "to *make sense of our lives,* to see things as comprehensively and connectedly as we *reasonably* can and to *guide our conduct"* (8:103). This is what he believes is "the most *reasonable* thing to do" (8:90). Why? Because this will "transform philosophy into some form of critical social theory with an *emancipatory* intent" (8:90).

In summary: Nielsen wants to make life rational in the most reasonable way. If this is his position here, I doubt he has avoided what he wants to avoid. His rejection words may apply to his expectations. Let me give reasons for my doubt.

The Hidden Prejudices

The *operant* tradition within Nielsen's *adopted* position harbors a prejudice in favor of the ultimacy of reason. This introduces the arcane and mysterious into his thought, in spite of their unacceptability. Because he did not unravel the mystery of rational prejudice, reason is still the overlord he wants to avoid. Reason provides the norm for our actions (8:99), in spite of Nielsen's opposition to an epistemology with justification at the core of its being (8:94). The ultimacy of rational justification hides the lack of justification for this ultimacy. Hence the Enlightenment prejudice presents as a clarity what in fact is a mystery. And inside the mystery Nielsen's god's-eye views remain hidden to him. It is not easy to find an expression for "God" that has a chance of being recognized by Nielsen. But if I am right that in his Enlightenment faith our appropriately functioning reflective judgment is "judge of all, though judged by none," I would be quite satisfied with the divinity of reflective judgment.

The *official* tradition Nielsen rejects is the foundationalist *version* of his basic commitment to reason as rationality. But that *commitment* underlies his *adopted* position as the *operant* tradition. Things he rejects in the official tradition, however, such as its autonomy and absolutism, are features that cling to founda-

117

tionalism not as a *version* of commitment to rationality, but because of that *commitment itself*, underneath the foundationalist version of it. This is what Nielsen himself identified as "the deep underlying rationale" of the tradition (8:94). His rejection of the official tradition's claim that we will "finally come to know and to understand" what thus far "no one has ever been able to know and understand," namely how to live the right and the good life, is precisely what critical theory also promises (8:94). The commitment underneath is what functions as the operant tradition. Foundationalism and WRE as critical theory are *different versions* of the *same* "deep underlying rationale."

Nielsen's "deep underlying rationale" is the strong refusal to relativize rationality or reason. But then his opposition to autonomy and absolutes will not convince. His adopted position turns out to be precisely what he wants to avoid. It is an ideological distortion, a pursuit of absolutized and autonomous reason behind the relativization and de-autonomization of all else. What is arcane, mysterious, mythical, tendentious by the criteria of Nielsen's adopted position? Only whatever cannot withstand the scrutiny of critical theory, of the WRE version of an unconditional surrender to reason. Descriptions of the ideal speech situation give a good indication (9:385 and 10:17/18). Distorted and ideological become properties by definition of what is not within the bounds of critical theory. But whether whatever is rational is normative is not a matter open to question. The commitment to rationality is, therefore, not open, certainly not open ended. Many of the claims made for that commitment do not stand up to scrutiny.

So philosophy is still overlord. Admittedly overlord of society rather than the universe. But that's overlord enough (21:450). Reason is a mystery because its self-evident superiority makes it impervious to critical examination. It justifies everything, but itself needs no justification. My criticism here is not that for Nielsen philosophy or theory or our beliefs should be rational. I agree they should be. My agreement here goes very far indeed. All that Nielsen has to say about critical theory as WRE I find truly admirable. But only as origin of insight and understanding, perhaps even as source of widespread agreement; not as my only hope in life and death.

My criticism is that philosophy as critical theory becomes the origin of the normative framework for the good and happy life and thus the supreme test for life and culture, the individual and society. Religion can have no place in such a conception. But it is not recognized that by thus replacing the religious function, the devotion to reason is itself religious. *Reason and science,* we might say, improve our *understanding.* Quite differently, *faith and religion* fan the flames of *hope.* If we place our *hope* in *understanding*—and why should we—we have given it a religious function. In addition, such a move will lead to submitting all religion to the hopes of rationality.

But suppose reason were not to be final arbiter. How reasonable would it then be to demand that religion either be rational or be dismissed? The rational approach to experience is far from illegitimate. Science, theory, and philosophy are all endeavors that should be rational. But why religion? To ask that religion meet the same demands as a good theory is treating religion like a sort of competing theory, a competing account of things, a rival belief system. If religion were in fact a belief system, to demand that it be reasonable would itself be reasonable. However, the view of religion as belief system is a Christian perversion—due to its capitulation to rationality—of Biblical religion.

To demand of religion as a source of hope that it meet the criteria of critical theory makes as much sense as demanding that numbers be colored or spaces have weight. Space, number, color, and weight are properties of things. They are not things having such properties. Rationality and religiosity are also properties. Of course, *things* can be numbered, dimensional, of a certain weight, and a certain color *at the same time.* But these qualities of things do not themselves have these properties. Just so, *people* can be both religious and rational. And it makes sense to ask that religious people *simultaneously* be rational people. But to ask that their religion be rational makes less sense. Unless they make their rationality their hope. But then they should be willing to admit that there is no rational justification for this.

The hope that *persists* is religious. Fundamentally, that's all that religion is about. And only to believers in the hope of

119

rational judgment is this hope so rational that its element of hope is usually lost. And given all religions' tendency toward exclusivity, it is to be expected that a person committed to WRE will find only ideology and distortion outside of WRE. Nielsen, however, *expresses* the fruits of WRE as a *hope*. That, I believe, opens up conversation.

The Blindspots
I now wish to indicate how the hidden prejudice in favor of reason affects Nielsen's adopted position.

One. In spite of his deep desire to be humane, the operant tradition makes Nielsen's rhetoric elitist and excommunicative. There is an unqualified trust in the modern, rationally enlightened, educated, and scientifically informed sophisticate. The deep convictions of the majority of the human race are threatened with censorship by WRE. If not censored they are put down with a call to rational emancipation. Rationality here does not serve as a power for the unfolding and opening up of human experience, but as an enclosure, as a limit beyond which we dare not go. I think it is far from clear to Nielsen that when he suggests the route of rational consistency as a remedy for resolving our differences with other cultures (or for the present incompatible belief systems within our own culture?), the very idea of rational consistency may be the "central belief" that needs to be "modified or abandoned" to resolve the conflict (21:446).

"Beyond reason" is experienced as "beyond rescue," rather than seen as a possible expansion of legitimate experience or, more importantly, as a possible avenue of transcending the impoverishments of our reduced sense of reality due to the autonomy of reason. The actual human practices we are trying to emancipate are not themselves belief systems and cannot be reduced to them. As Hubert Dreyfus remarks, "the pragmatic background cannot be understood as a belief system" (17). And when we do try to objectify these practices into belief systems, the practice of doing that very thing is not itself open to propositional objectification. In the words of Dreyfus: "No science can objectify the skills which make it possible" (19). That holds for WRE as well.

120

Two. Nielsen's adopted position on what is rational becomes deeply problematic in the operant tradition. Either rationality is, when all is said and done, taken as logical-conceptual, as whatever can be inferentially justified, confined to Sellars' space of reasons, of logical possibilities. These reasons and possibilities will be conceptual-propositional, linked by inferential relations. This could never lead to real emancipation, but only to enclosure and confinement of the human spirit, because reality and human experience are only for a very small part propositional. And the road from propositions to and from whatever else is real is not itself propositional and does not need to be validated by rational standards interpreted as canons of logic. It appears that, at heart, rationality for Nielsen is logical, theoretical, conceptual. Perhaps not in his *adopted* position. But the *operant* terms are "rigorous, conceptually clear, argument based" (21:450), "rational consensus" (19:241), "canons of correct reasoning" (18:23). Rational coherence and rational consistency are, ultimately, matters of logic.

Eugene Lashchyk reports Einstein's persuasion that the relation between concepts and sensory input is "not of a logical nature" (155). Einstein believed concepts are "not derivable by ... [inferential] methods from experience," and he believed the same about "laws and axioms of theoretical systems" (156). All of this, if true, would leave large areas of human experience as trans-rational, given that we think of rationality as largely limited to inferential practices.

If, on the other hand, rationality is taken in a much wider sense, such as to include the orderly, the well-founded, the justified in more than an inferential way, the consistent, efficient, observed, and so forth, we need to ask the question: why *call* that rational? What *makes* that rational? How do all those apparently unconnected senses of rational get connected? The suspicion is strong that, in the final analysis, the wider sense will be nailed down under the surface by the narrower sense. Nielsen sometimes denies that rational equals logical. But he also denies that rational could be replaced by meaningful, sensible, acceptable in a wide sense (v. 36-39). Of course he does, because that would open what is reasonable to the

121

common sense of common people whose most significant criterion for meaning is some religious authority.

If the commitment to reason is in fact a prejudice, its unavoidable hidden nature will also obscure our understanding of what in fact we are committed to. It will not be exposed to self-critical examination. A defense limited to *explicit denials* will not be convincing unless it is accompanied by a different explanation than I have given of the *language quoted* from his writings. To me that language appears to indicate a different story.

Three. The scope of Nielsen's position gets regrettably reduced by being channeled through the filters of reason. The authentic nature of other people's positions, the contributions of other disciplines, and the meaning of other experience are at risk to be misinterpreted. Charles Taylor's view that the problems of the epistemological tradition are linked to moral and spiritual issues of our times and culture aims, I would think, at more than would be accessible within Nielsen's WRE (472, 485). Could Nielsen acknowledge and respect, for example, that there are modern, educated, and scientifically informed people who, precisely because of their modernity and their deep understanding of rationality would not, like Nielsen, reject or fear the mysterious in the universe, but would accentuate it?

In spite of his arguments for Marxism's intellectual respectability (24) and in spite of his sympathies for the emancipatory claims of feminist philosophy (16), Nielsen's commitment to class struggle and his vision for socialism as the only hope (24:11) clashes with the "reason as only hope" of WRE, and though he grants feminist philosophers much when it comes to unmasking autonomy, universality, and impartiality, I do not yet see him make room for the legitimacy of intuition or faith in our experience.

Four. Nielsen's understanding of normativity becomes identical with his understanding of rationality. I do not object to rationality as a norm. As I said earlier, theory formation, for one thing, needs to be submitted to the norms of rationality. But the reduction of what is normative to what is rational leaves huge areas of human experience without their own real norms: emotions, historical development, hope, religion, justice.

Nielsen himself argues that immorality does not necessarily violate norms of rationality (3:317, 10:19, 17:220, 18:20, 19:245-246). I agree. What does that do to the status of reason as supernorm? This problem, in my view, is endemic to the entire rationality tradition and remains unsolved in MacIntyre's *Whose Justice? Which Rationality?*

Miraculously, reduction of normativity to rationality also destroys real relativity. No longer can we be satisfied to insist on the norm of rationality as only relative to theory formation and similar cultural products. Instead, our whole future, wellbeing, and hope is focussed on rationality. In spite of all the talk about historical relativization, *hope in rationality* absolutizes reason again. From history we know, however, that reason is reductionist (in our rational world reality has shrunk for all its being emancipated!). If all knowledge is subject to the norms of reason, scepticism about the senses, about intuition, about faith, and every other a-rational form of experience will run rampant. Having norms of their own, they need not meet norms of rationality. No wonder reason will find them wanting.

Five. Most regrettably, the decision as to who can be genuine partners in the conversation about our future will be prejudiced in favor of those whose "unprejudiced" positions are less prone to ideology. Those who are obviously ideologically impure from an enlightened point of view will be tolerated on the streets, but not in the official intellectual discussion chambers. In this manner genuine openness will be precluded whenever a hidden prejudice masquerades as the only possibility for objective, justified, and open communication.

As our own North American Indians will tell us, consensus is a very good way to go for solving problems. They have done it that way for eons. But they are deeply suspicious of the democracy of Enlightened rationality. Consensus is not necessarily rational consensus. When commitment to rationality is a hidden prejudice, it will lead to the naive claim that the people so committed are doing no more than being reasonable. We have in our time understood as vacuous a similar claim by analytic philosophers: "We have no tradition, we are just doing philosophy the way it's supposed to be done." Nielsen has called it "just a conceit" (8:97). How reasonable Rational Man is should probably not be answered by Western enlightened intellectuals, but by Western women or by non-Western women and men.

It All Depends

There are various ways to go for an Enlightenment believer. The purpose of this paper is not to dismiss Nielsen or even the Enlightenment. Rather, I intend to challenge believers in rationality to be more reasonable, more open, more critical. Nielsen's legitimate fear is that modernity is threatened with lack of a supra-arbitrary norm with which to call humanity to its senses when we cause suffering, when we oppress, when we cause injustice. Emancipatory interests are vital to our culture. But how much of the non-emancipation of women, blacks, gays, workers, and others is due to the non-emancipation of the Man of Reason? I agree that not only the tribal sensitivities of liberal Europeans should be revulsed by apartheid, but all of humanity. But I fail to see how a commitment to rationality will help us escape such a predicament.

To overcome arbitrariness we do not need absolutes, universal immutables, or the rejection of prejudice. If we acknowledge the thorough relativity of all human experience, we acknowledge that whatever we say or do "depends" on something else. In order to escape from arbitrary dependence or utterly individualistic subjectivism, we need to know, if all depends, what it is that all depends on. I am not sure I am right, but it seems to me Nielsen says approvingly and with great emphasis in relation to Marx: *"What is esential here is the self's need to be defined, not its need to do the defining."* And he quotes G.A. Cohen's contention about Hegel's importance for our need to "find something outside" of ourselves, something we "did not create" but "that created" us instead and with which we must "be able to identify" ourselves (10:26). He is talking here about our social reality. About that same reality he later remarks that, though it shaped us, "that does not justify our accepting its *authority*" (19:244). In yet another place "There are no Self-Identifying Objects. It is we ... who sort the world..." (20:7). The tensions here seem evident to me. The escape from relativism coupled with an escape from God's-eye views poses consider-

124

able problems. In Nielsen I see it end up with a hidden absolute origin, the hope in rationality.

If all truly depends, we need have no fear of relativism, except if it all depends on nothing, or on the individual-subjective, or on what is purely arbitrary. Absolutism and arbitrariness come to the same thing here. But no one believes things are thus relative. The claim that all depends on reason makes reason an absolute, contrary to the deepest impulses of the Enlightenment. Hence we have the combined *denials* of autonomy in the *adopted* position and the *operant* tradition's *affirmation* of rational prejudice. Critical theory is not expected simply to make "a" contribution, but is the source and foundation of universal humanity. Nielsen optimistically speaks of the ever "expanding cricle" slowly but steadily moving "toward a more extensive consensus" (10:21, also 12:111). If we persistently seek, we will find "a more adequate and more comprehensive view ... a consistent and comprehensive web" (21:447).

The alternative, however, need not be the total rejection of reason, but can be rationality specified and relativized. The power of "is rational," if that means normed, orderly, sensible, or permissible, lies in the hidden connection with logicality. If not, then why call it rational? Why then should human problems be solved rationally? That is the emancipation tradition. But what pleads for it? Experience? History? Devotion to rationality as in the Enlightenment, though having contributed to emancipation, has also served to make us sceptical, has reduced our world, has created the false hope of scientism, and has much to do with male superiority in our culture. If we drop the idea that the orderly or the normed is the same as the rational we can start looking for other norms. And whether or not some norm justifies our actions will not automatically be an evidential-logical matter of argument.

We have learned, in our time, to reject reason as a source of certitude. And, interestingly, have taken that to be the end of certitude. If reason could not provide it, then what? The implications of earlier rational certitudes had already rejected any security in trust or faith. At the same time, we can acknowlege the powers of rationality for generating important levels of agreement in communication. No matter what status we give them, none of us disagree that the universe does display certain general features and that conceptual-inferential procedures are geared to the discovery and articulation of them. The features change and are mostly general rather than truly universal. Nevertheless, Davidson is surely right that "communication proves the existence of a shared, and largely true, view of the world" (168). Science has in fact given us historical proof how effective reason is in laying bare long-lasting, wide-scoped structures. And when these structures are expressible in quantitative terms and found in physical reality, they enable us to have a great deal of control over nature and to predict events.

Critical theory and WRE may be well suited, by learning from science, to indicate to us ways in which we can become more aware of what is sharable by all of us. But that still does not set up reason as ultimate judge. *Pace* Nielsen! I know it's not in the *adopted* position. But the *operant* tradition knows only this. WRE as an instrument for reaching agreement on important matters is promising. As an all-inclusive framework for human happiness, eliminating all incommensurability and relativity on this score, it is a totalitarian ideology, a distortion of what is reasonable.

What we have not yet learned is to regain respect for and acknowledgement of the human capacity for trust or—as it is also called—for faith. And trust need not be typically justified by reason. Nor does one need to be a religious person to appreciate the role of faith in life. Atheist Jeffrey Stout seems to have no problem recommending faith as a theological virtue (272). Even then, some people will continue to invest rationality with ultimate hope. It is in reason they will trust. That will lead to a pre-rational judgment, a decision, a *pre*-judice. Such prejudice needs to be acknowledged as such, exposed and admitted. It will not automatically, just by being acknowleged as a prejudice, become illegitimate. No prejudice becomes illegitimate simply and only by not being rational. Unless, of course, reason remains neutral and autonomous. But even a modern believer in the Enlightenment such as Nielsen no longer believes that would be a good thing. And individualist concepts of autonomy are rejected by him as well (16:386-387).

The advantage of exposed prejudices is lessened ideological distortion and promotion of truly open discussion. Exposure differs, however, from emancipation. And emancipation from faith seems impossible. Those committed to rationality might take note of Karl Popper's moving address to the 18th World Congress of Philosophy in Brighton, England, as reported in *The Guardian* of August 29, 1988. He opened with the words: "I wish to make a confession of faith..." (8). If we could acknowledge such a faith, we could at least begin to explore just what sort of human function faith is, how it differs from reason, and what legitimate contribution it makes to knowledge. How, for example, do we *know* something is immoral especially when our immorality is not irrational?

If foundationalism in Enlightenment Humanism is similar to fundamentalism in Christianity, Nielsen's form of belief in reason may still retain some features of Enlightenment prejudice after the rejection of foundationalism, the way Christianity retains features of Biblical religion after the rejection of fundamentalism. Enlightenment rejection of God, revelation, faith, absolutes and the like may be less successful than its followers think. A rejected God may reappear as Reason (even when appearing or disappearing in the disguise of historical rationality). The authority of revelation may find its equal in a naive trust in reflective experience. Faith in the salvific directives of religion may have a double in the guidance of WRE as Critical Theory. Just as God in Christianity is the reliable source of normativity, Reason in the Enlightenment is the reliable origin, beyond criticism or doubt, of our relative truths. If reliability is rationally admissible, how really does it differ from certitude? Even religion's preacher may return to the stage as philosopher, preaching rigorously developed folk wisdom as life's most reliable pathway, privileged with the task of developing and proclaming critical theory. After philosophy, wisdom remains rigorous philosophy (21:450). If wisdom is critical theory, it is no more than traditional philosophy by another name. Why this is reasonable, beyond the prejudice of an emancipated community of believers in the Enlightenment, remains a mystery to all who are not such believers.

Nielsen at this point likes to speak in terms of arcane myth. My point has been to alert ourselves to the fact that all of us,

127

unavoidably, hope and live by "commitments which will not be extinguished" as well as that all of us fail to live by our commitments the way we hope. Christians have undermined their commitment in violent crusades of all kinds. And the Rational Man, whose gender is clear in this case, has much to account for to our mothers, our sisters, our wives, our daughters, and our women friends. Nevertheless, our commitments remain. Sometimes the commitments of others deeply offend us, as when the Ayatollah Khomeini hates Salman Rushdie with a deadly hate. But from that tragic story the Enlightenment believers among us may perhaps learn anew that religious offense is not in the same league as jokes about Santa Claus.

Especially when it turns out that we all have commitments that will not be extinguished and whose justification is rationally always self-referentially incoherent, even when reason is the hope that fans the flames, we all need to relativize our commitments. At the same time, if the prejudice against prejudice is going to die as a result of postmodernist self-reflection, what we will have won is renewed respect in philosophical circles for commitments. I am prepared, drugged though I may be with the opium of the people, to respect atheists, Marxist or otherwise, in the conversation of the West. At this late hour we would certainly do well to examine respectfully a proposal for WRE. But the right to full partnership in the conversation must not be reserved only for those whose ideological prejudices and distortions will survive the prejudice of rational consensus. In that case the humanity, rationality, comprehensiveness, normativity, and openness of WRE will have been sadly compromised.

Kai Nielsen the person will not easily be imprisoned by the built-in limits of critical theory as WRE. As in this very exchange, he will be humane, reasonable, wide ranging in his views and interests, respectful of genuine norms, and truly open to those who differ from him. I have learned much from carefully exploring his thought and my respect for WRE is a fruit of that. But it takes only few people of lesser stature, caught by the vision of WRE and blind to its prejudices, to want our universities and other public institutions closed and intolerant to all who do not believe that democracy is only the democracy of reason, within the boundaries dictated by the Enlightenment.

128

Already it is hard enough to find people for whom openness in scholarship includes openness to one's own religious roots, or even people who will acknowledge the legitimacy of such openness in others.

This somewhat passionate ending may perhaps show the depth of feeling I believe must attend this sort of discussion if it is to go to the roots of things. My deep respect for Nielsen and my trust in the authenticity of his humanity encourage me to be somewhat vulnerable in this attempt at conversation.

6. ON BEING BLINKERED
Kai Nielsen

Rationalism

Hendrik Hart's insightful, probing and careful examination of my views, for which I am grateful, has set me thinking afresh on topics I had set aside. He has perceptively raised questions about what may be unwittingly hidden agendas for me and has gently chided me for being a too rationalistic child of the Enlightenment. I hope it will be neither too churlish of me nor further evidence of my blindness for me to resist his blandishments.

Generally—the Wittgensteinian in me coming to the fore— I am in sympathy with the claim that philosophers tend to be too rationalistic, vastly overestimating the powers of reason.[1] (Sometimes this is more implicit than explicit.) And I am surely dubious, to put it minimally, of talk of Sovereign Reason. To find that very sense of things turned against me is both disconcerting and gives me considerable pause, given my belief that this is a characteristic philosopher's malaise. But all the same I shall resist the idea, pressed hard by Hart, that I make a god of Reason.

I am, and quite happily so, a child of the Enlightenment, though, coming late on the scene, I am someone who has also been chastened by the powerful critique of the counter-Enlightenment. Wittgenstein and even, though to a lesser extent, Kierkegaard, have been formative figures in my intellectual life. It is not just Marx, the pragmatists, logical empiricism and selected strains of traditional analytic philosophy that have structured how I see the world. This comes out most forcefully in my once obsessive repeated return to writing, from all sorts of angles, about what I have called, perhaps infelicitously, Wittgensteinian fideism.[2] Hart misses this strain in my thought and as a result makes me out to be far, far more of a rationalist

130

than I am. I shall, after recapitulating the core of Hart's criticism of me, show where he misreads me and then, and more importantly, try to say something of what a defender of the Enlightenment, who has taken to heart the counter-Enlightenment critique, should say about the place of reason in human life.

Think of me, if you will, as a person of Neurathian or Carnapian sentiments who has come to be deeply, though not uncritically, influenced by the work of Wittgenstein in the phases *after* the *Tractatus*. If Hart had seen this, he would not have criticized me in the way he did. His taking a Christian turn and my not so turning would have, if this had been seen, had a different opposition. It would have been seen that *on both sides* there are things, and *inescapably*, that are taken on trust. Then there would have been the search for some way of ascertaining—if that can indeed be done—on reflection and in keeping before us a diverse range of considerations, which of these systems of trust are the most worthy of being trusted. (But *some* of these things inescapably to be taken on trust would be shared things and that, I believe, provides an opening for wide reflective equilibrium [WRE] *neutrally* utilizable by either Hart or me.)

However, let me first turn to Hart's criticisms of me.[3] I have, Hart has it, this Enlightenment conception that rationality can emancipate us from prejudice (v. 108-110). Adherence to this tradition blinds me to the fact that rational justification or at least belief in its efficacy is itself a prejudice. I have the typical Enlightenment prejudice against prejudice failing to take note of Burkean insights about such matters. Where a philosopher is a philosopher of vision, as Hart avers I am, this blindness is indeed debilitating.

He takes me as being committed to the Enlightenment belief that no belief is authorized unless it has been rationally justified. For me, "rational justification" is pleonastic (v. 110-111), and while in rejecting foundationalism I officially give up the quest for certain knowledge, yet with this belief in reason a kind of foundationalism sneaks in by the back door. Underneath the temporarily reliable beliefs certifiable by WRE there is, Hart says, an "everlasting source of indubitable certitude"

131

(v. 111), namely an "unfounded absolutized belief in rational autonomy" (v. 111). But this, he rightly remarks, is just an Enlightenment myth. I, true child of the Enlightenment that I am, Hart would have it, take rationality as a supernorm in accordance with which our cultural life—indeed the whole of it—is to be assessed. "All other culture," Hart tells us, "is submitted to the judgment of reason which adds up to reason's ultimatization, totalization and absolutization" (v. 112). This is rationalism gone wild.

Hart rightly stresses that WRE starts with tradition, with considered judgments, with prejudices, in the broad sense in which he uses the term "prejudices," but then in Enlightenment fashion WRE tries to launder them, moving from *positive* morality to *critical* morality, and with this to the removing of their prejudicial character.

Hart resists this move. What I am blind to is "the possibility that some knowledge is impossible, some prejudice impenetrable to rational criticism or rational justification" (v. 112). My rationalistic prejudice is supposed to be the belief that all convictions, to be acceptable convictions, must be convictions which must come before the bar of reason. "...WRE is, in the final analysis, the self-legitimation of critical rationality, made possible by a fundamental prejudice in favour of critical rationality, which can itself neither be legitimated any further nor easily recognized as an uncritical prejudice" (v. 113). It is crucial to recognize, Hart argues, that the "acceptance of rationality as an autonomous, totalizing, and ultimate norm is not the objective or justified outcome of a process of empirical theory building subject to rational justification. It is, ultimately, a choice, a commitment" (v. 113).

I believe in the ultimacy of reason, Hart contends, and I also assume that "everyone knows what rationality is all about" (v. 115). I want, the claim goes, "to make life rational in the most reasonable way" (v. 117). But he tells us he looks in vain "for any attempt on my part *to justify* rational justification" (v. 117). I just take rationality, the argument goes, as some fundamental, and fundamentally unproblematic, conception that requires no justification. That we are justified in so appealing to reason is somehow just self-evident. What comes to a prejudice in favour of the ultimacy of reason is a belief that I harbour. Though it is a belief which I am not clear about. It is something I do not argue for or self-consciously assume. But it is, Hart claims, nonetheless actually *operative* in my way of thinking. I just have, that is, an unthinking rather blind "prejudice in favour of the ultimacy of reason" (v. 117).

My official position is anti-foundationalist but unwittingly, Hart contends, I make a foundationalist appeal to reason. Because I am unaware of my prejudice in favour of the ultimacy of reason, reason insinuates itself as the very kind of *a priori* overlord of culture that I wish to repudiate. Reason provides the norm for our actions. By following it we can come to know what is the good life for human beings. Moreover, this is not a conception of reason or rationality which is at all relativized or even historicized. Rather I go, Hart has it, in pursuit of an absolutized and autonomous reason. But this is pure dogmatism on my part.

I think of myself, he rightly remarks, as being a fallibilist but, he adds, the belief that whatever is rational is also normative is not an open question for me. What is through and through and, everything considered, rational just is normative for me. My commitment to rationality is categorical. But this is a commitment which I like a religious fideist just plonk for. I do not argue for it and indeed I could not prove it, give evidence for it or in any non-question-begging way establish it as something we *should,* let alone *must,* commit ourselves to. It is just an uncritical article of faith of the Enlightenment. It is, Hart would have it, my substitute for God. That is why he calls what he takes to be my belief in Reason religious.

Reason and Religion

Since this is so, religion gets, Hart claims, a new lease on life. It is not as vulnerable as I believe to my criticisms. It is not something to be set aside with the realization of what the Enlightenment signifies. Whether we take an Enlightenment turn or a religious turn, we must live with the acceptance of prejudice, the taking of things on *trust* and with the necessity for making existential choices. We can perfectly rightly question whether reason is or indeed even can be the final arbiter. And, if it turns out not to be or only *arbitrarily* so, then it would not be very reasonable indeed "to demand that religion either be rational or be dismissed" (v. 119). But it is just this demand— or so Hart has it—that I make of religion but it now appears at least to be the case that this rationalistic rejection of religion is unjustified. Indeed "unjustified" is too weak a term here. What I rely on here is a religiose dogma of secular humanism.

The unreasonableness of this demand on my part should be further apparent when we take to heart the fact that "the actual human practices we are trying to emancipate are not themselves belief-systems and cannot be reduced to them" (v. 120). Probing my Enlightenment beliefs and convictions, Hart asks:

> Why...should human problems be solved rationally? That is the emancipation tradition. But what pleads for it? Experience? History? Devotion to rationality as in the Enlightenment, though having contributed to emancipation has also served to make us sceptical, has reduced our world, has created the false hope of scientism, and has much to do with male superiority in our culture. If we drop the idea that the orderly or the normed is the same as the rational we can start looking for other norms. And whether or not some norm justifies our actions will not automatically be an evidential-logical matter of argument (v. 125).

The demand that we solve all our problems rationally is unrealistic and unjustified. Such rationalism has been a very mixed blessing. It has in many ways reduced and cramped our lives. We should not see WRE as in effect setting or, more accurately, trying to set, reason as ultimate judge. WRE, Hart grants, is a promising procedure for reaching agreement on important matters but then he wrongly claims that I take it to be something more, namely, as he puts it, "an all-inclusive framework for human happiness, eliminating all incommensurability and relativity on this score" (v. 126). He then says, rather extravagantly, that it becomes in my hands "a totalitarian ideology, a distortion of what is reasonable" (v. 126). But even if it were a distortion of what is reasonable it would not thereby become "a totalitarian ideology." I see no justification at all for saying that it is. Hart here is himself being ideological and *parti*

134

pris about who is being ideological and how.

But what is more important to realize is that I do not take WRE, nor does John Rawls or Norman Daniels, as such an all inclusive framework.[4] Rather it has the much more modest role in moral methodology that Hart gestures at. It is a device for assessing moral theories and for helping us, starting with our considered judgments—our prejudices if you will—to come to some resolution about which of our moral beliefs, including which of our considered convictions when they conflict, are justified. I, Hart claims, invest rationality with ultimate hope. I place my trust in reason and thus make reason my God. But this, the claim goes, is just to adhere to my Enlightenment prejudices and to set them, dogmatically and arbitrarily, against religious prejudices. What we need to learn, and what my rationalism shields me from, is the need, against Enlightenment ideology, "to regain the human capacity for trust" (v. 126). We must learn to cherish our prejudices and not just automatically set them aside as *illegitimate* because they are not rational. (They may, of course, be a-rational or non-rational without being irrational.) There can be no emancipation from trust, from reliance on some of our prejudices. God reappears in my appeal to Reason. "Just as God in Christianity is the reliable source of normativity, Reason in the Enlightenment is the reliable origin, beyond criticism or doubt, of our relative truths" (v. 127).

Trust

I want now to turn to showing—attempting to show—that Hart's critique of me is misdirected and that I am not the rationalistic fellow he takes me to be. He maintains that I believe—and very centrally—the following eleven propositions. In point of fact I do not believe or believe in any of them nor does my account, either officially or operationally, commit me to them. The eleven theses are:

1. Reason is our only hope. All depends on reason.
2. The normative is reduced to what is rational.
3. Reason is our ultimate judge or arbiter. Reason provides the norm for all our actions.
4. We must have no unfounded assumptions.

5. No belief is authorized unless it has been rationally justified.
6. True belief is a supernorm for the rest of culture. All other culture is submitted to the judgment of reason.
7. Rationality is an autonomous, totalizing, and ultimate norm.
8. Anything a-rational in the field of ultimacy is unacceptable.
9. We should believe in nothing except what is clear, open, grounded, argued, justified.
10. Reason has a self-evident superiority to all other human elements. It justifies everything but it needs no justification itself. With such conceptions in place or assumed, philosophy remains overlord.
11. It is reason, and only reason, in which we must trust. It is the source of normativity which is itself beyond criticism or doubt.

These are all characteristically rationalistic theses, some expressed by typical Enlightenment figures, and it seems to me, absurd to believe or believe in any of them. Hart should have been on to the fact that I would not so view things from the repeated use I make of the following three slogans:

1. Many things we reasonably believe we do not believe for a reason. (Alan Donagan)
2. It is difficult to recognize the extent of our groundless believing. (Ludwig Wittgenstein, Norman Malcolm)
3. The heart of rationalism is irrational. (Fredrick Waismann)

Anyone who could stress, explicate and defend such slogans could hardly be a believer in the eleven rationalistic theses Hart sets out as things we should definitely not believe in. They are indeed great rationalistic myths: the convictional and *irrational* side of rationalism.

WRE, however, stresses the need to start with tradition, considered judgments, prejudices (if you will); and in thinking about what is to be done and how to live stresses the need to repeatedly, on all levels of abstraction, appeal to considered judgments and to return to them in our various life commitments. Specific considered convictions can and should be criticized and sometimes set aside but there is just no way at all in which we could step outside our web of considered judgments—our prejudices—and decide what we ought to do and what reason requires.

We learn, or at least should have learned, from Wittgenstein that there is a myriad of framework beliefs or hinge beliefs that are so deeply embedded in our forms of life that we, at least in any even remotely normal circumstances of life, do not know what it would be like to doubt them: to bring them in question and to ask if they match up with reality.[5] Thus I am certain that I am a human being, that I have a head, that I will not turn into a sparrow and then turn back again into a human being, that I had a mother, that there are other people and that the earth has existed for many years before my birth. We have not the slightest doubt of such propositions—nonanalytic though they be—and any evidential propositions taken as propositions to establish their truth or falsity would be much less certain than such framework propositions themselves. They are propositions we are certain of, though, not knowing what even in principle would disconfirm them or infirm them, we do not understand what it would be like for them to be false or probably false and thus we do not understand what it would be like for them to be true or probably true either. So we do not know that they are true though we take them with firm intersubjective certainty to be something to be taken on trust. More than that, we have no understanding at all of what it would be like to doubt them. Doubt does not even come into the picture here. If someone tried to doubt them we would think he had gone mad.[6]

They surely strike us, to understate it, as reasonable to be so taken, but hardly as products of "pure reason" whatever that means. To doubt them is plainly insane. But they do not seem to be self-evident certainties of reason such as "All red things are coloured." They do, however, square with our experience of life and with what we can make sense of. Their denials seem in some practical sense unintelligible to us. Yet there is no proving their truth or finding evidence for them. (Any evidence we could give, let me repeat, would be less certain than the beliefs themselves.) And if we tried to provide a transcendental proof of them we would be less certain of the soundness of the proof than of the acceptability of the propositions themselves. I have followed Wittgenstein here, and whether Wittgenstein's views here are well-taken or ill-taken, with the stress I put on them it should be clear that I do not take the rationalistic turning that Hart attributes to me.[7]

A further way of driving this home should be evident from some parallel things I say about morality. There are moral beliefs—beliefs I have called moral truisms—that have a status similar to the factual framework beliefs mentioned above. That suffering is a bad thing, that integrity is good, that truth is to be respected, that persons are to be respected, that autonomy is a good thing, that needs should be satisfied, that satisfaction of desire is good, that love between human beings is to be prized, that human beings need to learn to cooperate and to coordinate their behavior are all things that are required to make sense out of the moral life or, more broadly, our lives together as human beings. We are as certain of these things, or at least nearly as certain, as we are of the factual framework beliefs I mentioned. But again we can hardly prove these moral beliefs. Indeed we are utterly at a loss as to what this would come to. But it is equally evident that they are not self-evident *a priori* true propositions. Yet we do not know how to verify or falsify them. Notwithstanding all these things, we are certain of them. We have no doubt about them at all and indeed all doubt here seems feckless. They are articles of trust and not axioms of pure practical reason. It is not a matter of what reason requires, establishes or even suggests but of what we on reflection trust. They are, if you will, matters of the heart, though they are also things that we reasonably believe, though we do not believe them for a reason.

They are part of what we reasonably trust but do not trust for a reason; they are a fraction, though a vital fraction, of our groundless believing, but not uncertain or in the least arbitrary for all of that. The heart of a rationalism that would try to prove the truth of such beliefs, show that they were *a priori* true or give evidence for them, would be irrational. They are objects of trust but, for all of that, of reasonable trust.

Such conceptions are central to my account and are prominent in my "Searching for an Emancipatory Perspective:

Wide Reflective Equilibrium and the Hermeneutical Circle" and in many of the essays on Wittgensteinian fideism reprinted in my *God, Scepticism and Modernity*.[8] The missing of this prominent strand in my thought vitiates Hart's central criticisms of me. I do not make a God of reason; reason in my view is not our source of normativity; it is not a supernorm for us; it is not our only hope; it is not our ultimate judge or arbiter—nothing is and that is not at all nihilism. The very idea that we can get to a situation in which we have no unfounded assumptions and in which everything is clear, grounded, justified, argued to an established conclusion is a philosophical myth. Wittgenstein longed for "complete clarity" but he also came to realize it was an incoherent ideal. We must rely on practices and while we can explicate and criticize any of our practices we can never perspicuously display them all. There will always be practices that remain an unarticulated part of our background of belief and action.[9] We will never get the whole picture there before us. Indeed we do not even have any good idea of what "the whole picture" would come to so that we could recognize it if we had it.

Reason in Practice

So I stress this underlying role of tradition and trust, in part following Wittgenstein. Yet I also say I am a child of the Enlightenment: a believer in suitably chastened Enlightenment values. How does this mix go together? Or does it consistently go together? I think if I in some detail work with an example—translating into the concrete—I can perhaps make some headway here. In doing this I shall depart from my usual practice of using socio-political examples and use an example from our personal lives which will have at least the merit of being something that is broadly familiar to most of us.

Suppose two people, a woman and a man, two women, two men—it does not matter which pairings—are in the process of deciding whether to live together and to share their lives. What kind of mix of reason and passion, reason and sentiment, should go together there? Is it reason or sentiment or neither which is the crucial source of normativity here? (This, of course, is putting it in a pedantic philosophical way.) Surely no one who had any sense at all would say that reason should be our only guide here. Feelings—contingently generated feelings—are certainly crucial but still they are feelings which would, if the people involved are appropriately human, be feelings that would withstand their reflective considering their lives together: their hopes, their self-images, their images of how they are to each other, their mutual understandings of each other, their motivations and the like. Here we have a complex mixture of reason and sentiment, hardly clearly isolatable one from the other.

A and B meet—a plain historical contingency not dictated by reason—and come to feel an initial attraction for each other. This initial attraction need not, of course, be *against* reason but it surely is hardly ever, if indeed ever, to understate it, *required* by reason either. Reason does not play center stage here. Indeed we are inclined to say—mistakenly I think—that reason has very little to do with it, but, even so, there need be nothing irrational here for all of that. Still, that picture is misleading, for these initial attractions will characteristically not be reason-free, though surely they are not anything like just products of reason. That is hardly intelligible.

A has a certain image of herself, a partially reflective conception of her life, of her world, of what she thinks human relations should be. This will surely limit the range of B's for which she could feel this initial attraction. Still, within this range there could be a B' for whom she had this attraction and a B" for whom she did not, and the difference here might not at all be rooted in reason. There might, that is, liking apart, be nothing in the facts or inferences derived from their statement which would favour B' over B". Furthermore there might be, as A and B' interact together, love each other and talk together, no reason (though there is a cause) for these feelings toward each other or for the particulars of their bondings beyond what was rooted in their particular likings. There is very likely to be, at least some of the time, a delighting in each other's company and a mutual liking of certain things: something hardly dictated by reason though not, for all of that, need it be at all contrary to reason.

Moreover, in the background, tradition, broadly conceived, is still unavoidably playing its role as well, for good or for ill. People's attitudes, deep primitive reactions, are very much structured by the traditions into which they have been socialized. There is scarcely likely to be much in the way of such a bonding between an unacculturated A from a preliterate tribe in the Amazon and a B who is a Stockholm professional. This, of course, is an extreme case but there will, though to a lesser extent, be very unlikely possibilities for bondings in less extreme cases as well. Tradition sets limits here though within ranges the limits are flexible.

There is a matter of trust and commitment which comes in here which is also not a matter of reason but which also need not be contrary to reason. A could be firmly and indeed happily bonded to B' while clearly realizing that but for accidents of history it could have been the case that she could have been similarly bonded to someone else. It could merely have been a question of her having met B' first.

Her sticking with B' is partly rooted in reason—what would a world be like that did not acknowledge the relevance and importance of such historical contingencies?—but A and B' would also already be linked in a love that was there between them and in a recognition of the importance of trust and commitment. But surely not a commitment that overrides any other considerations. Again, both reason and passion come into play, without reason having any clear, overriding, determinative role.

A and B in coming to such a decision will talk, though what is relevant between them will surely not just be talk. They will give considerations for and against deciding to stay together. What is involved here will characteristically involve a diverse range of considerations though certainly they will include the sentiments A and B' actually have, whether they form a compossible set, whether they are sentiments which on reflection, and in their continued interaction, will be sustainable and the like. Considerations that will be at the forefront will be feelings they have for each other, their understanding of their relations and what sort of life together they are likely to have if they live with each other in a certain way, their prior commitments to each other, relations (including commitments) to others (children,

141

parents, previous partners, perhaps even friends). They will, if they are reasonable, and in the fullest sense human, try to look non-evasively at these things, turning them over and over again, looking at them, as best they can, from all angles, and taking them to heart.

Of course, for a matter so complicated, and so rooted in feelings that are very difficult to articulate, and so subject to self-deception, this is very hard to decide: to feel through and deliberate through. Yet people decide such matters again and again—it is part of the stuff of human life—and they do it sometimes more impulsively and less humanly or appropriately than at other times. We do not all settle such matters equally well. In saying that they sometimes do it "more appropriately than at other times" I am giving to understand that some decisions are (a) better than others and (b) that some are arrived at in a more reasonable and a more human way than others. And by (b) I do not mean that the decisions are derived from some "norm of reason"—I do not even understand what that means—but that, where they are reasonably made, they are made with all those considerations perspicuously displayed (including their causal connections)—or, more realistically, as perspicuously displayed as possible—and dwelt on in a cool hour. The doing of this will aim at a clear understanding—or at least as clear as A and B' can get, given normal possibilities— of the facts of the matter, including the consequences of their actions for themselves and for others. There is, of course, no algorithm that they can appeal to here. So when we say that some decisions are more appropriate than others we are not saying that there is some norm of reason that determines or justifies what is to be done independently of feelings, including feelings mediated through practices, traditions and commitments that the particular agents in question—in this case A and B'—will have.

Reason is not wanton here. There are ways of just acting impulsively or by burying plainly relevant considerations, or by not noting plain causal connections or ambiguities or possible incoherent conceptions and the like. These are all plainly criticizable. And there is also the fact that there can be too much a dwelling on things—a kind of Hamlet syndrome—

142

which is the opposite of impulsive or unconsidered action. Neither serves the ends of reasonable and human action, but before concluding that after all I am here responding as Hart's rationalistic, male chauvinist "Man of Reason," consider that what I am calling here "reasonable" could as well be called "a more reflective, appropriately human way of responding." And while over matters of considerable weight we will in fact often not know what this will come to, procedurally (to put it in a pedantic and possibly misleading way) we will know how such decisions are to be arrived at such that without being "Men of Reason" we can and will distinguish in such situations between decisions reasonably arrived at, made in an appropriately human way, on the one hand, and unthought-unfelt-through and just impulsive decisions, decisions which are hardly appropriately human decisions, on the other. In the former case the range of considerations appealed to will include sentiments, practices, traditions, at least putatively true beliefs about what are the facts of the matter, logical connections, probabilities and the like.

In short, as an inadequate concision of these diverse considerations, we should say that matters of reason and matters of passion always come as a package. Both considerations are invariably relevant in coming to such decisions and no pecking order between them has been established or is likely to be establishable. Moreover, I see no reason why we should look for such a pecking order or think we could find one.

There is plainly no claim here that reason is our ultimate judge, that reason provides the norm for all our actions, that reason is our only hope, that the normative is reduced to the rational, that true belief is our supernorm, that anything a-rational in the field of ultimacy is unacceptable or that reason is an autonomous, totalizing and ultimate norm. Nothing of Hart's making of Nielsen into a Man of Reason obtains. Indeed the view I urge here—though I have urged a more robust and quite possibly mistaken view of rationality elsewhere—is compatible with a view of reason traceable through a tradition running from Hobbes, Hume and Russell to Gauthier, where in the field of action it is finally our considered and informed preferences which determine what is rational.[10]

Be that as it may, I do not (*pace* Hart) treat reason as some supernorm or deny the importance of a-rational features in human life. I have illustrated how I believe we should reason in a familiar situation from the domain of personal life but I could have chosen instead a more politically and institutionally linked case—a more social case—or a case of reflectively trying to decide whether to remain or become a Jew or a Christian or to become an atheist or some other sort of nonbeliever.

Conclusion

I am without apology or ambivalence an Enlightenment figure in thinking that human decisions should be made reflectively and with attention to the facts, and that our considered convictions—our prejudices, if you will—should be critically inspected *where our lives actually churn up some doubt about them.*[11] In this weak way claims about what are acceptable convictions will come up before the bar of reason. But surely not in the strong way that Hart taxes me with, in which we can accept no unfounded assumptions and will accept nothing, if we are reasonable, except what is clear, grounded, argued and justified. That seems to me perfectly crazy. Our ungrounded beliefs are too extensive, too pervasive and too unavoidable. To demand such rationalistic criteria of acceptance seems to me to be accepting what Fredrick Waismann referred to as the irrational heart of rationalism.[12]

Like Wittgenstein I believe that in our actual deliberations, reasonings and actions there will be an appeal to a largely unarticulated—and indeed in *entirety* an unarticulatable—background of practices, forms of life, traditions, some of which we just unavoidably must trust. However, I also believe, as I think Wittgenstein does too, that there is (some very deeply embedded framework beliefs aside) no practice or tradition or even form of life which could not, in theory at least, in certain concrete circumstances, come to be questioned. But this is not to say that we can possibly put in question the whole lot together and that we can escape in our reasoning and acting a trusting of our practices and forms of life. Some part of Christianity, or even Christianity itself or perhaps even religion more generally, might rightly be critically rejected, but not all our forms of life together. Something, as Wittgenstein liked to put it, must stand fast for something else to be critically assessed.

But that does not at all mean that there is or even can be any one thing, some of Moore's and Wittgenstein's framework beliefs aside (for example, "Live people have heads"), that can never come up even in theory for critical assessment.[13] These possible exceptions aside, there is nothing (no single belief) on a Wittgensteinian view that is immune to critical inspection and the possibility of rejection. But the idea of all at once massively rejecting the bulk of our framework beliefs and taking nothing on trust is incoherent. That, however, is also a core element of the methodology that my critical theory employs and it is not at all to make a god of reason, where trust and tradition can be set aside. There is no prejudice here in favour of the ultimacy of reason; there is no prejudice against prejudice, though there is a kind of Austinian fastidiousness about talking in that manner.

NOTES

[1]Ludwig Wittgenstein, *On Certainty* (Oxford, England: Basil Blackwell, 1969); Georg von Wright, *Wittgenstein* (Minneapolis, MN: University of Minnesota Press, 1982):165-182; and Kai Nielsen, "Wittgenstein, Wittgensteinians and the End of Philosophy" (*Grazer Philosophische Studien,* forthcoming).

[2]This comes out in all my books on religion (*Ethics Without God* aside) but most fully in my *An Introduction to the Philosophy of Religion* (London, England: The Macmillan Press, 1982) and *God, Skepticism and Modernity* (Ottawa, ON: University of Ottawa Press, 1989).

[3]Hendrik Hart, "Blind Spots in Nielsen's Vision," which is chapter 5 in this volume. The citations in this chapter from Hart are all from chapter 5.

[4]Kai Nielsen, "In Defense of Wide Reflective Equilibrium," in Douglas Odegaard (ed.), *Ethics and Justification* (Edmonton, AB: Academic Printing and Publishing, 1987), 19-37; Kai Nielsen, "On Needing a Moral Theory: Rationality, Considered Judgments and the Grounding of Morality," *Metaphilosophy* 13 (April 1982); Kai Nielsen, "Considered Judgments Again," *Human Studies* 5 (April/June 1982); Kai Nielsen, *Equality and Liberty* (Totowa, NJ: Rowman and Allanheld, 1985), Ch. 2; Kai Nielsen, "Searching for an Emancipatory Perspective: Wide Reflective Equilibrium and the Hermeneutical Circle" in Evan Simpson (ed.), *Anti-foundationalism and Practical Reasoning* (Edmonton, AB: Academic Printing and Publishing, 1987); Kai Nielsen, "Reflective Equilibrium and the Transformation of Philosophy," *Metaphilosophy* (1989); Kai Nielsen, "Philosophy as Critical Theory," *Proceedings and Addresses of the American Philosophical Association* supplement to 61:1 (September 1987), 89-108; Kai Nielsen, "On Sticking with Considered Judgments in Wide Reflective Equilibrium," *Philosophia* 13:3-4 (1985), 316-21. See also Marsha Hanen, "Justification as Coherence" in M.A. Stewart (ed.), *Law, Morality and Rights* (Dordrecht, Holland: D. Reidel, 1983), 67-92; John Rawls, *A Theory of Justice* (Cambridge, MA: Harvard University Press, 1971), 19-21, 48-51 and 577-87; John Rawls, "The Independence of Moral Theory," *Proceedings and Addresses of the American Philosophical Association* 47 (1974/75), 710; Jane English, "Ethics and Science," *Proceedings of the XVI Congress of Philosophy;* Norman Daniels, "Wide Reflective Equilibrium and Theory of Acceptance in Ethics," *Journal of Philosophy* 76 (1979); Norman Daniels, "Moral Theory and Plasticity of Persons," *The Monist* 62 (July 1979); Norman Daniels, "Some Methods of Ethics and Linguistics," *Philosophical Studies* 37 (1980); Norman Daniels, "Two Approachs to Theory Acceptance in Ethics" in David Copp and David Zimmerman (eds.), *Morality, Reason and Truth* (Totowa, NJ: Rowman and Allanheld, 1985); Hilary Putnam, *Realism and Reason* (Cambridge, England: Cambridge University Press, 1983), 229-47; and Richard Rorty, "The

Priority of Democracy to Philosophy" in Meryl Patterson and Robert Vaughan (eds.), *The Virginia Statute of Religious Freedom* (Cambridge: Cambridge University Press, 1987).

[5]See the references in note 1. And see as well Norman Malcolm, "Wittgenstein's 'Skepticism' in *On Certainty, " Inquiry* 31:3 (September 1988), 277-287; Peter Winch, "True or False," *Inquiry* 31:3 (September 1988), 265-76.

[6]Wittgenstein, *On Certainty,* and Malcolm as mentioned in the previous note.

[7]I try to show they are well taken in my "Wittgenstein, Wittgensteinians and the End of Philosophy."

[8]See my "Searching for an Emancipatory Perspective" and my *God, Scepticism and Modernity.*

[9]See the citations in notes 1 and 5.

[10]See my "Principles of Rationality," *Philosophical Papers* III:2 (1974), 55-89; "The Embeddedness of Conceptual Relativism," *Dialogos* XI:29-30 (1977), 85-111; and "Reason and Sentiment: Skeptical Remarks About Reason and the 'Foundations of Morality'" in Theodore F. Geraets (ed), *Rationality Today* (Ottawa, ON: University of Ottawa Press, 1979), 249-279.

[11]See the references in note 4.

[12]Fredrick Waismann, *How I See Philosophy* (New York: St. Martin's Press, 1968), 138.

[13]*Perhaps,* as pragmatists would argue, even they can be doubted, but *vis-à-vis* my arguments with Hart this need not be settled, for even if they cannot be intelligibly set aside, as I am inclined to think, they, as Wittgenstein shows in *On Certainty,* are not a matter of knowledge. They are *vor Wissen,* not *Wissen.* See here the reference to Wittgenstein and von Wright in the first footnote.

7. WHITHER REASON AND RELIGION?
Hendrik Hart

Introduction

Discussion so far has focussed on Nielsen's view that belief in God is irrational and my view that he covertly depends on a pseudo deity. But integration of the six essays around this theme is not everywhere apparent. It is clear, at times, that we miss each other. In the first two essays, I am more concerned with what I call Nielsen's religiose rationalism. He seems more clearly focussed on the irrationality of belief in God. In the four remaining essays we address each other more directly. But they have another problem of integration. Because Nielsen sees metaphilosophy and philosophy of religion as quite distinct if not separate areas, while I see them as closely related and sometimes identical, there are again risks of missing each other. Finally, because Nielsen wrote his second response after his third, there is some discontinuity in the progress of the six essays, since my third does not take his second response into account. So we need a closing essay to tie the discussion together, as well as to assess the progress made, if any.

Since Nielsen has left it to me to write this closing essay, I should not misuse this as an opportunity to have "the last word" on each and every point raised in our discussion. So I will leave many unresolved points untouched. Instead, I will concentrate on some major themes, to see whether our discussion has made progress. Until recently I concentrated my attention almost solely on Nielsen's metaphilosophical publications as they appeared after his 1984 CPA address (2). But I can assess some points at issue between us more adequately by also taking his work in philosophy of religion into account. I have done so in this essay. Especially *God, Scepticism and Modernity* is very helpful here.

148

I am more convinced than before that my case against Nielsen's rationalism is not as straightforward as I had thought. I see more clearly now that he wants to reject all forms of ultimate reliance on reason alone, not only positivism or scientism. I also note his desire to work with dimensions of human experience like faith, hope, and convictions that lie deeper than reason and that function as sources of knowledge and guides on our journey. The frequent effective absence of these dimensions in the discussion of metaphilosophical issues, however, raises questions about their active integration in Nielsen's views. His own remarks about what he writes in this volume and what he writes elsewhere about reason give pause for thought here (v. 144/145). But the presence to his thought of dimensions of experience other than reason cannot be denied. So I am hopeful we can make headway in our mutual evaluation of reason and religion.

For Nielsen, our discussion has been in philosophy of religion. For me it was intended as metaphilosophy. However, I see all metaphilosophy as religiously loaded at some point. And given my new appreciation of the Nielsen who writes philosophy of religion, perhaps our different approaches can be conceptually reconciled as reflections on trusted horizons of our experience. Perhaps we can find common ground in the possibility that metaphilosophy and religion have a similar focus, if we see them as the secular/naturalistic and the religious forms of (reflection on) trust and ultimacy. If we ignore for the moment that religion knows a practiced cultic form of developing trust and certitude in rites and rituals, perhaps there is a shared thread in the argument which we can follow to advance discussion.

Advancing the discussion is, I believe, of more than personal interest to Nielsen and myself. At stake is the broadly cultural issue of conversation between North American communities whose present record of communication is not impressive, namely Marxists and Christians as well as atheists and Christians. It could be argued that communication between deeply alienated communities is one of the prioriteis of our time. Never before in Western history have differences been so deep that every attempt at bridging seems bound for failure.

149

Our present culture is characterized by chasms that do not augur well for our life together. Examples are pro-life and pro-choice groups, environmentalists and promoters of corporate progress, the peace movement and protagonists of nuclear arms, or in philosophy deconstructionists and foundationalists. The differences here are exclusive to the point of excommunicative, while the relentless pressing of each point of view continues in spite of the obviously destructive implications for living together in one world. It is clear that in our present situation successful appeals to "reality" or a shareable "alternative" are as elusive as the search for objective norms or universal truth. It seems that our future depends in a large measure on keeping the possibilities for genuine conversation between deeply divided camps open.

In this situation I think it would be preposterous to believe that Christianity requires hostility towards atheists or Marxists. I also believe that Marxism's strong emphasis on solidarity and Christianity's call to love contain a genuine ingredient for serious conversation. Nielsen, furthermore, has demonstrated in more ways than one that his conversation with those who reject his position is nevertheless respectful and open. Hence I offer my contributions in this last chapter as a sincere attempt to engender conversation that seeks to break the impasse in the contemporary depressing state of relationships between alienated points of view.

This closing essay has three parts. In the first I focus on remaining difficulties between us. In discussing these I'll unpack my lingering suspicion of Nielsen's remaining devotion to reason, I'll set forth what I don't mean by rationalism, I'll say something about the tradition of rationality, and I'll show how I see Nielsen fit in that tradition. In part two I will reflect briefly on reason in ordinary experience, reason in science, and reason in philosophy. In part three, on religion, I deal with the rehabilitation of religion after the collapse of foundationalism, with the ways in which religion is not rational, and with metaphor in religious tradition.

Problems

I believe both our agreements and our disagreements are

150

linked to two shared concerns. One is our postmodern suspicion of reason, the other our lament for lost norm universality. Postmodern suspicion of reason is the most widespread and serious incursion into our Western intellectual tradition ever made. The contemporary harvest of moods implanted in our culture by Kierkegaard, Emerson, Nietzsche, and Freud has led to widespread doubts among secularists about continuing the Enlightenment tradition. I need only refer to the "after philosophy" talk that prevails in a variety of camps. But just how Nielsen fits here is not clear. He, like Habermas, is a serious critic of reason and a strong advocate of reflections that serve the cause of humanity. But in what measure does he maintain an allegiance to the Enlightenment? Traditionally, that movement is not only emancipatory, but also strongly links its emancipation to rational criticism. For some philosophers today, however, emancipation must be detached from or only loosely linked to rational criticism, as for example in Derrida or Rorty. For others the contemporary critique of reason develops as an emancipatory agenda within the boundaries of rational criticism. The latter approach, which I see at work in Nielsen, presents special problems related to rational prejudice and rational self-critique.

The roots of our shared suspicion of reason are both similar and dissimilar. The similarity lies in a concern with humanity in our thinking. We are suspicious of anything that despoils our humanity and agree that reason in various forms (such as scientism) has harmed us. But at that very point the dissimilarity comes in. Nielsen embodies his humanism in Marxism, which as a form of the Enlightenment embraces the rationality tradition. My concerns are shaped more outside the Enlightenment, because as a Calvinian I am suspicious both of human autonomy and of reason as its vehicle. This is in spite of Calvinism's debt to the rationality tradition in other ways. William J. Bouwsma's recent *John Calvin* splendidly portrays the tensions between Calvin's humanism and his rationalism. These tensions have mostly disappeared in Calvinism in favor of a dominant rationalism. But in Calvin himself, Bouwsma convincingly argues, the humanism was stronger. And just as in my case influences from Calvinism feed my suspicions about rea-

151

son, even within Calvinism itself, so I suspect humanist impulses in Marxism play a similar role in Nielsen's thought.

The second shared concern is our lament for the loss of universal norm consciousness. Normativity and rationality have been so closely intertwined in our culture that the contemporary critique of reason often seems to many like a critique of normativity. Norms and concepts of norms have been conflated. As a result, when we mean by normativity that a genuine norm is universal, we find it hard at one and the same time to reject the rigidity of a permanent rational framework as well as to maintain a sense of norm universality. Both Nielsen and I believe that not just a given tribe is called to justice, but all of humanity. And we are both concerned that the contemporary critique of reason threatens this universality as well as that of other norms besides justice. Add to that the factual divisions and conflicts about normativity that plague our culture and we have a serious problem. For now, both in the Christian religion and in the Enlightenment, the rationality tradition is withering and does not seem available any longer to provide a common ground for appeal in conflicts about norms.

Our shared concern for the preservation of universality at some deep level of our norm consciousness, our shared worry about contemporary divisions crippling our culture, our shared views of the importance of rationality in relation to normativity, and our shared suspicions of reason do not imply we both fear relativism, nor that we both fear incommensurability. I do not believe relativism is a real practical danger, because I believe it is not a view seriously held by people. Relativism seems to me a name people attach to problems of normativity tied up with relaxing the links between normativity and rationality. A relativist is then a person whose position is characterised as such by someone who too closely identifies norms and standards with conceptual frameworks. I do not share Nielsen's apprehensions here. Nevertheless, we agree that an arbitrary or nihilistic or sceptical approach to normativity which would grant legitimacy to practices or views which by our standards turn out to be destructive and false is worrisome.

Nielsen, on the other hand, does not believe conceptual incommensurability is a genuine threat, because he follows

Davidson in using the evident possibility of continued communication as ground for regarding global incommensurability as a pseudo-problem. It seems possible that his rejection of possible incommensurability and my rejection of real relativism are sides of an underlying agreement that the real world puts real limits on our ability to distort it.

If there is to be universal norm consciousness with necessary conceptual dimensions, we agree there has to be a claim to universality in some of our own views on some of our own grounds. Perhaps we agree that to be human is to be aware of norms and that to be aware of norms is to acknowledge that a common humanity requires a common norm. Perhaps we also agree that no such norm can be articulated except with the involvement of rational analysis. And perhaps we even agree that at some deep level no articulation of rockbottom normativity is possible except with the understanding that the norm intended in that articulation be universally regarded as a norm for all. But we do not agree that our views are always relative to our own position. Nielsen does not accept, as I do, that in an ultimate disagreement between two positions, nothing outside those positions will settle the issue neutrally or objectively. If that is relativism, then I embrace it. For we all believe in the rightness of our own positions at some point, even when we also acknowledge their historicity and fallibility. Nielsen has hopes, however, that the impossibility of global incommensurability can overcome relativism with WRE. But we both worry that in our times the multiplicity of ultimate positions and their alleged incommensurability pose a serious problem. Yet I do not see how solutions to this problem are possible with a return to reason as, in the final analysis, the arbiter. I see such a return as just a strategy for maintaining the dominance of one position in our culture, that of the rationality tradition. I read Nielsen as saying the road to agreement via critical rationality is the only road available and saying it in such a way that it is more to him than just one position. On the positive side, we agree there is but one reality and that its hold on all of us is powerful, that our access to it is undisputed, and that this being so provides some comfort. Though that one reality may not be neutrally or objectively shared, this does not mean there is more than a single, common reality.

The core issue here seems to be: can any globally significant conceptual view be held as right, if right implies *universality* on the one hand, while it is held to be right in a *given* historical context at the same time? No one believes "anything" goes. But is there an articulable universal on which we can all agree *today,* beyond platitudes like "the sun rises in the east?" Was Jaspers mistaken about the *chiffre?* Grounds are accepted in our culture as good grounds. But there is no appeal beyond our grounds to arbitrate between ourselves and others. Some people believe differences must be settled with an appeal to reason. They will likely proceed to settle their own differences in this manner and will attempt to persuade others to do likewise. But beyond this living of the life of reason by believers in reason there is no appeal for them. Some people in our culture believe differences must be settled differently or do not need to be settled at all. Nothing outside our own appeal to grounds will arbitrate among grounds or will further ground our grounds. So our modern question is: given the proliferation of views, the loss of ability to feel secure in our own universality, and the apparent visciousness of some widely held views, what are we to do? Although I do not believe that an acknowledgement of this reality commits us to relativism, I do agree that we face a very serious problem.

At Yalta, Roosevelt, Churchill, and Stalin appealed to reason to settle their conflicts. In Calcutta, Mother Teresa has a different way to resolve our conflicts. I believe that the discussion between Nielsen and myself revolves around this difference. I also believe that, as a pragmatist, Nielsen is open to the idea that conversation between Yalta and Calcutta is not just a matter of theoretical debate but of efficacy in action. The debate, of course, is necessary as well as salutary. But its finality is subordinate to the judgment of what we experience in action. He writes eloquently in this volume about trust that goes beyond matters of universally shared fact, as well as about the situatedness of our concepts in our actions (v. 131,137-139, 143). And his most explicit positive reflections on trust as our action oriented basis for philosophical reflection in his recent paper on Wittgenstein (26), which is more openly appreciative

154

of Wittgenstein in this respect than any of the earlier essays (for example in 30), show considerable movement on Nielsen's part. With this in mind I will try once more to address some of our disagreements.

Whether our agreements are substantial enough to even begin to significantly resolve some of our problems, depends in part on getting greater clarity on our disagreements. So before I explore the potential of our agreements, I will concentrate on unfinished business in our exchange on my case for Nielsen's rationalism. I have greater clarity as well as greater appreciation. But not all my unease has been removed. Perhaps it can be more fully removed, but it is also possible that we will find some stubborn differences.

Unease about devotion to rationality
In spite of his disavowals in all three responses, I remain troubled by Nielsen's expectations of theory, rationality, critical theory, and WRE. I continue to read his metaphilosophical essays as claims that, at bottom, in the final analysis, and ultimately, we will remain in the mess we are in unless we are prepared to allow "reason" to lead us out. His most recent essays on critical theory (27, 28) only reinforce this interpretation for me. I cannot suppress my image of Nielsen as hoping in reason, as manifesting a deep trust in grounding our culture in empirical argument, as making an ultimate appeal to reason as last resort: if reason fails us we have exhausted our available resources for resolving the human predicament. This hope may be historicized and relativized, and it may be held in a sincerely fallibalist attitude, but if I am right in detecting it, I remain puzzled about how that is not rationalism. Though he appeals to considered judgments and in so doing makes allowances for the influence of tradition, habit, prejudice, and many other potentially non-rational factors, the relationship of critical, rational assessment of these judgments to their being acceptable gives reason a powerful priority. In the very latest material I have been able to consult, Nielsen not only continues—in spite of his own recognition that the mainstream of thinking is no longer with him—to dwell primarily on the *logic* of religious *belief* in God as a *rational* concern. He does not seriously

consider that if faith is not irrational but nonrational, there may be inherent limits to the validity of a rational assessment of faith. He also recently claimed in an argument with naturalistic theology—contrary to his recent Wittgensteinian inclinations as far as I can see—that practical considerations play second fiddle to theoretical ones. "Of course, if belief in God has some theoretical plausibility you can then add pure practical necessity as a nice ancillary reason" (34:35). As I see it, this minimally points to insufficient integration in Nielsen's views.

I can perhaps address this by asking: in Nielsen's view, is "rational people" a pleonasm or is it a term expressing priority of some human capacity above others? Does he mean something quite innocent by rationality, namely our capacity for arguing to correct conclusions? Or does he mean that in seeking guidance in life, we should primarily be guided by that capacity? Does rationality provide the mark of authenticity for other dimensions that contribute to our reflection? I know he rejects a narrow positivist or scientistic reading of rational. But in what way does he accept boundaries to reason? Rational, as Nielsen has pointed out on more than one occasion in the preceding chapters, is not just another word for meaningful, sensible, orderly, non-arbitrary for him (for example, v. 36-39). But why does he hesitate to tie it to specifically logical-conceptual boundaries?

If we take the pleonastic view, the Ayatollah Khomeni was rational simply because he was human. If we go by an old definition of what it is to be human, namely rational animal, he could not have been both human yet not rational. But it could be argued that this human being was considered by us to be inhumane in some of his important actions and that our considerations had to do with his not being as rational as he should have been.

No matter how much the Ayatollah may have been a "rational animal," his total picture, his outlook on life, was not that of the Western "rational" man. There is definitely a difference between Iranian culture and Western culture in terms of the place of reason in human life. I agree with Nielsen that arranging our lives or any culture by following the ways of the Ayatollah is destructively misleading. But a problem between us

156

is whether or not "Western"—precisely in terms of the place we give to reason—is *universally* human or whether it is *just a tradition.* I read the Enlightenment as traditionally saying that ultimately rational emancipation is the only way for us to cope. Though Nielsen as a contemporary adherent of the Enlightenment will acknowledge that the place of reason is in fact a matter of tradition, he continues to subscribe to that tradition as superior to others now known. But he has no appeal except from within the Enlightenment to demonstrate that superiority. And I, standing outside of the Enlightenment—if that is possible for a Western Christian—have as little faith in the Enlightenment's emancipation as in the Ayatollah's ways.

Further at stake between us is whether anything beyond our culture's having taken a firm position in rational emancipation can justify our view of reason as having this cultural priority. We have lived the life of reason and we speak from within that life. We are not likely to take issue with Alasdair MacIntyre's claim in *Whose Justice? Which Rationality?* that our tradition is a rationality tradition. And the Ayatollah's tradition is not a rationality tradition. But both traditions are in trouble. And Nielsen's attachment to WRE or critical theory strikes me as not sufficiently aware of the impasse of the Enlightenment precisely in its attachment to reason. After the rationality tradition has fairly well exhausted itself in finding secure grounds for a warranted or justified reliance on reason, these grounds are now widely accepted to be less secure than was thought. Ultimately, the rational justification in general of rational beliefs in general is theoretical narcissism, a self-refuting form of self-justification.

Nielsen is enough of a pragmatist to agree that our beliefs originate in our actions and that their ultimate justification is also in our life of action. I take it that he refers approvingly to Wittgenstein's notion of *Vor-Wissen* as having to do with "pre-propositional certainties of action." And immediately following that he makes the significant observation: "Our quest for justification comes to an end not in 'self-evident knowledge' or necessary truths or 'truths of reason' but in *praxis,* in action" (26:7) And, I might add, our justifications start in the same way as they end. By having lived the life of reason, by having acted out our priority, we have come to believe that we had best so live. But our problem in Western culture is that our active life is as such a life of reason, our action is rational action. If the rationality component is at the same time the problem of our day, how can we trust action inspired by the problem to tell us where the problem lies?

One result is that in our culture people need to *be right*. Especially men are not only fierce about having to be right, but also lost about being wrong. And if we are right, others *must agree* that we are. Nielsen discusses *normativity itself* as a matter of *being right* and lets that depend on our *reflective judgment* as a final and *last test*. The role of critical theory in this context is nothing less than an "inescapable starting point and endpoint" (27:5-8).

Being right, I agree, is arguably first of all a matter of general-conceptual-rightness. In our culture being right can be correctly stating the case as a fact, or correctly stating a rule, norm, law, or regularity as a belief. We are bent on intellectual-moral justification of what we believe to be a fact or what we believe is to be done. And we want agreement on this. But it could be asked whether we might not profit more if we turned from justifying beliefs by *rational self-justification* to justifying them by *doing justice* to what our beliefs are about. The rational justification of rational beliefs is obviously very different from a justification of beliefs by their efficacy in allowing us to treat with justice the realities about which we have our beliefs.

Being right is not essentially tied in with *doing justice*. In Aristotle there may have been a relationship; in our time there is no necessary tie at all. In the Bible being right before God has much to do with being just; in orthodox Christianity it has become connected with having the right beliefs. From Aristotle to the Enlightenment and from the Bible to modern orthodoxy there are roads that more and more have come to associate "right" with conceptual correctness. In the process truth has also changed from what it meant in either Greek society or Hebrew writings. But even in purely intellectual terms, truth as abstract and formal intellectual warrant differs from truth as doing justice to what we grasp intellectually in and through concepts. We can be right yet do wrong, be wrong yet do right.

Doing the right thing may be enhanced by being right, but there is no necessity here. Would our concept of religion not be different if our primary aim were to do justice to religion, rather than having religion meet the standards of intellectual rigor?

Nielsen is fully aware of versions of Christianity in which belief is not treated as a rational-conceptual matter of empirical truth determination (see 30:98-100). He more or less dismisses that as unorthodox. But why should traditional orthodoxy be a standard for Nielsen's assessment of religious faith? It may well be the case that Christians who wish to remain loyal to their own sacred writ will always be tied to certain minimal conceptual beliefs, such as that God transcends creation and becomes known to us in a process of revelation significantly related to the written tradition of the Bible. But that still does not mean that these beliefs can be assessed in abstraction from the wider context of appropriation of that tradition. If being right in matters of belief is crucially related to how those beliefs allow us to be just, it may well be that Christian orthodoxy's record on doing justice puts its beliefs in doubt precisely by Biblical standards.

I agree that the rational-conceptual life is crucial to normativity and universality and that agreement on these matters is crucial to community. But rationality is clearly not all there is to normativity, universality, agreement, and community. Nor do I believe that rationality is the primary element. Operationally, however, I continue to read Nielsen as tending toward this view, as I indicated at the beginning of this section. I am not convinced that rational responsibility for him goes significantly beyond internal rational considerations. Though his recent developments certainly seem to make him sympathetic to concerns such as are outlined in Lorraine Code's *Epistemic Responsibility,* his actual treatment of our responsibilities with regard to beliefs still appears to be slanted toward an inwardly rational concern. His favorite appeal to considered judgments strikes me as a willingness to allow other than rational factors into the rational arena for rational consideration, but not a preparedness to submit rational criteria to the constraints of these considered judgments.

His protestations to the contrary nowithstanding, Nielsen

159

appears not to see his view as one view and rationality's contribution as one contribution. The very idea of critical theory is for Nielsen tied in with its salvific place in culture, or in his terms, its emancipatory role. His claims for critical theory do not formally differ from claims made by Christians for the gospel, though he would stress that his claims relate to observable matters and those of Christians to an unobservable revelation. I believe, however, that the correctness of his stress is not immediately clear. Claims to emancipation and claims to living a life of love can presumably be checked out in similar fashion. When I read his interpretation of Raymond Geuss's list of distinguishing features that give *critical theory* a "special standing as guide for human action..." (28:4), the place of critical theory and the place of the gospel in Western life may be equally plagued by as yet unobserved results.

Unlike Rorty, Nielsen uses language that fits the context of ultimacy. He continues to talk of a last stance, an ultimate appeal, a final argument. This last, ultimate, final reality is reason, historicized and relativized though it may be. That he considers his appeal revisable is at this point not very convincing in distinguishing his claims from religious claims, because he would at this point be at a loss to point out what a way of life that is not rational would come to. Indeed, the combination of finality and historicity makes Nielsen believe "that we are caught up in something that is question-begging and it is not clear to ... [him] what way there is out here, if any" (27:8). Add to this his evaluation of religion fundamentally on the ground of its rationality in believing and his unqualified rejection of incommensurability, and we have an indication of evaluating other traditions from within his own.

It is again important to stress that whether or not a form of life is religious or a form of literature is mythical does not depend first of all on traditionally recognizable properties of religion or myth, but on the function they have in life. If the role of myth is even loosely identifiable as Eliade has analyzed it, materialism is both religious and mythical. If you are not a materialist, the trust that all forms of life are forms of matter is nothing short of magical. Such a trust is certainly not rationally explainable if you do not already have it. Both Critical Theory and Wide Reflective Equilibrium are in that sense forms of magical trust that without human rational control we are doomed.

Of course, if he takes his position in a rationality tradition, then on *that* position he *can* only be right. If "right" is a matter of rational-conceptual determination and if "knowing what is right" supremely determines our life, then theory, especially critical theory, will be our supreme guide in action. But even if Nielsen claims he is right about our having to be right *in* being normative, then he might still acknowledge this as a matter of adopting a certain tradition. There are many ways of relativizing the need to be right. Many forms of life are not forms of being right. Artists do not typically try to be right. Yet we can meaningfully speak of artistic truth. Many feminists point out that the "need to be right" is typically rationalist, male, and misguided (see Code, Mullett and Overall). Psychopathologists bear out this judgment. Mother Teresa is engaged in relieving suffering in a manner that differs significantly from *being right about* suffering. If our beliefs are operational platforms, these operations may be more telling about the truth of belief than internal rational considerations.

Once we can relativize being in a rationality tradition, rational evaluations of other traditions must bear the relativizing marks of such an acknowledgement, lest the conversation between traditions be prematurely closed. But Nielsen's belief that the rationality tradition is a superior tradition is so strong that such relativization seems at this point unacceptable to him. Yet consideration of the relativity of rationality is precisely what marks current metaphilosophical disputes in which we argue about who is right. It is plausible that the assumed importance of "being right" sets up the problem from the perspective of one tradition. And perhaps the other traditions should resist the temptation of arguing that point. Because if the proof of the pudding is in the eating, if the active life finally justifies our positions, and living the life of rational justification and finding it important to establish who is right is one such life, then if we do not believe we should live this way, entering the argument about who is right makes playing by the rules of that life unavoidable. More importantly, it will prevent us from living

161

our own life if we are in another tradition. It is not clear to me whether Derrida relativizes reason altogether or whether he just refuses to be bound by any current rational achievements. But is seems clear that in any case he is struggling with reason as a potential tyrant rather than liberator.

Of course I affirm that in matters of *theory* the core thing is being right. But you can be *theoretically right* in the affirmation that *being right is not* "the" guide to living. You can *be right* in affirming that wanting always to *be right interferes* with getting on with our lives. You can be right in having a theory which affirms that priority needs to be given to justice, love, and self-sacrifice and that a prior need to be *right* about justice, love, and self-sacrifice can seriously interfere with our efforts at *being* just and loving. And thus you can be wrong in having a theory which affirms that theory is the high road to an emancipated society. Nielsen explicitly denies there is any such high road, though implicit in his claims for critical theory are hopes that seem far too high.

Though as a Calvinist I was raised in an intellectualist tradition I have never felt entirely comfortable in that tradition precisely because Calvinism has also always had powerful reason-relativizing impulses. And from that position "outside" of our Western attachment to reason, from that evaluative "outside" I come to the conclusion: if we believe reason must deliver us from distortions, rationality must give sense to our lives, theory must be our source for shared norms, then we cling to reason in rationalist ways; especially if we also use reason to establish the universality of norms and to escape the relativity of each culture's normativity.

In sorting all this out there will be conceptual as well as semantic confusion. A fundamental questioning of the rationality tradition requires that many unquestioned assumptions will be questioned. This is not arbitrary redefinition. In his philosophy of religion Nielsen often complains about stipulative redefinitions or low redefinitions of reason or religion. But in our postmodern era we do well not to assume large, shared traditions on reason or religion or morality. Instead, we witness a renewed attempt to come to grips with old problems that will not go away. Our problem lies in lack of definition. To our

162

modern awareness too many realities protrude beyond our current definitions. If we acknowledge this we will try to use our terms in imaginative ways. Whenever someone claims in this context: but I am right, we are likely not face to face with a widely shared point of view, but confronted with someone having taken a position. There is nothing wrong with that. But when the positioning is not acknowledged, the position becomes ideological and distorted. With this in mind I want to explore a bit more my continuing unease that Nielsen is a rationalist, that is: someone who self-consciously stands in and cultivates the rationality tradition as The Tradition of the West.

What rationalism is not
Rationalism, as I perceive it, is not the same as a healthy respect for rationality, logic, and empirical arguments. Here I agree with Nielsen. We should be willing to give reasons for our conceptual claims, present evidence for our rational assertions, and make our propositional statements coherent. To do so is not to demand that we become rationalists. Beliefs—at least in most Anglo-American philosophy—are our expressed, stated, or articulated acceptance of the reality value of our concepts or propositions about our experienced world. Rationalism is not the demand that these conceptual/propositional beliefs should be empirically grounded and arguably coherent. If we truly believe what we conceive, we will be prepared to act on what we believe. That acting will justify or falsify our believing in so far as it allows us to do justice in and to our experienced world. And when our statements or our actions are challenged, we should be willing to defend our beliefs empirically and rationally. In short, I affirm rationality as a pervasive good in human life. On this point we do not differ.

I also want to assert, though not in the manner of scientism, that science or theory-formation as the institutionalized or professional form of accurate belief formation is a human, social good. This does not mean that what science cannot tell us we cannot know. Nor does it mean that beliefs of ordinary experience are in principle less reliable than those of science. It does mean that the most expert, professional, developed, and responsible procedures for belief formation are exemplified in science, in the theoretical enterprise broadly (not positivistically) conceived and therefore including social theory, hermeneutic interpretation, reflection, and self-reflection. To believe this is not, in my book, to be a rationalist. No one is a rationalist simply for believing that science does enrich, has enriched, and continues to have great potential for enriching the world.

Though rationalists believe in the universality of norms, that belief is also not what makes us rationalists. Nor is the demand that we must be reflective about norms. Though justice, the norm that guides us in seeking to be just, is not the same thing as our concept of justice, I nevertheless accept that without a concept of justice we shall not do justice very well. And to have a good concept of justice, one that is contemporary, that allows us to be just in our times, requires a great deal of sophisticated logical analysis, rational reflection. Such a concept will also have to be right by conceptual standards. Though I hasten to add that social agreement on a single right concept of justice is not required for a society to be just, nor is agreement of this kind the same thing as uniformity in being just. And I add as well that determining whether or not we are right by conceptual standards is not a matter of *simply* or just *conceptual* procedures. We reflect and argue as human beings and all of our humanity is in play when we do so. That is what constitutes Code's *Epistemic Responsibility*.

I can affirm my positive appreciation of rationality in yet another way. I believe there are things we can accomplish only by being rational and that without these accomplishments we would not be able to be human. There are, of course, vast areas of reality whose independent existence does not depend on our rationality—the rest of the astronomical universe outside of our earth, plants and animals on the earth, even phases of our own human existence. Today much of that existence does depend on whether or not we will take better care of the universe. But that only highlights the fact that without us, vast stretches of existence would have a better chance of continuing to exist. That aside, however, most of culture is not only unthinkable without human thought, but cannot exist without it. Without our concepts of them as essentially constitutive

164

elements, human relationships, social institutions, cultural enjoyment, the pursuits of peace and justice, and many other realities would simply vanish.

Having said these things, not much has yet been settled. The crucial issues are the cash value of "empirical" and the extent of the authority of "rational." If empirical is tightly hemmed in by "sense experience" there are serious problems, because no laws, principles, or norms are empirical in that sense, though the focus of our rationality is precisely these realities. These are unobservable in a manner that is incomparable to the unobservability of theoretical particles, namely in principle unobservable. A similar problem plagues our rational need to be definite. What justice is cannot be defined. Knowing justice is not identical with understanding its concept, getting to know it is not exhausted in trying to conceive it rightly. In the life of justice we get to know justice. But so to "know" is not only more than science can tell, it is also more than we can clearly define. At key points, knowledge "transcends" rational-empirical definition and description. When these affirmations about being empirical and rational are allowed to play a role in discussing our issues, we may get a handle on whether subscribing to the positive value of rationality takes on rationalistic overtones.

In this context I have a special interest in the extent to which human trust plays a role in knowing. T. Govier's paper shows both that we have hardly begun to explore this important area and that a better understanding of it seems promising. Nielsen acknowledges ungrounded trust as an important factor in the life of reason. However, at times he limits it to trust of rational-empirical facts and concepts that are widely and probably universally shared, such as: I know I have a head (26). But at other times he goes beyond that. At this point it seems clear that not all that we trust is also rational and empirical for Nielsen. But it is less clear whether in concrete instances he would allow for the significance of trust in knowing. A prime example is the trust of unobservable principles to which some of our scientific propositions point. An everyday example is my trust of the situation when I walk halfway across Jarvis street in Toronto during rush hour at an intersection without traffic lights. I wait in the middle while two lanes of traffic rush by on either side of me. That trust may arguably and empirically be ungrounded. It also is not significantly connected with any conscious beliefs. Yet I in many situations I must and do trust in this manner, or I would never cross the street. In the latter case I suspect Nielsen acknowledges the legitimate role of trust. But I am not sure he allows for it as well in significant phases of science such as that of the knowledge of laws.

In my view trust in the final analysis "transcends" rational-empirical boundaries in the sense in which the stricter contexts of science demand rational-empirical foundations. But it is also a crucial factor in what we call experience; especially the experience of action as distinguished from the experience of contemplation. And since all of experience finds its support at its extremities in trust, trust itself requires a basis in something else; something we consciously decide to risk giving ourselves to in trust, such as reason, or sense experience, or God. It may not be immediately apparent that even the routine experiences of life are surrounded by trust. Is trust involved in my seeing that the ink on this page is black? Obviously few normal people would be aware of that. But psychopathology teaches us that severe insecurity undermines even the most secure details of simple observation. Trust indeed seems vital to all experience. And at the intersection of trust and reason I begin to test for rationalism.

The tradition of the West
"Rationalism" may not be the term everyone would want to use to name Nielsen's views. I don't mean rationalism in the old and now discredited sense in which rationalists were different from empiricists. An empiricist like Locke is in my sense a rationalist as well. Rationalism is a tradition which does not exclude empiricism. It can have intellectualist or conceptualist as well as empiricist exponents. I use rationalism as a name for self-aware adumbration of the rationality tradition. It may not be simple to define that tradition, but for the moment I can simply identify it as the only tradition in world history known for its peculiar trust in reason, its privileging of rational insight. In that sense it goes all the way back to the Greeks. The Greeks

166

viewed this world fundamentally as cosmos, by which they meant a world rationally ordered. Knowledge of truth for them was the rational disclosure of that order. The true human being was the being with rational access to rational order. Physical, biological, or political order, natural kinds as well as normative principles, were all a matter of rationally accessible rational order. For the Greeks, reason and the rational order to which it corresponds were comprehensive, total, all-encompasing, universal. In this climate rational order as super order and reason as super judge were born. In our modern culture this gave rise to a self-conscious defense, a sophisticated espousal, a philosophically articulate acceptance of what MacIntyre presents as the rationality tradition of the West. Rationality is that core of our Western tradition on which the Enlightenment capitalized to achieve emancipation. And in this context it is undoubtedly tied to the logical space of reasons, to arguments whose validity depends on propositional relationships ordered by logical canons. That side of our humanity is, of course, entirely legitimate and so is its development. But in our culture it has been privileged, prioritized, given a place of superiority and pre-eminence. Rorty has referred to that special place of reason as the place of supreme judge of culture. That tradition is what I have in mind when I speak of the rationality tradition.

The Enlightenment's basic doctrine of human emancipation is the assertion of human autonomy based on human rationality, on the excorcism of tradition and authority in favor of rationality. Coming to terms with the crude cartesian form of this doctrine has, of course, been at the heart of the history of philosophy ever since Descartes. Foundationalism was a widely adopted form of it. But even after foundationalism, philosophers who self-consciously want to preserve the Enlightenment also try to preserve a privileged place for reason or rationality in human life. Habermas's critical theory as the high moral ground on which we escape distorted discourse is a classic modern version of the Enlightenment. Rorty's confinement of truth and knowledge to the Sellarsian space of reasons gives credibility to his claim that he continues the tradition of the Enlightenment.

In the life of ordinary people the priority of reason is

detectable in our culture's preoccupation with the single, simple, clear truth or norm; with having to be right; with what is the case; with rules, facts, and intelligence. In Western religion, notably Christian orthodoxy, it is detectable in the priority of doctrine over practice. Acceptance of and agreement about the right creedal formulation as well as subscription to a body of norms or rules far outweighs any other dimension of Christianity in significance. The diversity of major worldviews in our culture (Capitalism, Marxism, Christianity, Humanism, and others) in all of their forms (individualist or communist, subjectivist or objectivist, relativist or absolutist, nominalist or realist, and others) share a common intellectualism and moralism, the rule of a conceptual framework as guide to life. The appeal to the role of a common life world or of considered judgments, rather than undermining intellectualism, is more likely a modern way of maintaining it. Male dominance is not peculiar to our culture, but the male who dominates in our culture is typically Lloyd's *Man of Reason*. Webs of belief, conceptual systems, propositional networks have a position in the West that they have in no other culture.

In the sophisticated climate of the university the Enlightenment's influence requires that not only our theories, but all of our beliefs, truth, reality, what is essential, normativity, good grounds, justification, trust, and so on, have rational-empirical grounds as their primary and privileged framework of legitimation. Someone like Nielsen sincerely claims that any such thing as finality, ultimacy, a last word, or even totality is now suspect. But he also claims that in order to cut off relativism we cannot do without them and that in a fallibalist sense we can still use them. It is therefore difficult to understand sometimes how he can both "relativize" (historicize, contextualize) reason and still use reason to cut off relativism. In any case, the earlier forms in which the Enlightenment's visibility was recognized are now no longer dependable recognition points. But, typically, Enlightenment respect for and hope in reason and rationality does not thereby cease, even when the logical ideals once embodied in the movement for an Encyclopaedia of Unified Science have long since faded. Davidsonian arguments against incommensurability still seem to feed the hope of some

168

that with a solid set of theories the human predicament is in principle solvable.

If the Enlightenment's cohesiveness between Descartes and Habermas has any continuity, its character as a movement—or an ideology, a religiose position, a cultural tradition, a worldview, a typical way of being civilized—can perhaps best be expressed in its emancipatory hope and in critical rationality as the most visible embodiment of that hope. Or, perhaps better, critical rationality as the best route toward ever embodying that hope. Positivism as well as critical theory express this hope, Carnap as well as Rorty, Ayer as well as Jaspers. The best way to tell whether we're faithful to the Enlightenment is to determine whether we are rational. In that way rationality functions as supernorm in the Enlightenment, even when its believers are thoroughly historical and relative in its application and grant that reason requires context to make sense. It is not meaningful to characterize our Western tradition as a rationality tradition unless that actually says something which essentially colors that tradition from the Greeks to today, and which has privileged connections with the priority of logic.

Of course, the continuity will go side by side with discontinuities, the times of triumph with times of hardship. Human emancipation and rational autonomy have always been related in a tense dialectic. When autonomy means self-determination and self-reliance, emancipation sometimes requires stress on freedom to the extent that reason is experienced as hemming in our liberty. At other times the same emancipation requires stress on control that seems impossible without reason. Derrida stresses autonomous freedom, Habermas autonomous control. Both may be making their claims as at bottom the most rational thing to do, not aware that underneath the claim lies a dialectic of self-determination in which reason and freedom can be in serious conflict.

Kant's *relegation* of religion to a place *within* the bounds of reason clearly indicates the tradition's estimation of reason. And the modern *rejection* of religion *within* the bounds of reason is a clear consequence of the (unacknowledged) recognition that no religion tolerates another within its bounds. If the adumbration of reason in our tradition is at bottom a religious adumbration, faith in reason could not make room for religions whose faith would not bow to reason. If philosophy demands that it be essentially closed to religious argument, its ultimate trust is arguably confined to reason within its own limits. And that move is all that is required—not rites or rituals—to make the tradition religious. The non-natural, the spiritual and the sacred, or God may traditionally characterize religion, but that says nothing yet about the presence of functions of religion that now cling to reason in secularism or naturalism. As Nielsen says in this volume, religion is significantly a matter of attitude. And he clearly allows that attitudinal stances take human vision beyond being just a belief system (v. 43). Of course, a stance's being attitudinal beyond its being a belief system does not make it a religion by itself. But there is at the same time no inherent reason why a secularist cannot have the same attitude to nature as a Christian has to God. Conversion, rebirth, and reconciliation are key Christian attitudes. But without them one does not necessarily lack religion. The progression from primitive myth, through rational theology and metaphysics, to critical theory is one which does not lack continuity in providing solace in our quest for guidance in life.

If we link the trust in reason to its earliest connections with realism and we link realism with the trust of the perfect form as a divine reality in Greek culture; if we further link rationality's strong connection with the immutability of these forms and today's attempts to safeguard normativity with rationality; and if, finally, the closing down of language into literal meanings as the first order real meanings of words is connected with unchanging essences, then we can see how key dimensions of earlier forms of religion are still clearly visible right inside the Enlightenment. Eliade would surely recognize them as degenerate forms of original myths. And the way I see it, the right move to make would not be to rid ourselves of the mythical elements once and for all, but to return to an acknowledgement that no life is lived without its myths about what the eye cannot see but the heart perceives as very real.

The lasting inheritance the Greeks gave to our tradition is, positively, our yearning for freedom and reason in our lives. These are crucial to our ability to be critically responsible agents. And without critical responsibility no agent can fulfill the task of being human. But critical responsibility is not the same thing as autonomy. Hence my judgment that our yearning for freedom and reason interpreted as emancipation toward autonomy has its negative side in our rejection of authority and faith. Human autonomy interpreted as Protagorean humanity, the human species acknowledging no higher law than that which (human) reason imposes on us, is impossible if authority and faith are accepted. But such autonomy, in turn, limits and shrinks what we can know and what can be real. Autonomy does not open up our universe but closes it to a material horizon comprehensible by reason. To acknowledge that most of the universe is beyond our control would radically affect what we know. To submit to transcendence would be revealing. But our culture is essentially and unavoidably secular, naturalistic, and humanistic in its search for autonomy.

The uneasy conversation between Western tradition and Biblical religion has many weaknesses. There is the rationality tradition's inability—given with its inner organization—to see the rejection of faith as a disguised faith in reason. Another is that tradition's rejection of authority as a disguised authority of reason. And so is its rejection of revelation as a disguised revelation of reason. On the other side there is Christianity's inability to extricate faith from its submersion in the rationality of doctrine. Added to that is Christianity's consequent loss of trust and reliance as human acts which transcend all fact, history, objectivity, and propositionality, though not disconnected from them. The Greeks gave us philosophy as the source of sense in our lives, as the solution to what John Dewey called "the problems of men," to which I will refer as the human predicament. In so doing our Western tradition ascribed to philosophy the role which precisely religion played in other traditions.

It is hard to fault Rorty's analysis of the traditional role of philosophy as substitute for religion and revelation, as super judge. This unmasking of philosophy is an embarrassment to secular thinkers who for the first time understand that the "authority of a tradition" they believed our culture had denied and rejected for centuries, we actually had covertly harbored all

171

along. So in the "after philosophy" postmodern climate, there is a strand of philosophers who cling to the Enlightenment as the best continuation of the Greek inheritance, yet want to absorb all the postmodern critiques of reason and the Enlightenment. The hope for undistorted discourse only through critical theory is a form of that and so is philosophy transformed as redeemer in the human predicament. I see Nielsen subscribe to both. The transformation of philosophy in his case is not a move away from philosophy's redemptive visions, but an attempt to strengthen that vision by shedding some of the current vices of philosophy.

Many philosophers realize that the philosophical tradition has been distorted and ideological. But there remains a puzzling naiveté about how philosophy's role is *as such* distorted and ideological; not just as it has been invaded for centuries by all sorts of isms. Philosophy in its role as covert or pseudo religion, as the comprehensive rational grasp of reality which replaces revealed religion with a comprehensive belief system, aims to perform a service that has traditionally been the service of religion.

There is much empirical evidence that our Western trust in rational control has given us a world-picture which invites us to exploit creation. There is very little evidence to suggest that a closed, secular, materialist universe has added primarily to human flourishing. The view of guiding norms that associates them with conceptual-semantic dimensions of reality has not earned an unambiguous record of guiding us to happiness and healing. There is clearly something in the continued trust in reason and rationality in our culture that transcends the evidence of sense experience and valid argument. The "more" is precisely what the rationality tradition rejects as distortion and ideology in other traditions, namely faith, myth, and a leap of faith.

Many philosophers are quite willing to give up realism, permanence, absolutes, Archimedean points, and the like. But there is strong resistance to accept what is called relativism or incommensurability. This is more than the legitimate ideal that philosophy as the most general conceptual framework of reality's most general structures should strive for a unitary conception.

I see behind this a resistance to relativize the role of philosophy and of reason as the vehicle of the religious depth-functions of the Enlightenment. Relativizing is a process that pertains to conceptual systems, not to whatever it is we form concepts of. The same holds for incommensurability. It is conceptual bodies that may be incommensurable, not the world understood in terms of these concepts. It would be folly both to project conceptual properties onto the one world in which we live, and at the same time to reduce the world to these projections. It is just as much folly to simply transplant the one world wholesale into our conceptual systems and deny that this one world is present also in conceptions we do not share. The truth lies in between. The web of beliefs is human, we form it. But we do not create what we understand. The one world puts severe limits on both relativity and incommensurability.

One of the limits is that relativity is relative *both* to our subjectivity *and* to the one world. As a result it is easy to carry relativity deeply into morals, where human subjectivity is obviously vastly more pervasive than in our assimilations of the physical universe. And because quantitative relations in the physical world are stable to the point of seeming immutable, it is almost impossible to bring the same relativity into simple number systems. It should not be difficult to appreciate that as a whole two moral systems could be incommensurable in their totality, though in spite of that the shared world would continue to make discussion possible. It is only the tyranny of rationality that could even make us *conceive* of the possibility of communication as proof for the impossibility of relativism and incommensurability.

The Western tradition, especially in its Enlightenment form, can among other ways be characterized as advocating a privileged position for reason and theory *vis à vis* norms. It is not easy to articulate what this comes to over and above seeing it at work in practice. No particular characterization of this tradition is universally acknowledged. But we could say that in this tradition other norms, say those of justice or love, do not fully come into their own as norms irreducible to the norm of rationality. I see Nielsen as coming close to acknowledging this irreducibility, though I also continue to see the norm of reason

173

as superior among the others in his view.

Reason, of course, *should* play a role in our experience of other norms, in trusting and finding them, in shaping and in conceptualizing them. But on final analysis they must have their own access. Considered judgments and moral sentiments should not merely inform reason, but should also limit it. The norm for justice is primarily found in the doing of justice. The norm for rationality is found in being reasonable. Being just and being reasonable are irreducibly different as well as related. On the one hand it makes sense to say: our doing justice must not be unreasonable or irrational. On the other hand it makes sense to say: rational justice is like colored distance. Concrete entities can be both distant and colored. But distance is not colored. Human beings can be both just and rational and they can be that in relation to one another. But justice is not rational. They are irreducibly different and they are differently known as well as differently authorized.

Being just requires a concept of justice as well as a sense of justice, a way of rationally understanding it as well as a way of intuitively sensing it. But, as we know from ethics, good concepts and sound intuitions do not yet make us moral. We can be highly rational and deeply sensitive creatures and yet be immoral, though we'll not likely be as moral as we can be if we are irrational and insensitive, as Nielsen clearly agrees.

In the Enlightenment, with its emancipatory sense of rational criticism, what finally determines—in the final analysis so to speak, though no analysis needs to be embraced as finally final, just as the end for the moment—whether or not our justice is normative is the appeal to reason. Reason can take many forms: theoretical analysis, free inquiry, undistorted discourse, critical thinking, reflection. The autonomously emancipating community will want to let its *critical concept* of justice, acquired in wide reflective equilibrium, settle our disputes in the course of empirically grounded argument. In that argument nothing will be accepted as legitimate unless the process of argument itself has legitimated it, unless it has been rationally justified. More is at stake here than simply allowing reason to give us a sense of the coherence of our considered judgments and our moral sentiments. Before the court of

174

reason, neither our sense of justice, nor any tradition, nor an authority, nor any revelation, nor a grounding trust can have the finality of appeal that reason has. In *Communal Certainty and Authorized Truth* I have shown in great detail that the role of reason in the work of John Dewey, in spite of his relativising of that role and notwithstanding his situating reason in practice, remains an unmistakably privileged role.

My sense of undistorted discourse within critical theory is that of a round table discussion in which justice, love, taste, decision, enjoyment, and others can all participate, though reason chairs the discussion according to its own rules. More seems to be going on here than the making of a contribution to the discussion by one of the partners. Or at least it is not clear to me that what I described as the legitimate role of reason at the beginning of the previous section is the same thing as being the arbiter in human discussions. And that is what I have meant by rationalism in my ascription of rationalism to Nielsen's philosophy. Needless to say, I should at least once more present some evidence. With that I will close this preliminary clearing up of difficulties that remain in our disagreements.

The evidence
When discussing "belief in God," Nielsen never fully allows believers to take a mystery as something incomprehensible. It is not that he does not acknowledge the mystery. But it is inconceivable for him that the sense of mystery has the sense of pervasive incomprehensibility. Even though he is aware that faith is not reason, rational coherence remains a significant condition for trusting a mystery. I would not myself refer to God as an infinite individual transcending the universe. But even if I did, I would take that as a metaphor and not as a genuine concept. In fact, "genuine concept" as a reality which transcends metaphor is not a reality we should matter of factly assume as obvious. Quite literally, no language may be literal that is not also metaphorical (Hesse).

I think, in fact, that in the area of trusting mysteries whose reality transcends our experience, we will have to be content with metaphors in principle. "To say it is all a profound mystery" writes Nielsen, "is just to throw up our hands and give up"

175

(34:12). But I do not accept that at all. A child may hear a story, know that the story is just a story, and still hear the telling of a reality. I am not saying this to make the point that faith is like that, but to underscore that in grasping the meaning of a narrative there is no need to know literally what it means. The language of faith can be fully metaphorical without thereby losing real meaning. To see the distance between the language of faith and the "non-metaphorical" language of factuality, it would be instructive to read Schaberg's account of the birth of Jesus as told to faith and as it may in fact perhaps have happened. The distances are immense. But that need not create any problems for faith. For it is entirely possible that an insistence on what we mean by "literal" is what undermines the possibility of faith, because it is entirely possible that the world of faith is open only to those who understand metaphor on its own terms.

If a person is not self-consciously religious, it maybe difficult to understand what Eliade means by the reality of myth. Yet for a person who owns some sort of faith, the reality of that faith is so self-evidently real that questions of "literally" real seem inappropriate without affecting the reality in question. The myth is temporally-historically real. But the time is "all time" and the history is "all history." What happens, happens all the time. If what happens all the time also happens in what happens now, we need different levels of language to get at that. The story, the narrative of universal time is told in language whose symbolic or metaphorical chracter is hightened. The insistence that truth can fundamentally or at bottom only be true if literally true is not merely a form of rationalism, but also a form of secularization that closes human experience. Paradoxically, the literality of truth becomes a metaphor of its own, a peculiar form of myth.

True, orthodoxy in Christianity is correctly identified by Nielsen as in part a belief system. But he acknowledges that it is also more. Why is it that this acknowledgement so seldom functions? Functionally speaking it seems like a throwaway remark, rather than an effort to place the beliefs integrally within the more that Christianity is. The beliefs receive their meaning from the more, not *vice versa*. By this I mean that if we attach religious significance to a narrative, the beliefs we form as a result of this attachment need not in any way be based on or dependent on an objective-empirical, factual basis within the narrative. The narrative could be completely fictitious, yet I might believe that the reality it reveals compels me to act in certain ways. The beliefs about my actions will be based on the fiction, yet the actions for which I have this basis can be very empirical and so can my beliefs about them.

What "reality" in the fiction compels me? Perhaps a depth of wisdom about life that is so authentic and credible in its relation to actual life that it compellingly inspires the believers. I am, again, not saying that all of the Biblical material is of this sort. I am only saying that there is nothing "metaphysical" about faith's narratives having to have a "factual" foundation to be believable. So why, if Christianity is more than a belief system, go on to treat it abstractly as any other belief system, without letting its context characterize the beliefs? It may well be so that a Wittgensteinian fideist like D.Z. Phillips, when Nielsen debated with him almost two decades ago, was not situated in mainstream orthodox Christianity (30:94-101). But that proves nothing with respect to a discussion of what is possible for faith in God without being incoherent. To me it looks very much like Nielsen needs religious faith in God to be a species of rational belief, in order for that faith to be reachable as a target for arguments about the irrationality of religion. He is correct about many forms of orthodoxy. But there seems no need to dismiss as inauthentic the untraditional views of modern Christians who struggle with orthodoxy the way Nielsen struggles with foundationalism. Why reject their redefinitions of religion or even their stipulative redefinitions of reason? Why can these not be descriptions and approaches offered in the face of the many difficulties all of us discover in postmodernity?

Nielsen can deal with Christian faith's irrationality only if it has a common denominator with ideologies, metaphysics, or science in being a belief system. But the importation of religion into the network of a belief system—inappropriately I believe— is a Western attempt to make out of religion something that can meet the criteria of rationality. For believers that was done— unsuccessfully I believe—in order to fit the cultural climate of the West. By non-believers it is done so that it can then be shown to be false. Liberation theology is for that very reason not first of all interested in a theology of liberation, but in a liberating practice: emancipation if you wish. But not emancipation by means of another belief system. Liberation theology is to be understood in part as liberation of Christian religion from theology, from being contained within a system of doctrine. Why is it not possible that these new developments be seriously entertained? In that context religion is not *also* a set of practices, but *primarily* if not *only* a way of living.

I agree that the liberationist's Christian faith is not orthodoxy. It is not even orthopraxis, because liberationists are suspicious of the "ortho" in these expressions, the attempt to "be right." Liberationist Christians are more interested in living justly than in being right. That changes the entire perspective. Our discussion as a discussion between an atheist Marxian who pursues emancipation and a God-oriented Calvinian who hopes for all creation to be set free from its groaning might well benefit from an acknowledgement that orthodox Christianity as well as Marxism are indeed belief systems and as such do not do justice to the emancipatory and liberating impulses they also present.

But Nielsen's argument with religion suggests that his rejection depends primarily on the rightness of adjudicating faith as belief and belief as conceptual assent. That seems to me what he means by his assertion, also in this volume, that otherwise we can all gently be led into belief in God, religion, accepting revelation, and so on (v. ch. 2 note 47). Belief in God is for him dependent on minimal factual truth claims. It is clear to me, however, that in Jaspers' doctrines of transcendence and *chiffre,* the success of his doctrine depends on his claim that none of the claims about transcendence can, in order to have any truth at all, be truth claims in the traditional sense of analytic philosophy. And again, I do not claim that Jaspers gives us a description of Christianity, but only that Nielsen's claims about what is required are simply the claims of a certain philosophical tradition. Jaspers is not a theist, but in fact a philosopher of reason. What he demonstrates is that even a philosopher of reason who rejects revelation can acknowledge what Nielsen claims is manifestly incoherent.

For Nielsen the conceptual incoherence of the concept of God is indeed what is first and foremost at stake. It is a never ending theme, also in this volume, that "the logically prior question of the legitimacy of the very concept of God" is for him "the central question to be dealt with..." (v. 21, see also 18/19). But why, if not because that places religion within the bounds of reason? And why is not the inisistence that religion be treated within the bounds of reason an ideological approach? Why is that not false consciousness? Is that not, in fact, self-deceivingly ideological because it requires that religion be a belief system as well as that it deny its own character as a chosen position?

What would happen if we would speak of "concepts" of God metaphorically? If we cannot, in correct religious par-lance, "shake the hand" of God in spite of the fact that we do speak of "the hand" of God, why insist that when we speak of "the concept" of God we should be able to "understand" it? Because to be a concept it must be understandable? But should the hand then not also be shakeable? If I were to speak of a concept of God, I would simultaneously take that as referring to something "beyond comprehension," just as the hand of God is "beyond shaking." And just as the "hand" metaphor communicates, so does the "concept" metaphor. It is com-pletely beyond sense only if making sense is a privilege of rationally clear and fully understood concepts.

Another favorite target for Nielsen, also in this volume, is religion's exclusive truth claims through revelation (v. 27, see also his important 25 and his 34:29/30). He points out that although religions claim to have the truth revealed to them, there are so many competing claims that to think one of them has the inside track is both arrogant and without rational foundation. I will momentarily discuss the rationality tradition as the context for this contention. But first I want to remark that it is not clear how religion differs from philosophy here. Philosophies present truth claims to us, traditionally claims about how the world hangs together in a most general sense or about how the human predicament can be resolved. It presents those claims as having been arrived at in the most reliable manner, namely rationally. Does not the very same thing apply

179

here as in the case of religion? Why is it somehow different that competing truth claims have gone without resolution for two thousand years in philosophy, claims of monism and dualism, realism and idealism, rationalism and empiricism, essentialism and nominalism, spiritualism and materialism, intellectualism and voluntarism? Is there any *evidence* to suggest that the latest promise in the form of critical theory or WRE will finally achieve what has never been achieved in philosophy? Is it arrogant to take positions here? Is it mistaken to speak of truth here? Does the variety of philosophical traditions constitute enough evidence, after millennia worth of effort, that reason is bankrupt? I take it Nielsen and I both think this is the case. But then how does philosophy differ from religion on this score?

That aside, however, I am more interested in the question: why must the expression "truth claim" be taken in the sense in which the rationality tradition takes it? Again, Christianity as orthodoxy has taken it this way. But at least the Bible does not speak of truth in this sense—I would almost say: ever. Quite characteristically, the Apostle's Creed does not make a single *claim that* something is *the case*. That's to be expected, because it did not occur to its formulators that any "truth-claims" (in the sense of the rationality tradition) were being made. All the statements articulate what believers have *faith in:* I believe *in* God, *in* Jesus, *in* ..... A Christian who confesses is meant to be saying: in my actions I seek to give evidence of my confidence in the healing (saving, redeeming, liberating, emancipating) that occurs when I trust God, Jesus, God's Spirit.

It is often said that faith in God presupposes belief that God exists. But that can also be turned around. It is possible to say that faith in God enables us to say that God exists. In that case the faith would determine what it means to say that God exists. And it is possible to say that God exists in faith without thereby making the claim I am making when I say that my Macintosh Plus computer exists. In fact, the truth of beliefs that express faith may well suffer from being taken as straightforward empirical claims.

Such "truth" is not intended—though alas it has become that in the history of the church—as stating assent to certain conceived facts. Rather, truth here is disclosure (*aletheia,* revelation) of shalom becoming evident in the consequences (fruits of faith) of trustfully journeying along with the church in its following of Jesus. The trust is a confidence that the power of evil gets broken in the following of the self-sacrificing Jesus, in relying on the radical renewal of life in this trust, in confidently hoping life does not end in this trust. Jesus' saying: "I am the way and the truth and the life" is a promise that in following him this disclosure will occur, that his life shows the way, that his way leads to life. In this context truth means: in the life so lived the meaning, reality, or truth of salvation and liberation will be made manifest. Revelation and truth have irreducibly different meanings here from how Nielsen takes them. Nevertheless, as I remarked earlier, the beliefs about my life of faith can be very ordinary empirical beliefs without any problems of incoherence attached to them.

Given Nielsen's own adumbration of some of Wittgenstein's key insights into trust, why does he not explore in greater depth that WRE is itself, ultimately, a matter of trust? Wittgenstein teaches and Nielsen agrees that we share common trusts: I have a head, I have ten fingers, my mother is a woman. If you think that through, what it comes to is that for our senses to inform us we must trust them. Reason's former solid basis in sense evidence now points to a deeper basis in trust. And for our arguments to convince us we must trust them. Reason's once self-assured reliance on self-evidence is, on deeper analysis, a matter of trust. And though in some places in this volume Nielsen appears to limit his adoption of Wittgensteinian trust to universally accepted platitudes (v. 137), in other places he connects it with deep ultimate choices and decisions (v. 131) and with moral convictions (v.138). That being the case, it would certainly appear to be *reasonable* that our access to ultimacy, origins, destinies, and similar realities that impinge on our living have its deepest foundations in trust.

What is trust? The sensing and the arguing we trust are not themselves, of course, acts of trust. What do we do when we trust our sensing and our arguing? I suggest that trust is taking a stand somewhere, taking a position in the world, making a commitment such that by confidently *living in* that position, *standing in* it (Luther fashion) we find the other phases of

181

human life coming together meaningfully. If the best example of trust is being confident that I have a head, trust is cheap. But if we begin to talk about unobservable principles and goals as the proximate conceptual embodiments of what at an infinite distance we trust to be our origin and destiny, we can have access to what Nielsen, correctly I believe, refers to as inaccessible realities. Their inaccessibility is, of course, a matter of being inaccessible to conceptual analysis or to sensory awareness. But they can be "seen" in trust and take on visibility in symbols and metaphors. The seeing and the visibility here are not the same as in a doctor's seeing an infection by looking at a red throat. But there is nothing bizarre about "seeing" when Christians believe that Jesus best made *visible* our origin and destiny. Just what is so irrational about that?

It seems to me that in his discussion of D.Z. Phillips (30:98-100) Nielsen at least has no problems with the *coherence* of such an *attitude*. He may even object that talk about origin and destiny makes it possible for atheists to become believers, because talk about these things is basically human. His objection then is that if an atheist can find it acceptable it cannot be religious. But I do not believe that argument goes anywhere. Religion is embedded in a culture. For some atheists what is objectionable to Christianity is related to how Biblical religion was embedded in the rationality tradition, embedded in certain beliefs that implied concepts of a clearly irrational nature. When contemporary Christians seek to preserve what is authentic in their religion without the bizarre trapping of that rationality tradition, it is hardly helpful to object that in this move atheists could possibly be led to believe. Maybe the move does open certain possibilities in Christian conversation with atheism. Why can't we just talk about that?

A fundamental issue we need to address, it seems to me, is whether or not it is meaningful to suppose that there is more to reality then meets the eye or is accessible to reason, and whether or not trust is a human capacity which allows us to have access to such reality. With the end of foundationalism we may be able to "see" that our culture and especially the Enlightenment has given trust to reason in a way that has made trust suspect. The Enlightenment has grounded itself on reason in trust without acknowledging the trust factor. If we can now disentangle trust from rational grounding, we may also be able to look at trust as access to reality which transcends reason.

There are no final arguments for relying on the benefits of WRE. And within the Enlightenment WRE is not the single poisition all have taken, but one of as many diverse claims as there are in religion. What prevents Nielsen from acknowledging that trust is the main ingredient that enables him to embrace a question-begging first-and-last position? He says that "it is not clear" to him "what way there is out..." (27:8). But if he can refer to the things we trust but can't prove as certainties, if he can call them *VorWissen* though their knowledge is not propositional, and if he also subscribes to the thesis that knowledge is more than science (all in 26), then why can he not adopt the position that trust is a form of knowing, though not a (propositional) form susceptible to arguments of rational coherence or empirical evidence? There will have to be some redefining, but it need not be stipulative. It seems entirely reasonable even at this stage of philosophical development to look at knowledge as perhaps always having a strong relation to conceptual awareness, though not being reducible to conceptual understanding. If knowledge is multidimensional and trust is one of its dimensions, then it is certainly thinkable that there are forms of knowing in which conceptuality dominates ("being the sum of three and four") and knowing in which trust dominates ("the destiny of the human race").

Why is it not possible to have our discussion between philosophy and religion—for the time being perhaps just hypothetically—from this perspective? Is it because Nielsen overlooks that the common denominator he wants both of us to acknowledge is peculiarly his own position in the primacy of rationality? And all his disclaimers to the contrary notwithstanding, if he claims that WRE is just using your head, is that not the same as what some believers do according to Nielsen: redefining the Enlightenment so that every believer can accept it? Is it not a distortion of the Enlightenment to suggest that it comes to no more than what I described in the opening paragraph of the section immediately preceding the previous one (*What rationalism is not, v. 163*)?

183

I think it is fair to speculate that Nielsen as Enlightenment loyalist and certain believers as Christians are both beginning to distance themselves from an embarrassingly unrealistic reliance on our rational powers. It may well be that Nielsen's rejection of rationalism and some Christians' rejection of orthodoxy can be understood as an opportunity to bring Biblical faith and the Enlightenment in a genuine discussion. Perhaps Enlightenment believers could acknowledge what is in fact a *trust* in critical rationality. Perhaps Christians could honor their faith as a life more than a doctrine. That would give both sides a more critical self-recognition even when both would relativize rationality in being thus critical. It would also initially widen the gap between them as the gap between a rational framework based on trust and a faith which surpasses rationality. That very distance, however, could break the current deadlock of incommensurability, because it would open us to the common presence of trust and to a more common use of relativized rational discussion. It would not be a discussion in which reason showed faith to be irrational, but one in which trust in God and trust in critical rationality would be compared and evaluated in the life to which these trusts would lead us. If there were to be a resolution of the question of which tradition would recommend itself as superior, the criteria would not be those of superior rationality but of greater human flourishing.

Marxists at the 1988 World Congress of Philosophy acknowledged that Christianity could provide hopes that are not available in a theoretical system and that dying people need such hopes. After forty years of Marxism in Iron Curtain countries religion fares well there. It may be that the time has come in philosophical Canada for Marxists in the Enlightenment tradition and Christians who profess their faith primarily as hope and comfort to engage in conversation rather than mutual dismissal.

Such a move might also allow Nielsen to relativize his negative language about positions which do take other dimensions of experience into account. It may allow him not only to *say* that he, too, makes room for them, but also to *functionally* demonstrate, operationally give evidence in the metaphilosophical essays, of the integration of these other dimensions of human experience and their norms into his position. Perhaps we will then see extra-rational functions identified on the record as playing a key role *within* the development of WRE, not solely subject to rational control. Reason would play a role, of course. It would be the role I have described and to which Nielsen subscribes as I do. But reason would not be the guarantor of superiority, nor the privileged guardian against arbitrariness. To subscribe to human flourishing as an overall mark of being on the road of true humanity may not be "rational," but it surely is not arbitrary.

Reason
Discussion of this kind is difficult. Nielsen's ability to relativize his own views and his genuine attempts to listen to others as they speak from within their own worldviews encourage me to stick with it. But I have no illusions about making great steps forward. At best I can hope to have opened up enough problems to forestall premature closings. If I can fairly ask Nielsen to listen to me beyond my arguments, to "hear" me in more than just a conceptual way, perhaps the above exploration of our differences can lead to an exploration of areas of agreement.

I hope that I have learned from Nielsen. Now that I have identified many disagreements I also want to record my respect for WRE. As a strategy for discussion among people with widely different approaches to our human predicament, open to whomever wants to participate in that discussion regardless of attitudes to reason and rationality, it strikes me as a helpful tool. The only condition for entering into the discussion would be the desire to participate and to participate genuinely. Such participation would require acceptance of conversation and discussion as activities in which people listen to each other, are open with each other about themselves, expect to be changed in the process, and have hopes for greater community and happiness in part through such discussions. No one would need to suspend any commitments brought into the discussion, whether to reason or to revelation, to evidence or faith. But participants would have to be willing to enter into each other's understandings and reflect upon each other's commitments from out of these understandings; as well as be willing to hear each other's commitments and reflect on their understandings from out of these commitments. Enlightenment believers would have to be open to the claim that religion is not first of all a belief system—though it involves beliefs—as well as to the claim that belief systems are grounded in trusts that lie beyond those systems; though they may be sceptical about such claims. Religious believers would have to be open to the claim that if they do state conceptual beliefs and make propositional claims, they must be willing to be held rationally accountable for such beliefs and claims; though they may be sceptical about inflated expectations of such accounts.

In such a discussion there may well be common ground, especially within the Western tradition in which all of us have at least learned to value rationality. We don't have to accept Taylor's choice at the end of his essay—*either* the irrational will to power *or* the rational will to truth—to acknowledge the value of rationality, the contribution that rationality makes to knowing and to truth, and the power of rationality to lay bare common ground for agreement, general conceptual frameworks in relation to which—if not within which—we can assess divergencies (482-483). Reflective and thoughtful, critical and wide open argument on perspectives and norms can only contribute to our mutual respect. Reason plays its role in human life as one of the factors that contributes to our flourishing. Rationality can also be accepted as a special norm, namely in philosophy, theory, and science. But we can learn from the feminist critique even within science, that a focus on reason and logic alone will cause theoretical blindness. We should expect to make progress if we allow other perspectives besides that of reason to inform our theories.

Against this background I will give three forms of rationality special attention. I see them as special, limited forms of rationality; where rationality is itself already a special and limited form of experience. By stressing rationality as a special form of experience I stress that no special form of experience can by definition contain, limit, or be the one norm for all the rest of experience; as well as that other forms of experience will then be acknowledged in their own right and not evaluated in the light of reason. And I refer to experience, of course, in a

186

vastly wider sense than that limited sense in which it is used in the expression "reason *and* experience." I use it as in "experienced help wanted." In the latter sense reason is a phase of experience. Hence I offer these reflections as contributions to our discussion on both the legitimacy and the limits of rationality, understood as an aspect of human experience which can only be legitimized by the integrity of its role within that experience.

Reason as ordinary experience
When I talk about forms of experience I can use many expressions to get at what I mean: points of view in experience, dimensions of experience, layers of experience, language games, horizons of experience, and others. I have in mind the familiar phenomenon of perspectives of human experience that are mutually irreducible. An example would be rationality and morality. I take it these cannot be contained within one another, cannot be seen as subsumable under one another. As Nielsen has often argued, you can be as rational as you need to be and yet not be moral. In and by being rational you are not therefore also being moral.

There are a good number of these diverse perspectives. Justice and morality also differ in that way. The abortion debate illustrates that legislation intended to do justice still says nothing about whether what is legal is also moral. Nielsen's most recent essay on Wittgenstein demonstrates well the irreducibility of rationality and trust (26). Our basic trusts are neither rational nor irrational. They are trusts. Our rationality depends on trust but is not yet present when only trust is present.

Yet another example is the economic point of view. Debates about finance minister Wilson's new federal tax in Canada show that satisfying economic requirements will not automatically do justice in the land. Margaret Thatcher's behavior in the Commonwealth shows that the economic point of view can obscure moral obligations. The classic opposition of intellectualism and empiricism shows that the conceptualized and the sensed in experience are irreducibly different as well.

Enough examples to illustrate what I have in mind: human experience displays a wide variety of points of view, all of which are in some sense autonomous, or irreducible, or unique: trust, morality, justice, frugality, rationality, sensitivity, and more. In *Understanding Our World* I discuss this more fully (149-202). At the same time, no human experience is simply, singly, and uniquely of one kind. Legislators may be particularly obligated to do justice, they cannot ignore the moral point of view, they neglect being rational at their peril, without trust they would never come to a vote, if they did not figure in the cost their laws would be unrealistic. And the *cannot* is more here than just a *should not,* because the should is fundamentally a form of can. We should not tinker with norms because our getting away with it is an illusion. *Genuine should* differs from *can* only in the time it takes to get to the destruction. We cannot swallow poison and live. For the same ontological reasons we cannot transgress moral norms and live. They are norms precisely in that their transgression leads to destruction. And that, in turn, is one way in which we are guaranteed that so-called arbitrary behavior even in morality will only last longer than arbitrary behavior in physical-organic dimensions of life. But the former, like the latter, cannot last.

Though points of view are uniquely of their own kind, concrete experience is an intermixture of acting simultaneously on all of these various levels, from all of these perspectives. So let's say human experience displays a broad spectrum of interrelated angles of experience and one of our challenges is to conduct ourselves as integrally within this spectrum as we can. Such conduct provides an important social model of integrity. I will use this model as a plausible approach to understanding the complexity of human life. But I need to observe one more characteristic of this complexity. Although the angles of experience are irreducibly different and although we attempt to integrate all of them as much as we can, it is also important to recognize that in different sorts of situations different points of view seem to dominate the complexity. Smart business people know that without paying attention to social justice, to environmental concerns, and to morality in advertising they will in the long run not do well. Yet the prevailing point of view is an economic one for them. Legislators who ignore economic reality—though unfortunately ours are overly concerned with it—or who turn a blind eye to morality will not be politically sucessful. They demonstrate that their relationship to the polis is out of whack. Nevertheless, within the political community their primary or dominant concern—though it's not clear that legislators see enough of that today—is that of public justice.

Society as a whole, of course, has no mechanism to oversee and integrate the total picture. In a very pluralistic society such as ours that creates immense pressure, because we are forced to live with legislation many of us consider injust and immoral, with markets that do not respond to justice and morality, with socially unacceptable forms of personal behavior that are pervasively destructive, and hence with a public which feels increasingly marginalized and without power.

Now I have enough of a picture to continue. Here is the picture. Our experience arguably displays a variety of irreducible angles. All perspectives plausibly play their own role in all experience. But typical experiential wholes such as our familiar acts (writing a play, researching a chemical structure, managing a grocery chain, being leader of the opposition) can usually be understood as integrated from the point of view of one of these angles. Finally, many of these angles are institutionalized in our culture: the state (justice), the university (rationality), the market (economic), and many others.

Against this background let me make some remarks about the place of reason and rationality. It is a given that we humans are reasoning, analyzing, arguing, understanding, logical creatures—at least are capable of functioning in this way. But this is just one strand in the network of human experience. Its peculiar contribution is that in excercising this gift we become explicitly aware of structures of reality, patterns of experience, law-like webs of interrelationships among entities and properties. We regard them as law-like because they seem to universally condition the entities that display them. Entities, so it appears, depend on displaying these structure for their successful existence. These patterns we experience as general, common to the entities, properties, and relations in which we detect them. Our rational, intellectual, reflective awareness of this is conceptual and propositional. This awareness results in a web

189

or network of conceptual understandings which, when we accept them as sufficiently reliable to act on them, become our noetic belief system.

Our noetic belief system is characterized both by stability and fluidity. It is stable enough to support present experience, fluid enough to move along with us in history. That the earth moves around the sun has been a stable and almost universally shared belief for several centuries. That women should have the full experience of total equality with men is a recent belief only slowly gaining acceptance. Since the generality of the rational point of view is in principle common as well as unified, our fruitful excercise of this human level of functioning has an immense potential for shared, common experience. One single true belief brings a host of individual variety within the grasp of agreement by many people. Institutionalizing rational experience results in the availablity of definitions, shared descriptions, laws, and theories which historically enter into the fund of general, shared, common understanding of a culture. This fund makes agreement, shared methods, and common strategies possible and so contributes to community.

Because we have in our culture refined our "isolation" of these structures so much in the development of theory, we seem tempted to view these structures as well as the concepts and propositions in which we grasp them as themselves "independent." We are beginning to appreciate more and more, however, how much both the structures and our understanding of them are related to other realities so thoroughly that we can with justice speak of the relativity of these structures and of our concepts of them to these other realities. In fact, we have come to understand that the more we isolate them and act on them in isolation, the more we endanger ourselves. Only in integration, contextuality, and interrelationship can our rationality function properly. And the most immediate locus of integration is our language, which is the soil into which we implant our understandings, in which they grow and develop, and via which we relate our understandings explicitly to the realities we conceptually intend.

Language is the vehicle of communication. On one side of its reality language gives us access to our shared conceptual

190

understanding. It becomes our shared vocabulary and grammar of "literal" language. However, language is used mostly to refer not to the shared structures embedded in it, but to the variety of concrete and individual realities which do display—but which also transcend—their common structures. And because the same word refers both to the shared structure and to the endless variety of meanings embedded in the concrete variety of actualities, language is also very metaphorical. Each word is literal in its dictionary meaning which captures the shared structure, and metaphorical in its capacity to take on the richness of the concrete and changing realities to which the language refers.

The literal dimension of language is heavily dependent on conceptual understanding. On the metaphorical side language requires hermeneutic interpretation. Conceptual understanding and hermeneutic interpretation differ as the grasp of general structures differs from the intake of individual meaning, though both can be shared, both can be expressed in words. Both kinds of knowing are necessary for the so-called natural sciences as well as for what we call the human disciplines (Hesse). And it is crucial to remember that conceptual meaning is on the one hand like a snapshot in that the captured meaning does not keep up with the developing reality from which it is abstracted when we paste the snapshot into our theoretical library. On the other hand it is an agreement which demands continued conversational community to be maintained as agreement.

I do not believe that some words in and of themselves have literal meaning and some metaphorical. Rather, in our use we can sometimes focus more on our shared conceptual understanding and be more literal, sometimes more on our creative individuality and be more metaphorical. In the world of theory, where we use language as much as possible in its shared conceptual meanings, we try to be as literal, as univocal, as definite as we can. In the world of literature our sharing requires hermeneutic interpretation. Yet in neither world is our knowing purely of one kind rather than another, but only more of one kind than another. Of course, the one "more" characterizes the whole of our knowledge in a given case as typically different from knowing characterized by the other "more." Literature and science are differently experienced.

Knowing Shakespeare and knowing the law of gravity are not without continuity even though they differ qualitatively. The dictionary records what a given people at a given time in fact agrees to mean literally. But articulate and effective language users will even then always make use of the metaphorical overload of potentially all words. Lingual communication is impossible without shared conceptual understandings. But the language itself is already richer, because of its metaphoriocal load, than the concepts embedded in it. The reality of which we speak, furthermore, is infinitely richer than what even metaphorical language can capture. In order to know the reality in which we live we must converse with one another and thus share concepts and thus have a common rationality. But all the other dimensions in which we experience that reality are equally indispensable to our knowing of that reality. And these other dimensions are not rational. They are not irrational, but just other than rational. And the rationality of our experience just evaporates without the other dimensions. One of these dimensions is trust, without which we cannot know and which itself is not rational and is not expressible in terms of rational experience.

If we can for the moment accept this account hypothetically, as a plausible approach, I think I can get at some of the differences between Nielsen and myself and try to flesh out some agreements. The rational point of view, the logical-conceptual input into the complexity of our experience provides us with access to structures which in turn provide us with critical ability, comprehensive approaches, and common or shared understandings. Rationality produces critical, comprehensive, common experience.

Critical experience is produced, because the detection of general structures allows us to have concepts which provide stability and give guidance in considering improvement and change. Genuinely general structures have law-like or normative qualities. They indicate conditions for continued existence. In *Understanding our World* I have dealt with this very extensively (1-84). Without a correct conceptual understand-

192

ing of, for example, the complexity of the interdependent structures of the environment, we would be without means to help us out of our present mismanagement, partly based on misunderstanding, lack of insight.

Comprehensive experience is produced, because insight which is genuinely general-structural insight has the potential of covering the entire range of individuality in which the law-like patterns do their structuring. Putting our finger on just one minute chemical interrelationship in a gene allows us comprehensively to redirect immense areas of human suffering. Common experience is produced, because the universal interlacement of structural patterns is not as vulnerable to the individuality, subjectivity, and rapid change of concrete experience and concrete reality *in* which these structures are observable, but which are themselves incomparable and hence unanalyzable. But the structures can be temporarily arrested and isolated and, because of their relative stability, continuity, and law-like universality, used as criteria, as tools for critical experience called thought.

Our Western temptation has been, however, to overrate the grip we have on reality from the irreducibly unique point of view of rationality. Understandably, because it is easy to overlook the fact that a comprehensive and common view is nevertheless a unique kind of experience. So we can be tempted to believe that knowledge can be reduced to conceptual awareness, that truth can be reduced to conceptual adequacy, and that historical concepts of temporal structures can be projected onto an eternal and unchanging world of essences, natures, laws, norms, forms, necessities, or principles. The temptation here, I believe, lies in the lure of generality combined with stability, which can give our logic the illusion of timeless control rather than of temporal limitation. Especially if we let numerical abstraction—in which our control becomes calculably precise—be our guide and model, we are easily misled to crown reason sovereign.

Rationality is and should be present in all experience. But it should be allowed to have a dominant focus only when we self-consciously reflect, when we "think" in the way Dewey taught us *How We Think*. Reason and logic provide us with the common structures of thought, while thought itself gives us access to *other sorts* of common structures. But these latter are not themselves rational structurers. Reason discloses them, but only reason itself has a rational structure. And reason, as Dewey made very clear, is relativized by its origin in contextualized experience and by its reference to further experience for its validation. And here I am talking about reason in ordinary experience. The even more isolated theoretical use of reason itself needs the validation of its concepts in the web of beliefs of ordinary experience, in order even to be testable. All this relativity does not take away, however, the immense power of rational criticism. It only relativizes that power.

Fed by the desire for emancipatory autonomy, however, the power of rationality is not merely immense but becomes tyrannical. Since the structure of our conceptual frameworks is a logical structure, we are also tempted to conceive of the network of structures we filter into our concepts as themselves logically structured and to act as though their universality of presence inhabits the entire universe with logical necessity. Hence we can give our (isolated) conclusions the potency of ontic necessity. Though philosophers slowly begin to appreciate that reason and logic are limited to concepts and propositions, we are yet reluctant to interpret this as a limit on rationality. For that to happen we first need to learn to appreciate that the relation between two times two and the product four is a structural numerical one and not a logical one.

Of course, we can use logic, structure, or order as strictly synonymous if we wish. But in that case "logical" as in "a proposition is a logical structure" means something different than when we speak of "the logic of inter-galactic space" and mean that only to stand for the structure of that space. But I use "logical" in the restricted sense of having to do with the structures and laws of propositional-conceptual relations. The only thing logical here is the proposition in which we formulate the general conclusion of our analysis of 2x2=4. It is not the world of numerality that is logical, but the world of numerical propositions. And, of course, these "worlds" are not unrelated. The fact that some philosophers are beginning to appreciate this, however, is far from identical to the undoing of the damage the Enlightenment has done in feeding our cultural delusions about unprejudiced rational autonomy.

I find it entirely plausible that Greeks were bewitched by this rational-logical point of view, overwhelmed by their concepts as though they gave access to the "essential nature" of things. It is entirely plausible, given the peculiar relation between language and concepts, that the "discovery" of theoretical isolation by the Greeks can in part be explained by their alphabetization of language, as Havelock points out. They seem to have yielded to the temptation to project onto the actual world another world of rational realism, enabled to do so by semantic tools that made it possible to symbolize elements of the universe with elements of language. Given that misguided picture, it was no wonder that the Rational Man of Greek philosophy (women and slaves were certainly considered less, if at all, human) was born, the superjudge of culture, not a substitute for God, but something much better. If you treat language in its "literal" meaning as having correspondence to eternal essences—words as names for fixed realities—males in possession of the logos surpass the gods in power. The arbitrary rule of capricious gods in a world of fate yielded to an improved universe in the grip of eternal and immutable rational control. Nielsen, I know, has yielded the eternal and immutable, but I see his use of WRE and critical theory as a hanging on to rational control in ways that differ from Rorty's continuing respect for reason, namely as the privileged vantage point only for human discourse.

So enamored were philosophers with the rational point of view that they not only disqualified trust and feeling as unreliable, but suppressed them completely as reliable forms of knowing (which Nielsen seems to do as well) and even as reliable sources of knowledge (which Nielsen does not do). Having equated order with logical order, they now rejected the notion that outside of logic there was order or structure at all. Hence beyond rational order and conceptual truth the world was chaotic at worst, contingent at best: unreliable and devoid of stability.

These developments—if that's what in fact they are—are crucial to our discussion on religion. Religion is normally the

195

institutionalized form in which we ritually cultivate the human experience of trust to enable us to rely on our intimations of transcendence and ultimacy to order our lives; transcendence, that is, in the sense of surpasing understanding and not in the sense of being beyond the universe. But the major tradition of the West, inspired by its philosophers who became the secular replacement of priests, prophets, and preachers, was religiously enamored by reason. However, not only did that tradition obscure and denature faith and religion, but so did Christianity as the Western form of Biblical religion. It misinterpreted revelation as a supernatural dictation of concepts and propositions, which it called revealed truths. It lost sight of faith and revelation as unique perspectives on the world gained from storied traditions of fundamental trust. I will come back to this in the closing section on religion.

Perhaps one of the more hopeful avenues we have of regaining access to full experience in philosophy is feminist epistemology. The Western socialization process excluded women from power. The "privilege" of access to rational domination was not extended to women (Lloyd). Co-education as a late phenomenon may have been a blessing in disguise. For in women the wholeness of experience, perhaps especially as a consequence of centuries of suffering, has been much better preserved. Women still can speak unproblematically of knowing with their bodies, of the truth of experience, of the validity of sensed reality (Belenky a.o.). This can be patronizingly spoken of as women's intuition or women's emotions, but we see more clearly today that in women's experience we have a significant preservation of experiential wholeness and integrity. Women are not devoid of reason. Rather, they have probably better preserved reason as a contextualized human capacity, integrated in the rest of their experience (Code). In that sense we may say that perhaps only women know rational integrity. The feminist debate in science will undoubtedly teach us that even in the institution where rationality legitimately prevails, the academy, we will produce better theories when we will open up our minds to the many other dimensions of human experience. We will at least learn to appreciate that a theory understood only in the isolation of conceptual abstraction does not yet qualify for either truth or untruth, but at best for logical coherence or experimental confirmation (Code, Mullett, Overall).

It is less likely that religious experience will recommend itself to Enlightenment believers. In that kind of experience, however, the revealing value of dependence, transcendence, and trust remains real for those who enter into that world in spite of the secular and naturalistic trends of our culture. The materialism to which naturalism and secularism tend to lead us and the inability of rational truth to lift us beyond that sort of a world have the effect of imprisoning us in an environment in which the meaning of spirituality remains hidden. Saying to a materialist that he is suppressing spirituality may seem question begging. But the extent to which, in spite of our rational life of centuries, we are losing control of our world may re-open us to the power of dependence, the safety of trust, the truth of trusting what transcends our immediate natural environment. The experience that seventy years of official, state enforced atheism has not dampened people's religious enthusiasm behind the Iron Curtain has forced atheist Marxist governments to acknowledge as a reality that the religious impulse, far from having to be an opiate, can in fact sustain human life under trying circumstances. That might occasion someone to think that in circumstances without trial and hardship, situations of flourishing and freedom, religion would just wither. But there is no evidence for that. We do have evidence that religion may wither where another experience takes its place, that is, fills the same need. But in that case it is debatable whether there is a genuine difference between disappearance and going underground.

If we can learn to experience religion not as a set of beliefs competing with science, but as trusting the revelatory powers of traditions of humanity in which dependence and transcendence have been part of human experience, our alienated environment may again become a familiar universe. Religious truth is not the adequacy of conceptual grasp, but rather the power of symbols to reveal the meaning of our surrender in trust to the ultimate mystery of our existence, made familiar in traditions of ritual celebration. Religious people are willing to let such revealed truth at the extremities of our experience guide us also at the limits of our rational exploits. We can, of course, choose to define truth as propositional and conceptual. But the word history of "truth" alone would make that seem seriously arbitrary.

MacIntyre's *Whose Justice? Which Rationality?* has argued convincingly that a rationality of justice is impossible without a justice that transcends and is not reducible to *concepts* of justice. Only when our conceptualization is humbly open to a *life* of justice that is more than rational will we succeed in being rational about justice. Viewing reality rationally is encompassing and universal, yet all of its concepts are utterly dependent on the input of other dimensions of experience. Justice in action, moral life, economic practice, embodied trust and other experiences need to *in-form* (that is: have a formative role within!) our analysis in order for us to have useful concepts of justice, morality, frugal care, and credibility. In ordinary experience the rational perspective is not only one of many, but also one that for the most part silently runs underneath the surface, because in most social situations the points of view that dominate and prevail are those of justice, morality, frugal caring, vulnerable trust, and others. We do, of course, also reflect and think and analyse in ordinary experience and when we do, the criteria of rationality dominate. But when we do, the other dimensions remain part of the picture, just as rationality is not absent when other criteria dominate. The only place where reason rightly dominates in wholesale fashion is in the institution whose framework may well be called the culturally organized space of reasons, namely the world of the university, of theory, of science, of professional reflection and analysis.

Reason in science
Science broadly conceived is not only physics, but psychology as well; it is mathematics as well as economics, biology as well as sociology, logic as well as linguistics, ethics, and law. Science so conceived is the professional deployment of reason in all the pattern-and-regularity-discovering, generalizing disciplines. These are the most isolated because their focus is not only general, but also aspectual. They differ from disciplines such as

198

geology, literature, history, and perhaps theology, which are also general but interpret concretely individual realities; they differ as well from the applied and arts-like disciplines such as engineering, agriculture, and medicine. Science thus broadly conceived is the disciplined articulation of general patterns of regularity or of inclusive networks of order among properties and relations which in definitions, law-statements, and theories help us to understand, explain, indicate trends, predict things and events in our world, and in appropriate contexts act with precision and control. Science is the disciplined development of coherent comprehension of our world, developed—certainly in our modern world—not to satisfy our curiosity but to excercise power and control. Truth of science is truth of control rather than of necessary essence or immutable nature.

But if I was near the mark with my view of irreducible perspectives, we should not expect concepts of morality to have concepts of physics as a model. Patterns of simplicity and uniformity conceptualizable in exact terms and indicative of stable and lasting relationships are fairly well limited to those dimensions of the world in which change is extremely slow, individual variety at a low level of diversity, and the effect of our conceptualization minimal. So we should not expect the dependability and objectivity and precision with which we can tell exactly when a satellite will be where in the universe to be even in sight when we make statements about moral issues in a pluralistic society. Nevertheless, there too, we can do science. With careful analysis, we can detect universal depth structures of morality that will allow us to foretell that certain moral developments, if continuing, will turn out to be destructive to society. A picture of morality which is individualist, subjectivist, and voluntarist denies the reality of social-moral patterns simply because they are not the same as patterns of the galactic universe.

On the other hand, it is true that moral structures have a constitutional dependence on human rationality which galaxies do not. Our morality depends on our concepts of morality in a way in which the planets do not depend on our concepts of them. That's what we mean by logical objectivity in the a-logical or pre-logical dimensions of the universe. But just because moral concepts are not objective to conceptualization (because in part constituted in conceptualization) does not mean that there are no general structures of morality whose analysis leads to valid concepts. Nor does it mean we should strive for a unified physical theory, à la Hawkins, in which the whole picture of the entire universe is contained. If you are in search of this, it should be recognized as the quest of a faith called scientistic materialism.

All this adds up to science as professional and specialized rationality whose criteria cannot simply be used to evaluate the rationality of the world outside of the university. Yet the gift of science to the world, a gift uniquely contributed by Western civilization, is of inestimable value. Its conceptual instruments have not only enriched scientists, but our entire civilization. With the instrumentalities of science we can excercise more control over reality than has ever been possible in human history; control for our good as well as control for utter destruction. Science can contribute to the eradication of disease, hunger, and poverty. It can also contribute to the assurance of the destruction of the universe and the annihilation of the human race. Science, therefore, will never be adequately understood unless it is understood in relation to our own responsible role in our journey to our destiny.

But exactly here it becomes important to recognize the limits of science and the limits of rationality. And that recognition will be the more genuine and productive when we reflect on those areas of modernity in which we know that we have overstepped the boundaries within which this gift can be responsibly used. The environment, natural resources, the poor, non-white races, underdeveloped nations, women, homosexuals, the labor class, and many more are the only hope we have of teaching science and rationality where the limits of their power can be found. For in all of these areas we do not see the fruits of emancipation through critical rationality. Rather, in these areas the reductionism of a rationally controlled world has permitted vast regions of human experience to slip out of our awareness. In the context of our culture, saying that science has its limits is saying much more than science isn't everything. Scientism has pretended that it creates the only limits there are.

And scientism has been a pervasive force in our culture. Science is possible only if certain realities are "ignored" because science requires the isolation or abstraction of its material. But if these same realities are ignored in our understanding of the phenomena, science will contribute to ignorance. "The economy" names a reality vastly richer than "economics" can ever understand. Science occupies only a small corner of knowledge and does so in principle. It cannot "in time" hope to occupy the whole space of knowledge but at best only the logical space of reasons. Understanding necessarily is a limited form of knowing. It is knowing focused in conceptual understanding. But there is also knowing focussed in sensing, in trusting, in love, in justice, and in many more ways of being in the world. And this leads me to consider, finally, the place of wide reflective equilibrium (WRE) as a viable rational approach to human problems.

Reason in philosophy
WRE, as I see it, can indeed be another approach to philosophy. "Philosophy" designates an enterprise that has been sufficiently varied and flexible in history to allow for the sort of transformation that will make it serviceable in our time. If reason is seen as judge of culture and philosophy as supreme court, I reject philosophy. But if we see it as a reflective discipline which among other reflective disciplines provides conceptual integration both within theoretical reflection and for the relationship of theory to other experience, philosophy has a place. Philosophy can help bring to conceptual clarity or theoretical definition a general conceptual framework. Such a framework may serve us with a global and integrative set of concepts that will facilitate the global interrelation of the scientific disciplines with one another. Such a framework may also contribute to integrating an integrated theoretical enterprise with the rest of experience. In the form of WRE, philosophy can provide the conceptual unity, wholeness, inclusivity, generality, interrelatedness that is not available from any specialized disciplinary viewpoint. Philosophy as academic discipline is then the discipline which helps science develop conceptual tools for interdisciplinary integration and for the inte-

gration with culture which science should serve (not rule). It will then also be a discipline which keeps the rational enterprise open and moving, in touch with what lies beyond the limits of reason, preventing scientific abstraction from becoming alienating isolation. In such reflection, thought will remain dominated by rational criteria, but not be entombed—or enshrined—within them. If philosophy thus does a good job, it will also bring the theoretical enterprise in touch with its non-theoretical assumptions and prejudices, its human interests and aspirations, rather than build conceptual walls around theory which makes us *think* there is no other reality.

WRE so conceived can indeed have many of the characteristics Nielsen ascribes to it: serve emancipation, have normative significance, be a critical instrument, be comprehensive and widely shared. WRE will need to justify nothing except its own concepts and theories; other reality, existence, experience, knowledge, and belief whose specific focus lies beyond the specifically rational domain has no need for rational justification. If philosophy can accept what is real, can acknowledge, conceptualize, and interpret what it accepts as real and valid coming from other dimensions of human experience, and can provide concepts of integration for science in such a way that it provides a link between science and the rest of human experience, WRE will uniquely be able to contribute to the formation of a body of concepts that is critical, widely shared, and in touch with reality in an extensive as well as intensive sense. But whether or not WRE will be able to serve humanity with a unique and limited role in society will largely depend on its ability to let other experience be itself and to allow itself to be only one voice among many in the multiple languages of human experience. It cannot be the superjudge, the adjudicator of all culture that Rorty rejects. It can also not be "the whole truth" where all other knowledge is but partial truth. A comprehensive framework for science and for the integration of science into the rest of experience is very comprehensive. But it is not "the truth" about "the essence" of "reality." It can also not be our only or the most important resource for shared normativity. Nevertheless, we do not need deconstructive negativity. Philosophy can be a genuine practice with a genuine contribution that is comprehensive, common, and critical.

Nevertheless, for Nielsen WRE and its rationality is enclosed within a materialist, rationalist universe without ultimate origin or destiny. Hence his picture of WRE's world is not the simple, objective, universal fruit of undistorted discourse, though potentially it could be a fruit such discourse. If, on the other hand, he would be prepared to distinguish between WRE and the framework within which he uses it—which is not itself a fruit of it—then WRE discourse might not only allow for input from his materialist perspective, but from Christian, religious perspectives as well. Indeed, Christianity is, in Nielsen's view, one of the live options in our culture (34:31, *pace* v. 17). He also sees that philosophy does not give "philosophical underpinnings" to religious stances (26:30), and that it has no role "quipping away" (25:16) the human needs met in religion. It is therefore possible for religious believers, it seems to me, to develop greater rapport with Nielsen the atheist. He, of course, might be tempted to use WRE as the single method not only to evaluate competing beliefs, but also the validity of non-rational practices such as religious ritual. WRE itself, however, might be usable to help determine whether that is indeed a valid use for a method of analysis. But in order to get more clarity about what I have in mind here, I need to say something about religion and especially about how we will be able to relate reason and religion.

Religion

If we do have some agreements in what I have said so far, I may be able to make a case for three theses, at least plausibly present them as entertainable hypotheses. With these I wish to do more justice to an aspect of our discussion that has remained underdeveloped, namely my response to Nielsen's objections to religious faith. But that response had to be prepared first. For that reason the discussion has been dominated by my objections to Nielsen's rationalism. Perhaps now, however, the preparation has been enough and it is time I respond to his objections to religion.

One thesis is that the collapse of foundationalism as well as the Enlightenment critique should have profound implications for our evaluation and estimation of religion. For whether or not Nielsen is a rationalist, we agree that in foundationalism there was an unwarranted imperialism of reason. Hence it may be fruitful to ask whether evaluating religion from the point of view of this imperialism could possibly be a problem.

A second thesis is that it may be fruitful to view religion as in principle a-rational, though not irrational. A shoe or dandelion are examples of a-rational things, a concept or a theory examples of something rational. A theory is not tested for comfort in walking or for its response to periods of dryness; a shoe or a dandelion are not tested for logical coherence or for their factuality. Of course, our concept of shoe or dandelion is required to be rational. But then, of course, it is first of all shoes and dandelions that determine the rationality of our concepts of them. It would be foolish to require that our criteria of rationality would determine the acceptability of shoes or dandelions.

The third thesis is that if we allow religion to be religion, and faith faith, we may form an understanding of their reality in which, once they have themselves informed our concepts, they may turn out to be considerably more acceptable to rational people than we previously thought. But then it will be the rationality of *concepts* of religion we will be after, not the rationality of *religion.*

I will now briefly explore all three theses.

Religion after foundationalism

If I understand the reality of reason in our lives somewhat adequately, the rationality tradition's long-standing criticism of religion—starting with Greek criticism of mythical belief—may well be much less airtight than has been believed.

The traditional critique of religion stands or falls, I believe, with the assumption that in some very essential way, religion is a belief system. It may also be other things, depending on what you believe believing to be. It could be said, for example, that a religion is a set of beliefs *and* a set of practices. If you put it that way you imply—very problematically I think—that beliefs are not practices. But be that as it may, the discussion of Christianity at least has centered—certainly in Nielsen's case—on its beliefs, especially belief in God. And Nielsen acknowledges these days that his position that belief in God is incoherent is no longer widely shared among critics of religious faith. But he still finds it a singlularly important objection (34:7).

What is unavoidably correct here is that Christianity, certainly orthodox Christianity, is a *de facto* belief system, a system of doctrine. It may even be true that in Christian tradition the doctrine is essentially prior to the practices. But I want to argue that Christianity is itself a product of taking Biblical religion into the rationality tradition and that Biblical religion loses nothing of its authenticity—to the contrary, may gain in authenticity—in shedding its image as a belief system. The critique of religion which centers on Christianity could teach us that a developed religion cannot successfully survive an attempt to make it into a belief system. If we persist in interpreting religions as primitive "theoretical attempts to describe and explain the universe" (Hawking, 172) we will probably never understand religions. As well, if religious people try to succeed—in competition with theories—by developing their religion as a belief system, then evaluating the system by rational standards will show it to be deficient and rightly so.

Religion as an alternative to science, a rival of science, a different way of understanding than rational understanding, is doomed—as much as science trying to be religion is doomed. I believe we should resist both. So we should resist speaking of "the universe" and mean by it that dimension of reality appropriately described by physics. Reality is not, I believe (*pace* Nielsen 34:28), the same as physical existence. And we should not try to see physics as incomplete so long as it does not have a theoretical model that will serve, *à la* Hawkins, as a complete world picture. It seems possible to have a satisfactory theory of physics which would enable us rationally to understand the physical universe fully, without believing that this would amount to ending the quest of understanding "the universe."

If the universe would be identical with the physical universe, I would not be able to understand that except to say that, for example, psychiatry is a merely primitive approach to emotional illness, providing some help till physics has advanced further. Instead, I believe that physics is in principle incapable of even providing concepts for what emotionality really is. But even if we take understanding in a much broader sense than the understanding that is possible in physics, then if we could fully "understand" (rationally) the universe, that would still not be all there is to "knowing" the universe. All that we can rationally understand is concepts, and concepts do not exhaustively give us access to all that is real, nor do they by themselves fill out the complete picture of what it is to know.

If Rorty is right, our tradition has not only claimed that knowledge or truth claims should be adjudicated rationally, but that the rest of culture should be adjudicated within the web of our beliefs. Rorty also believes that rational people can critically review this tradition without loss of rationality. Part of such a review, I believe, should be considering the possibility that faith and reason are not competitors but irreducibly different. Science and religion, that is, ought not to be viewed as two rival belief systems, each with its own antagonistic truth claims. To make that intelligible, I must use the notion of forms of life that are not belief systems.

Playing soccer is not a belief system, nor is conducting an orchestra. We don't relate to a symphony by evaluating the beliefs of the composer, players, or conductor. They have beliefs, of course. They also have beliefs that relate to—intrinsically so—their artistic practice. But it would not occur to us to evaluate a performance or even the whole practice of writing, performing, and enjoying music the way we evaluate religion. The relevance of this does not disappear by remarking that religion seeks truth and truth is irrelevant to musical composition. That merely reflects a certain view of truth which not only I, but many other philosophers do not share. Truth need not be limited to conceptual adequacy, whether through correspondence, coherence, or whatever. Of course, if truth were a characteristic only of beliefs, and religion were not a belief system, then we should have to drop the relation between truth and religion. But the universe is not that simple.

It is possible that we have created a problem for ourselves by referring to religious people as believers and then taking that to mean their attachment to concepts. That's a late view of religious faith and a very Western one at that. Cantwell Smith's

Faith and Belief tells its story well. It is also one that Christians have participated in creating. Part of the program of making the following of Jesus acceptable in the West has been to make religion rational, because the tradition into which followers of Jesus entered was already a rationality tradition.

What would happen if we tried to re-interpret the empirically widespread form of life called religion? Only rationalists reject it, and I have advanced the thesis that this rejection is in fact a form of substitution without acknowledgement of this fact. If that argument were made only by Christians, it might be suspect. But Rorty's analysis of the rationality tradition strongly suggests that the West has made a religion of our relation to reason. This may mean that the one tradition completely unsuited for a fair analysis of religion is the Western rationality tradition, because it has not merely a prejudice against religion, but an essential one. It is, one might suggest, incapable even of recognizing the phenomenon.

I realize, of course, that when it is presented as a conceptual belief system, as it has been historically, Christianity is not capable of meeting the criteria of such systems. If believers try to conceive of faith as subscription to a rationally coherent and empirical-historical *doctrine,* the verdict can only be that it is irrational. But having made this point, I have said nothing about proper faith, authentic religion, the reality of God, or the authority of revelation.

If Reason is not superjudge, the rational evaluation of religion—legitimate enough—will need to take into account the possibility that religion is not first of all a belief system, hence not to be adjudicated primarily as though it were one. A rational concept of religion needs to respect the reality of religion first and foremost. If religion comes in a great variety, that needs to be noted, not necessarily sorted out into what is and what is not religion. If some forms of it seem incompatible with others, that may require choices. If some forms are not acceptable, that does not need to mean all forms are.

If religion itself need not be a competitor of reason with a religious doctrinal belief system, other evaluation schemes become available. Religion can be as different from the life of reason as the life of art or sports. Within the same religion, interpretations of key elements may differ widely. Within Biblical religion the interpretations of what the Bible itself is and how it is to be read, views on immortality and the resurrection, and views on the divinity of Jesus sometimes differ in such a way that the interpretations are not always recognizable as interpretations of a similar referent. For some, philosophy could fill the function others find in religion. Nielsen himself uses that terminology lately, though to indicate forms of philosophy of which he disapproves, such as metaphysics. It is always possible to relate to philosophy as a religion. But it is difficult, because as we know from our history, that tends to make for bad philosophy and for the exclusion of the religious self-recognition of such philosophy. As well, it makes for non-recognition of religions that are not belief systems to the extent that these are treated as though they were belief systems. And that, in turn, is understandable, because the exclusivistic nature of a religion as a belief system would also exclude the possibility of a developed religion that was not a belief system, even though its development as a belief system undermines it as a religion.

A crucial issue for Nielsen is, of course, whether religion is a belief system at all and if so in how far, how the beliefs relate to the rest, and how they are to be assessed. Let's take as an example the story of how Moses came to accept his vocation as leader of Israel's liberation from slavery. On the one hand there can be no doubt that the story is related to what modern historians would call documented historical events. In that way Biblical religion is historical religion: Abraham, Moses, Samuel, David, Jesus, Peter, Paul, and John were real people in real history. And whatever the Bible tells of them relates to that history. But what the Bible tells about them and these events cannot be documented in a way that historians can access, but only as the Bible accesses it: stories of their trust of God's presence in these events and what that would lead to.

The reality trusted as God's presence is accessed in that trust via visions and dreams. The stories about what these visionaries—prophets, for example—saw and heard have their own inner continuity and development. Their logic is a logic of trust, their evidence an evidence of trust. Together they have a coherence of experienced trust. I trust that our children were given to my wife and myself by God. That doesn't mean bypassing intercourse and pregnancy. It does mean trusting that there is more going on than intercourse and pregnancy. The more is connected with the Biblical stories. But if you interpreted the more as a historian would, it evaporates. The reality of the stories is real only in the stories as trusted. What you can tell of the reality beyond those stories is exactly nothing.

The inner connectedness of the trusted reality in the stories has enough coherence that within the accepted interpretation—which will differ from community to community and from time to time—it is possible to tell what is and what is not authentic. "God eats soup but not yoghurt" fits no religion that I know. "God protected me from worse" when I got hurt but not killed in a mishap belongs to almost every religion I know. Who or what is God? Beyond and outside the stories that are trusted there is neither knowing nor telling. Every person who is religious *knows what* is accessed in the stories and the trust to the extent of *knowing what to do* in response. The trust in the reponse comes in terms of trusting that the promise attached to trusting the story leads to what is hoped for: liberation, salvation, justice, peace. Outside of that there is no reality. But that does not mean there is no reality. For the religious person trusts that in the trust a sure road to redemption is accessed, a road that is real, a road that is empirically walkable, a road that leads to empirical consequences. And the reality in response to which these roads are experienced as real is called God. And God is brought into our experience via stories that tell what happened to people—what was revealed to them, as we say—as a result of that trust. The language of those stories uses almost any natural phenomenon to refer to "God:" rock, fire, wind, spirit, love, and so on. Christians believe that God became as real as we will ever get in the way that Jesus related to and hence revealed God.

All the "beliefs," and there are "beliefs," have their reality within the stories in connection with the evoked behaviors. But perhaps it is better not to call them beliefs, because they do not articulate ordinary empirical concepts, even though without the use of concepts they could not be meaningful. They articulate trusts in terms of concepts of ordinary experience. But the trusts are not in what the concepts conceive but what is trusted as present beyond these. Nevertheless, these conceptoid trust-beliefs do form a coherence within which "believers" assess what is authentic about their lives of trust and what isn't. But outside of the trust the reality that is trusted is not available, will not be revealed, cannot be known.

This probably makes not little, but no sense when evaluated from within a "purely" empirical-rational-noetic web of beliefs. But that is as it should be, because these "beliefs" do not fit a system which takes that web as the limit of what can be believed. Nielsen may object to dealing with the irreducibility of religion to such a belief system as too stipulative a redefinition of religion. But this objection carries too little weight. In some cultures Christianity is unacceptable to people precisely because in their experience Christianity differs from a religion by being a doctrine, something to be intellectually appropriated. They are suspicious of a doctrine which tries to pass itself off as a religion. And there are other reasons for considering alternative definitions. In the postmodern situation resolving puzzles of this kind should not be confined within previously well defined conceptual boundaries, but rather directed at previously untried approaches, to be judged on their merits. The traditional rational prejudice of the Enlightenment must not have apriori advantage in the discussion, unless it can reestablish itself in a postmodern world. Religion is in trouble today, but so is the life of reason.

We can at least start on equal footing. To be rational about trust we need not set rational criteria first and then see if we can trust. To trust a genuinely conceptual belief system, that system must be rational. To trust Nielsen's WRE, we rightly require it to be rational. But if Christianity, now characterized as the following of Christ, as trusting his way to human flourishing enough to walk it, is not necessarily a rational-empirical belief system—though historically it became a belief system—we may also evaluate it as a possible practice. That the Bible refers to the *Christos* of Christianity, the man Jesus of Nazareth, as son of God, need not mean anything more than that in all his life he embodied the full reality of what it means to trust God in all of who you are. Jesus can remain son of God uniquely, yet not differently from the way in which it is the vocation of all human beings to be children of God. The following of Jesus will, in fact, be accomplished precisely in so far as the follower becomes such a child.

Naturally, a historically developed life of faith in God in terms of following Jesus will include an articulation of what this comes to. In so far as this articulation is distinct from other such articulations and has an inner coherence, it may be said that Christianity has a distinct "belief system." But such a coherent articulation need not be different in status from, for example, the articulation of how certain ideas and concepts were an integral part of Toscanini's performances of Beethoven. Such an articulation could certainly be achieved. But having it available would still make it quite silly to begin speaking of Toscanini's Beethoven as a belief system. Yet we could possibly speak of Toscanini's Beethoven as the true Beethoven without even then having explicit reference primarily to Toscanini's beliefs.

Both Nielsen and I know mysteries, acknowledge that we cannot explain everything and that there is more to be known than science can account for. Even where science is competent and qualified, there is much mystery left. We can acknowledge this by saying that within our awareness, layers of reality and experience transcend rationality and sensibility. Though they enter our experience, we do not speak of observing them with our eyes, nor of rationally comprehending them. Trust is one way of holding on to what we know without knowing how to explain it. One important role of religion is the cultivation of such trust. And there is no need to speak of trust only where knowledge stops. We can perfectly well speak of trust-knowledge where comprehension stops.

Trust is needed at all levels of experience. Given my own incompetence, I need a good deal of trust to benefit from reading Hawkins' *A Brief History of Time*. In the context of such trust I learn a lot. The same thing happens when we allow the reality of mystery to enter our experience in trust. I suggest that the meaning of the religious term "revelation" is first and foremost a way of naming what happens to our awareness if we

211

let mystery, transcendence "inform" us, play a role in our total knowledge field. We may speak of revelation as a process of mystery (the unexplained) and transcendence (what is beyond explanation or what cannot be accounted for simply by what is natural) entering into knowledge through trust. It seems likely that we all have this revelatory dimension to our knowledge. It would seem reasonable to investigate this.

I agree with Nielsen that the universe seen as a definite entity with a rationally conceivable definite origin and destiny is not a reality (34:30). But "universe," "origin," and "destiny" are nevertheless not empty words; not even when "ultimate" gets attached to them. Beliefs about these are not empirical-propositional, but articulated guides through history, ways in which humanity hopes, ways in which we trust the presence of the unseen. Traditions of storied wisdom, myths, and ideologies make our communal human journey in the universe between ultimate origin and destiny more meaningful, even though these stories can make no pretense to being rational-empirical accounts, factual-historical descriptions. At the same time, they count in history, help us make history, and help us in interpreting history religiously. Our ways of flourishing and our dealings with death and disaster are in fact rooted in them. They are real in that sense. And Christians believe that in the Bible we have such a faith-narrative that is reliable, which will in fact and truly give us well-founded hope.

In conclusion: in discussing religion we are not primarily discussing views or beliefs, even though they are in the picture. Our problem is not first of all one of radically different views, but of ways of living. If we do discuss views here, they are second order. They are not themselves about views or beliefs, but about ways of life; whether or not these are understood as religious. They are not beliefs internal to the narrative but descriptive of what we believe the narrative requires of us in response. The legitimacy of very different traditions may be feared as endangering the unitary approach of reason to truth. But realities and expectations connected with what transcends us, thoroughly relativize what is right or what is rational. If that is relativism, so be it, so long as this is not understood as a view which endorses individualistic and arbitrary subjectivism. Reason is at risk in the experience of mystery and that experience relativizes reason, much the way Jaspers relates reason to the *chiffre* of transcendence. WRE's inability to accept a relativized reason shows how precisely in that respect it is a form of rationalism. Our knowledge as such is not limited by bounds of reason, but only our conceptual knowledge, our rational comprehension, which though being a component of all knowing is not all there is to knowing. And reason within the wider context of knowledge as such is meaningful only within the context of, surrounded by, and limited by mystery.

The Bible knows only one "true" God, but it acknowledges "true" worship outside of the boundaries of both the Old and the New Testament traditions. In the context of a religious tradition, whether I'm right (as in determining what is the case or what is according to universal rules) is less important than whether a hurt gets healed, a burden lifted. Norms for flourishing, as all norms, are always unobservable. Norms are not facts, whether or not it makes sense to speak of the fact of normativity. We detect them first of all in not having followed them. Hence ways of life and their norms are evaluated in terms of the life to which they lead and in terms of the consequences we expect to follow.

An inquiry into the nature of trust and its effects on experience seems an important part of these considerations. Nielsen is willing to accept trust. If he can consider trust as access to what transcends reason and our senses, he may look in a different way at what religious people mean by God. If by "God" we mean what lies "beyond" all things as their origin, the impenetrable source of their reality, our guide to a destiny of flourishing, we can consider the use of any reality as a symbol for what is the mystery "behind" it. This is precisely what cuts out the possibility of doctrine conceived as a permanent underlying conceptual system. When we say, for example, that God is the incomprehensible, mysterious origin and unity of the ways that lead to happy existence, we are still speaking metaphorically, symbolically. Traditional images of God as creator, father, lord, redeemer, judge, the omniscient-omnipotent being of beings are all faith metaphors. They translate the incomprehensible and invisible mystery of God, through faith (trust!

213

remember, not "belief" in the rational sense and especially revealed), into symbols that give us something to hold on to. Trust in these symbols as a foundation for our hopes, symbols as realities that are not conceptual, makes it possible to treat them differently than the truth-claims of the rationality tradition. Such truth is not accuracy, factuality, correctness, arguability, objectivity, historicity, observability. Rather, it is a trustworthy symbol of mystery, which serves to provide a framework for action. It is accessible only in storied fashion, not in terms of a permanently conceivable what or who.

Religion and reason
How, then, could people raised in the rationality tradition of our culture view the relation of reason and religion more positively? In terms of my proposal of looking at reason and rationality as distinct kinds of experience, we can begin by acknowledging the limits of rational experience. Not all of our experience is or needs to be rational. It is enough that our concepts be distinct, our propositions clear, our definitions correct, our theories correct. Our rationality has enough challenge in fulfilling our intellectual need for definition, clarity, and explanation. These limitations still leave reason with considerable power. The rational-conceptual tools we produce give us a grasp of general structures whose definiteness and clarity gives us the power of explanation. Individual reality is conceptually experienced as fitting broader frameworks with law-like character. When we find the logical home of something within that coherence, its reasoned place in its conceptual context, we have explained it. These tools also give us the power of criticism. Any individual reality which does not fit the law-like context of real structures legitimately endures the judgment of reason.

These limitations leave rationality more than enough scope. The general and encompassing nature of conceptual tools implies that concepts are necessarily univocal. In principle only one concept can be the "right" concept of something and what we claim is "the case" will always be in competition with claims that differ. Thus a simple definition or theory which is "right" will be able to withstand the competing claim of others

214

as well as cover all concrete and individual reality intended in it.

These powers must not be interpreted as rational omnipotence. They should not confuse us into thinking that concept users become judges or creators of what they conceptualize, even when it is true that they allow us to be critical and allow us to be creative. Intellectuals as social critics are in their place. As supreme judges of reality, the way I understand Habermas, theorists overstep their boundaries. Except the products of reason, such as concepts, propositions, definitions, and theories, nothing in reality needs rational justification. About nothing that is not itself of a rational character does it make sense to say that it is irrational. The very concept "irrational" is irrelevant unless what we are evaluating is rational-conceptual in kind. Rational or irrational are conceptual characteristics. Most of our experiences, practices, and behaviors are neither rational nor irrational but just different. They may have properties, components, dimensions, aspects, or relationships that qualify as rational or irrational. But for the most part they will be of a different kind.

Economic theory is a good example. Theorists understand concepts about the economy. When we think that what they understand is the same thing as knowing economic reality, we start depending on their advice to solve real economic problems. The result is our present inability to manage the economy.

At this point let me review the tradition of religion as a belief system. Religious beliefs, in so far as they are not what I have referred to as conceptoid articulations of trust, are genuine beliefs. But they are beliefs regarding our practices. Religion as belief and doctrine is typically Hellenic. Consequently, such a religion sets itself up for evaluation of its trust mistaken as conceptual-factual truth claims. And since rational truth claims are exclusive, truth in religion will become strongly related to what is right; right understood as the right thing to do according to a single rule (moralism or legalism) or as the right thing to think or "believe" concerning what is the case (intellectualism).

When I reject this, I do not mean to say there is no role for

215

reason in religion. I do not want to say either that genuine beliefs within the bounds of religion cannot be rationally defended against challenges. But the role of reason is limited to grasping what religion in fact is, rather than prescribing what it should rationally be. Reason's role is not that of determining whether or not people should be religious (most will be anyway), but of trying to grasp conceptually what the peculiar role of religion in fact is. The mistake of seeing religion as identical with a belief system, trust as assent to doctrine, has its complement in seeing reason as super judge. The peculiar role reversal of reason and religion in the West has been to make reason the only religion (=the only way to human flourishing) and to make religion (other than that of reason) irrational and hence unseemly for (religiously) rational people.

Christianity has tried to maintain itself in the West first by making itself, by the eleventh century, acceptable to reason, then by using a propositionally infallible Bible to compete with science as fallible knowledge, as in the battle between creationism and evolutionism. This has had the disastrous result of not only deforming Biblical religion from journey into doctrine, but also of Christianity's becoming more and more unacceptable by the standards it allowed to become its own. There was nothing wrong with Christianity's attempt to situate itself reasonably within a culture devoted to reason. But Christianity did not recognize that the role of reason in religion is to be played within the bounds of what religion is.

In our·culture, adherents of the Christian religion did not sufficiently realize that adaptation to the rationality tradition was adaptation to a fundamentally alien authority. Kant's analysis of religion within the bounds of reason is a natural move within the West. If I say this role was incorrectly conceived by Christianity, I do not mean—I repeat—to say there is no role for reason in religion, nor that religion could not adapt to a rationality culture. Nor do I deny the historical conflict between faith and reason. But I am saying that the limits of reason's function within religion are set by religion. As within the state our rational analysis is limited by the experience of doing justice, so within religion our rational analysis of our role is limited by having faith. That does not make discussion

216

between faith and unbelief impossible, because such a discussion is in fact a discussion between faiths.

Religion is not without understanding. But we have long known that understanding itself is a phenomenon with many different colors. The understanding which surfaces in hermeneutics differs importantly from that in science. A similar differentiation needs to be made for understanding that is religious. Understanding as such is not religious in and of itself, or in abstraction, but because it is always the understanding of humans who in their ultimate commitments are religious. And intelligent human beings who acknowledge their religious position will also do their understanding in integral relation to their religious faith. If a certain devotion to reason rejects this as improper, reason simply becomes its own religion within understanding. But religion is then understood from its functional role rather than from certain phenomena traditionally associated with it such as the spiritual or the sacred. Hence I now need to say some things about what can be said about religion as an irreducibly unique form of life.

The core of religion, I believe is the practice of dependence. Actually, I distinguish between that distinct *practice*—the cultic practices, the rites and rituals of a faith tradition—and the actual *dependence of the total person.* Both can be referred to as religion. But for the moment I can dispense with that distinction. Dependence, of course, is another strike against religion within the Enlightenment, because that movement— in this way manifesting a deeply rooted Western tradition as well—not only made reason the encompassing horizon of experience, but also looked upon the process of emancipation not merely as a liberation in general, but specifically as a liberation *from* authority and revelation, and liberation *for* autonomy and independence. Hence there was a second reason to deny religion its role, because religion signifies dependence. But in fact we all depend on many things in many ways and most of our dependence is beyond our control. The San Francisco earthquake was a living reminder of that once again. And this dependence gives rise to the human quest for knowing how we can ultimately depend in a universe whose origin and destiny are an ultimate mystery to us. And any knowledge we

217

may have of this mystery will not be objectively factual, empirically rational knowledge, but trust knowledge. And trust knowledge is not an inferior form of conceptual knowing but an irreducibly different form of a knowledge practice.

Now, as I have said earlier, Nielsen has lately stressed—agreeing with Wittgenstein—the inescapable need for trust in knowing. Trust, I would say, signals our dependence, not just in knowing, but in all of life. We have made neither ourselves nor most of what we find in our world. To be at home in our world we need to trust. We need to trust our senses, our analyses, our legs, the sidewalk. Trust is the ultimate way we have of being dependent in fruitful ways.

What enables us to trust? We trust many things. But when we trust our senses, that's not the same as sensing. And when we trust our analyses, that's not the same as analysis. What is this trust? It is, I suggest, a human faculty which is irreducible to sensing or reasoning. And it is also a faculty which—as little as aesthetic delight or enjoyment (listening to a symphony, seeing an exhibit, tasting good food, touching our lovers), or play—cannot be taken as essentially a belief system. Trust is *sui generis*. It is possible to trust our analyses. Then we get a belief system. Belief—in this contemporary sense—is a trusted concept, definition, theory. But the believing of the concept is a trusting, an accepting. Neither empirical verification nor irrefutable argument are available any longer to let us off the hook, unless we trust them as such.

In this context it is interesting to notice that our increase in rational knowledge, our increase in conceptually understanding and explaining our universe, does not replace faith, but makes our dependence on faith-language alone much less. But it does not decrease our dependence. When we understand fertilization, gestation, and birth we can say more than: "God gives us children." But this does not mean: "We now know where children come from and we know that they do not come from God."

The trusting, the accepting without which we cannot live can, like all human capacities, be excercised. We can learn to reason, we can learn to sense, we can learn to be just. And, just as these other capacities have their institutionalized form, trust has that too. The institutionalized form of excercising our trust is religion as cultus. In religion as cultus people develop their trust by trusting their ultimate dependence via symbolic rites and rituals. They ultimately trust in something that, they trust, does not depend. By it they direct their lives in the deepest sense. It is called ultimate simply because it forms the foundation for all forms of empirical trust, such as trusting our senses, trusting our children, trusting the government, trusting the ice. In that ultimate trust people develop a sense, a symbol, a metaphorical understanding of their origin and destiny. Origin and destiny, like norms, are invisible. They are neither proximate nor observable. But through trust they come within reach.

The rationality tradition has given our dependence its ground in reason. But in such a manner that reason made dependence and trust seem a violation of our autonomy and hence unreliable, as Schouls shows very convincingly. Dependence and trust became suspect to reason. The rationality tradition is not a good one to trust when it comes to an analysis of trust, because in its analysis it distrusts trust, as Schouls makes clear (2:144-145). Today, of course, as the rationality tradition reinterprets itself after the collapse of foundationalism, not all adherents need to distrust trust any longer. In our time one of the direct benefits of feminism has been its exposure of the danger of rationality as the single road to truth and knowledge. Feminism helps us re-examine the notion of other trustworthy sources of knowing or at least of trusting reason only when contextualized and embodied. Gadamer has restored to us the notion of truth in aesthetic experience, which is not conceptual rightness. But we still need to come to terms with the authentic experience of truth as trust in religion.

Trusting is a practice (Govier). In it our deepest and most ultimate foundations for life become known to us. In our ultimate trust we also come to know our God, whose becoming known to us in this way is called revelation. The word "god" is simply a term for what we so trust. Such trust in reason is what divinizes reason. Modernity has placed such trust in reason and as a result the reliability of reason has been authoritatively disclosed, "revealed" to modern people. Biblical religion, both

Old and New Testament, is intended to place our deepest trust in service and sacrifice on behalf of others. Hence they speak of God when they name the "I am" which is revealed as present in the cross of Jesus. The fact that the humanism in Marxism is connected with human autonomy makes the service of Christianity and the service of Marxism very different in kind.

The control and domination that came with the religion of independence, the autonomy and naturalism resulting from rational emancipation, and the secularism produced by the rejection of authority and denial of revelation have fundamentally undermined our capacity to trust. In both publications Schouls provides a clear and convincing analysis of this in Descartes. Dependence on reason *as* trust is therefore never really acknowledged. This is even true for the Christian religion, the rationalized Biblical religion in which faith has become a belief system related to objective propositional truths and historical facts. In certain forms of orthodoxy faith as trust is even suspect.

Perhaps the best way to sort out the relation between the life form of trust and the life form of reason is to acknowledge that faith in God is in the first place a-rational. Nielsen and all who argue with him are right in exposing "belief in God" as "irrational" when those defending "belief in God" are talking in terms of ordinary, "literal," or "propositional" language. Treated as "belief" in this conceptual way, the trust in God is misunderstood. This is because, within faith, the role of beliefs is not that of accepting understood concepts. Rather, in proposition-like language the symbols of trust are being expressed. The "propositions" of faith are at best analogously propositional. But if that is so, "irrational" would apply only to genuine conceptual beliefs within a genuinely propositional belief system. In that way beliefs about God are not rational. Any view "from the outside" in which we present our dependence on transcendence has to be metaphorical and cannot be metaphysical. Much of Christianity now deals with "truths," empirical claims, historical claims, conceptual positions formulated in response to the rationality tradition. Christianity is Hellenistic. But that is not necessarily the same as Biblical religion.

In so far as all religion needs to enter into a culture

concretely, that is, needs to make its ultimate reliance a genuine basis for genuine experience, adaptation of God to that culture is unavoidable. But when the adaptation has replaced the mystery of the original source, reorientation is needed. The attacks on religion as irrational could mean: we must be rid of religion. But if reason is not a qualified judge in this matter, we can look at religion again. Nielsen's objections to Dilman on this score (30, 139-144) do not take into account sufficiently that when we come to know God in terms of appropriate responses to the God-stories of faith, that is not so much ignoring the question of what "God" refers to, but more a referring in terms of responding appropriately, rather than a referring in terms of definite concepts. And he also does not acknowledge the significance of responding to the sort of identity that the stories give God, for which reason the Christian responses are not in some general way the same responses as those of any highly moral creature.

Nielsen's attacks on religion are essentially attacks on orthodoxy. And orthodoxy in all its garbs is best characterized as a form of what becomes crudely known in fundamentalism, that is, the absolutisation of certain facts and concepts of religion. They are likely to be "facts" lifted from their religious context and projected into prominence because of their fusion with other religious forms in the culture. In Christianity some of these are the creation story and the flood story's historicity, miracles, the virgin birth, Jesus' divinity, the resurrection, the trinity, and Biblical inerrancy. In the wake of a recognition that rational attacks on these "rational-empirical" facts have some validity some Christians rethink Biblical religion. Perhaps this may stimulate Nielsen to think along. If, for example, in liberation theology an attempt is made to refocus the religious life on the twentieth century practice of redemption as liberation from oppression, rather than on the preservation of beliefs, it would seem appropriate for a Marxist to become interested, especially when Marx has in many ways opened the eyes of liberationist Christians to a rediscovery of Biblical elements of their faith.

Claims of exclusivity or claims that some belief is true should be relativized by our ability to *live* out of our faith, to

221

show *in life* whether truth in love *leads* to blessing. That would be a new empiricism: the truth of practice. In the New Testament the practice of following the crucified one is identified as unacceptable to "Jew" and "Greek." To Jew because it relativized a given practice. To Greek because it offended reason. "Jew" and "Greek" are religious identifications here, not racial or ethnic categories. They indicate a historic religious practice of which the New Testament already saw the rigidity and the irrationality. In Christianity both these obstacles have been interiorized in legalism and intellectualism, rather than overcome in a life of following. But in a true following, the untruthful claims and the rules that lead nowhere could disappear and be replaced by claims and rules which, energized by a life of following, reorient us in our claims and rules.

Nielsen wants not to be doctrinaire but pragmatic about pragmatism. He goes beyond Dewey in that, because Dewey's allegiance to the rationality tradition, as I have tried to show in detail in *Communal Certainty and Authorized Truth,* made him doctrinaire about intelligence. Postmodern philosophers, Nielsen too, are showing that they can depart from their own tradition to criticize it. Nielsen's 1984 presidential address to the Canadian Philosophical Association (2) was a declaration in many ways of a new beginning. Some postmodern Christians are showing similar developments. They can de-dogmatize their tradition as well, especially its doctrinal side. They favor a religion which, if it has to be right, is right in its orthopraxis. As a result of these developments I believe a conversation can take place in which mutual respect is possible, mutual contributions acknowledged, and the discussion conducted in a different framework. A discussion which is not offensively rationalistic but appropriately reflective would show the benefits of articulating and comparing the different ways of life.

In such a discussion Christians could abandon the need to be "right" without ceasing to be followers of Christ. Their form of Biblical religion known as Christianity can be abandoned, in order to make more visible their trusting that in Christ people live potentially more fully than in other ways. That is precisely the area in which Christianity has failed. It has proclaimed the *belief that* in Jesus we have life and has made that belief a doctrine to be understood and subscribed to more than a life to be lived: orthodoxy. But only life provides the arena in which "claims" of Biblical religion can turn out to be true. In that sense Christian tradition has misled people like Nielsen, by failing to represent Christ as the champion of all who labour and instead presenting him as the incarnation of a theology. Instead of living hope Christianity made better thinking the core of religious tradition. But since Biblical religion is not essentially a thought pattern, Christianity was destined to lose that battle from a religion that was essentially practiced as a way of thinking, namely rationalism.

Christianity, seeking to locate itself safely within the Enlightenment, has become a scandal, its doctrine irrational, its claims arrogant. And the sandal it has become is not, of course, the scandal it should be, namely the scandal of foolishness in the eyes of self-proclaimed wisdom and weakness in comparison to self-assumed strength. The humility and reliability of Jesus who wants to lift the burden from those who labor has by and large not been the hallmark of official and institutionalized Christianity.

The metaphors of faith traditions for action
I want to close with some remarks about a Christianity that does not need to apologize for being a meaningful, sensible source of hope and comfort, as well as a realistic guide for contemporary conduct, especially in the modern world of scientifically educated people. Christians today need to engage in the same self-critical re-evaluations of religion as the Enlightenment is engaged in with respect to modernity. The rejection of foundationalism and scientism, in so far as these have shaped orthodoxy, call for critical self-reflection in orthodoxy, which is rational-doctrinal religion in more than just its fundamentalist forms. They also call for a radical reorientation to Biblical infallibility, which is a rationalist objective guarantee of the risk of trust in more than just its inerrantist forms. The Enlightenment has promoted science as ideology and Christianity has developed religion as a belief system. What happens to Christianity when we acknowledge orthodoxy as rational distortion? Once dissolved from its Enlightenment origins I see no

objection to evaluate WRE by its own professed criteria. If indeed it is *no more* than an "undistorted" web of well developed and widely shared beliefs, for which we claim no more than its potential to contribute to our critical task as a society, and which is not necessarily tied to materialist rationalism, I am free to test it by its claims and accept it for what it is when it passes the test (26:30). Similarly, once dissolved from its origin in orthodoxy, I see no reason why we cannot do the same for Christianity. It should be tested by its aim to be Biblical religion. I will make some suggestions in that direction. I will not look at Biblical religion as a belief system, nor will I acknowledge crusades in the Middle Ages, persecution of Jews and homosexuals for a millenium, bourgeois capitalism, right wing authoritarian social structures, and other characteristics of Western Christianity as legitimate expressions of Biblical religion. I will, instead, focus on the role of Jesus in Biblical religion and see that role given body in modern followers such as Mother Teresa, Beyers Naudé, Dom Helder Camara, Oscar Romero, Martin Niemöller and others. And the presence of Jesus is not necessarily limited to embodiment only in the life of those who follow him knowingly. But for those who do, their life in part reflects the belief that they have entered into the journey portrayed in the Biblical story as a tradition with authority, told in the Bible as a story to be trusted. That is: they "believed" in terms of joining the journey in trust.

Their life reflects in a more Biblical way whatever claims of uniqueness and universality can authentically be made for Christianity. Their role has been uniquely individual, historical, culturally situated, and fallible. They "tell the story" of authentic religion with their lives, rather than "teach the doctrine" of Christianity in theological discourse. As such they have also been an undeniably universal embodiment of truth, a "timeless" incarnation of hope for life, an authentic expression of a way to travel of which none can rightly disapprove. They have been "exclusive" not in "excluding" others but in not accepting for themselves what they sought for others. Rather than to reject the testimony of others who, like Ghandi, were also embodiments of the presence of God, they accepted the condition of those whose lives they sought to improve.

224

If we could abandon attempts to fixate God's revelation in conceptual coherence in favor of hearing the crying of God in the poor and oppressed, we would perhaps drift away from orthodoxy, but come closer to Biblical religion. If faith is trust and if in Jesus God becomes incarnate in human following, then true faith can take on many forms other than conceptual coherence. That's not a matter of formulating a doctrine of the incarnation, but trusting that the only reality we need to accept as the reality of God is the way Jesus sojourned through life. And though Christians believe that God uniquely came to be present in Jesus, the Christian tradition does not prevent us from acknowledging such incarnation in others, even those who do not know Jesus.

One form that faith takes on this model could be trusting people who give themselves as messages that God will take care of us. Another could be trusting that the reality of God takes shape in us when we so live for others. For intellectual appropriation of such religion we can look at liberation theology. There is no inherent need in Biblical religion to fix "God" in some particular substance or in an individual entity, nor does transcendence need to be a "spatial outside of reality." The "all in all" of the New Testament allows for other understandings.

In such a re-evaluation of Christianity in the light of Biblical religion, we will have to critically examine why Christianity so easily identifies with whatever has power, whether the power of money, or arms, or ideas; rather than with weakness, poverty, hunger, and oppression.

Looking at Christianity as not a belief system—though there are beliefs in Christianity—also means looking at its uniqueness differently. We don't have to look for the exclusivity of a belief system now, which cannot cope with other truth. The Bible has enough indications that its religion never meant to be exclusive in the sense in which the answer to "what's distance between a and b?" is just one single answer. In the Old Testament the book of Malachi acknowledges acceptable worship of God outside of Israel. The focus on Jesus does not change that for the New Testament, notwithstanding his claim that no one comes to God but through him. Christians need to honor that claim and take it seriously. But Luke (in the gospel story of

225

Simeon's greeting of the baby Jesus in the temple and in the Acts story of the Roman centurion's worship of God), and John (in the story of the Samaritan woman) and Paul (in his treatment of Gentiles in Romans 2) give examples of emphases to which traditional Christian exclusivism cannot do justice.

Jesus' saying "I am the way" need not be interpreted in any other way than: what you see in me is that God will give life to whomever loves the other more than self, to whomever will give her own life in love for the life of another. That is exclusivism only if the recommendation to include others to the point of excluding yourself is exclusivism. It hardly seems like an offensive form of exclusivism, but more like an inclusive form of exclusivism. "I am the way and the truth" is at any rate seriously misunderstood if understood as an exclusive traditional truth claim.

Modern Christians can be both fully rational and fully faithful in leaving behind the rationalism in the orthodoxy of an inerrant Bible, in favor of the participation in the story of God present in Jesus, contextualized by the authority of the Biblical narrative. That story is not a doctrine and it certainly need not be a doctrine to make it possible for us to reflect on it. In *Setting Our Sights by the Morning Star* I have tried to give an account of such religion that will be recognized as authentically Biblical by the orthodox faithful, as well as in touch with our times by thinking people. There is nothing irrational about a tradition which seeks its comfort, authority, wisdom, guidance, hope in the stories of the Bible and in the life (and death and resurrection) of Jesus. Healing, trust, and deliverance are central to these stories and that life and they are actions that differ from being in a state of belief or intellectual assent. In these actions Christians trust God is present. Apart from and outside of these actions God does not exist, as the via negativa has always tried to express. The Biblical God is not an absolute, a substance in, of, for, and through himself standing apart from or over against all else.

I resist Nielsen's move that in order to be the God of Christianity, God must have the characteristics that make belief in God unacceptable to Nielsen. I also resist his move that anything he will accept cannot be God. But I accept his intimation that to be moral we need not be Christians. Jesus made it quite plain that to "do God's will" one need not be one of those who say "Lord, Lord." Atheists may indeed be among those who live to serve and to suffer.

This is not Godless Christianity or atheist morality graced by Christian vocabulary. The reality of God may not be conceptually identifiable, but the reality of God we trust in the stories of Christianity do give a truly identifiable character to the Christian life. Biblical Christianity is not just universal morality. But the mystery of God and the mystery of faith need to remain mysteries. Any articulation, if taken literally, will in time lead to idolatry and falsehood and in the long run to unbelievability. If orthodoxy forbids of God that she be our mother, orthodoxy has become heretical. In that sense articulations cannot be "understood" at all. But they can be trusted. And if trust is a legitimate form of knowing and not only a necessary contribution to knowing, God can be known and our knowing true, even if we have not understood. The language of God-talk has to remain the language of faith, the metaphorical language that seeks to express a primordial trust that God is whoever or whatever is with us in our suffering and that God is in us when we are with those who are suffering, when our understanding and our knowledge are the understanding and knowledge of suffering, understood and known only in our own suffering with those who suffer.

When a Christian couple professes after the birth of a child: "God gave us" this child—maybe especially when the child is deformed, helpless, and dependent for life—they do not profess ignorance of intercourse, fertilization of an ovum, birth, and so on. They, in fact, indicate that very process in the language of faith. In it they see the presence of God; both when the child is healthy and gives reason for great gratitude and when the child is not healthy and gives reason for the parents to be God's presence in suffering to that child.

Nielsen is afraid that with such a religion its truth claims cannot be falsified. However, that "nothing can count against" such faith, that nothing can "separate us" from a God who is "present-with," is faith language that is poorly interpreted as a traditional rational truth claim or empirical fact claim. The truth of the claim is claimed in faith and is talked about in faith and is meant to be experienced in faith. And that faith is trust. The truth of the trust is misleadingly understood if interpreted as the truth of the rationality tradition. Nevertheless, if "the life of trust" does not—historically, in the generations, communally—inspire the hope and the comfort in the midst of suffering that God's presence is meant to inspire, that then does mean the faith is not true, the trust has been put to shame, the hope was false.

Biblical religion is a hoax if and when the following of Jesus demonstrably dooms historical generations to a life of despair as a result of such following him. In as much as Christianity has seen forms of such despair, it is not true Biblical religion in those forms of it. We know today that Christian conservative orthodoxy is a proven breeding ground for sexual violence. Its sexual morality is, in practice, clearly immoral. Those who in Canada today accuse homosexuals of violence against children must consider that the violence is possibly induced by their peculiar Christian environment rather than by their sexual orientation. Concentration on truth as rational doctrinal truth prevents conservative orthodoxy from examining the truth of moral conduct as an indication of the presence of the lie.

For a believer, the faith talk does not get translated on a different level and then tested. Rather, all the other levels of human experience become enveloped in the level of faith. Nevertheless, what can be rationally tested is whether my claim—made from within my faith—that religion is non-rational rather than irrational, as I take it, is a plausible claim. Religion as reason does not work, reason within faith works well, unless reason is itself the faith. Within faith, "God-talk" will always remain metaphor, including talk of God's reality or existence. In our secular naturalist world God literally cannot exist at all, and by the standards of rationalism talk of God's existence is indeed without meaning, is incoherent.

Christianity as life made "rational" (propositional) in theological doctrines will turn out to be irrational. As a particular belief system or moral code, Biblical religion becomes deformed. The prologue to the gospel of John or Paul's letter to the Galatians clearly reject right doctrine or right practice if that means a Hellenic rationality of "ortho(-praxis or -doc-trine)." That's at best a legitimate phase in history, one meta-phor that worked for a while in a rationalist culture. No single "belief"—say virgin birth or resurrection—can have the func-tion of objective shibboleth. No norm in isolation—hetero-sexuality—can be stated abstractly and maintained as the truth. Trinitarian doxology can be liturgically celebrated, but not stated in a theological doctrine. The mystery of the universe is *in*all things and *is* not one of them. It "transcends" them all. But in trust the mystery of God-with-us reveals itself with authority as reliable. And today we read that mystery in the symbols of poverty. Rather than doctrines, the oppressed give us the language of presence. The symbols of theology, fact, and empirical reality have proven their poverty in their inability to cradle God's presence. The poor are a better representative of that presence. Because of our evil they will be an ever present representative, calling out to us to serve.

The stories of the Biblical tradition are stories we read as faith stories, told in the realitiy of the culture and trust of believers of that time. Hans W. Frei's *The Eclipse of Biblical Narrative* ably sketches how these narratives are historical. Their realism is not the realism of modern day journalistic accounts, but the realism of hope against hope. If we consider our life, its history, our symbols, and our contemporary dark-ness all together, then within that context we may adjudicate such specifics as norms and beliefs, even in WRE. Norms and beliefs also count. But not as "the norm" and hence "having to be right." They are neither permanent nor have priority. They have their place when they can be agents of light in our darkness, can heal wounds, can liberate from oppression.

God is "revealed" (that's not a supernatural dictation of propositions) in redemption as self-denial and self-sacrifice. For Christians, Biblically speaking, such redemption is to be lived before the "present" face of God (current hopes shaped by current darkness) in tune with a "trusted" face of God (Bible), focussed on a privileged face of God (Jesus).

From the point of view of orthodoxy the denials and reformulations in which I have engaged have by some and at times been regarded as heresy. Heresy is itself, however, a category of orthodoxy. The Bible, I am convinced, takes orthodoxy far less seriously than it takes itself. In my discussion with Nielsen I hope we do not need to take orthodoxy as a criterion I must meet. Rather, I want to invite Nielsen to evaluate my own claims as they stand. I meet God as present in Nielsen. I hope I re-present God to Nielsen. I have faith that God is present in me. That presence is all I need to know I am not God as well as that God is real.

The power of trust in God lies precisely in the access it gives to a reality that all of us need and hope for, but of which we all know that it is not present in anything empirical, physical, creaturely, or whatever we may call the reality accessible to science. That's just why there is myth. To believe that human reason, or human autonomy, or undistorted discourse, or critical theory, or wide reflective equilibrium can do what those who have faith in these agencies hope for is possibly very primitive. It is a modern form of magic, subscribed to by people who have allowed the spiritual (forces directing us), the sacred (what is totally different from anything we see around us), and revelation (access via trust to the mystery of the hidden) to go underground, but who still have all the expectations all human beings need in order to live, but now attached to ordinary things.

How is Habermas' hope in critical theory different from "primitive" faith in nature divinities? To say that this hope is critical, discussable, and revisable is only to say that it is in reason rather than in rocks. We know that ordinary rocks cannot deliver the flourishing we hope for. Why should ordinary reason be able to do that? Is postmodernism not precisely another form of what we have met throughout our history, namely the discovery that another "ordinary" reality—this time reason—will not deliver what we thought—in faith—it promised? It may well be that loss of all mythical consciousness is a far more "primitive" state of culture than historically developed myth that continues to be acknowledged as myth.

Myth is universal consciousness of universal time in terms of which individuals live here and now. It tells primordial stories of good and evil. Among the Jewish people myth became a driving force in its entire culture. In their history they began

230

to incarnate, as a people, the universal narrative. The Jewish people began to own the narrative as their own history, to direct their development as people through the myth and to reinterpret the myth via their own development. In Jesus this incarnation went even deeper and took on the character of personal ownership. But Christianity, too, is in danger of loosing its myths. It, like Western rationalism, has wanted to drown out the myth in "real" history. Western Christianity desperately wants to make the reality of revelation propositional and historical. It is precisely Christianity's "realism" and "historicism" that robs the central proclamation of non-violence from all the power it has in the preaching of Jesus. It is precisely the insistence that the resurrected Jesus was a resuscitated corpse that sets up the dilemma of either an irrational "belief" in the resurrection or a denial of its reality.

The Judaeo-Christian primeval myth is that of a God who creates the world as the scene for divine empowerment, love, and protection in our strugle against evil, a God who seeks our flourishing, a God who is willing the give up the divine life in order to restore the universe to flourishing and who promises that such a divine love is attainable for all who are willing to seek flourishing at such cost. Both Jews and Christians have always been tempted to localize, concretize, and fixate this God in our familiar universe: the Temple is God, the Bible is God, Jesus is God. And once such fixation has happened, the human struggle to incarnate the God who was "revealed" in Temple, Bible and Jesus becomes blasphemy and consequently no longer happens.

The challenge for both Christianity and the Enlightenment is the rediscovery of faith and myth. That would be the rediscovery of human flourishing in terms of trust or faith in a power, love, justice, life other than, different from, greater than (=transcending) any power, love, justice, life we have ever known. Through faith it is discoverable, knowable (=revealed) in mythical narrative in which such totally different (=sacred) love, life, peace, justice, joy, and flourishing are told as coming from, originating in God, in a way that is intended to direct us (=spirituality) toward incarnation of these gifts in our own lives. In the Judaeo-Christian myth this God was "present" focally (through faith) first in the Temple and after that in Jesus. The point of the story of Jesus was that there should be a body of Jesus remaining on this earth in which the God of Jesus would be incarnate, present through the faith (trusting life) of Jesus' followers.

I agree with Nielsen that it is "boring and unfortunate" that we witness in our day a "return to the old topics and the old theses of traditional Christian philosophy and natural theology" (31:8). But I find it plausible to surmise that after the collapse of the Enlightenment's unproblematic faith in human autonomy on rational foundations, a plea for continued trust in rationality may turn out to be equally unfortunate, that is, devoid of treasure or prosperity. Christianity inside analytic philosophy as well as critical theory inside the Enlightenment may turn out to be close relatives.

Marxism, on the other hand, challenged a dying Christianity with its own call to solidarity with the oppressed and countered the myth of the body of Christ with the myth of the utopian future, the necessary triumph of the labor class. Could a conversation between Christians and Marxians rekindle human enthusiasm for myths?

Conclusion

For a postmodern rationalist like Nielsen, reason is not only thoroughly fallible and historical, but also no longer super-judge, final arbiter, or only court of appeal; even in matters of truth and knowledge. Nevertheless, religion is still discussed in terms of its permissibility. And the criteria for this permissibility seem to be primarily rational. In this discussion we may have reached the point of considering anew what religion is.

Perhaps Christians can abandon attempts to make their religion appear to be a matter of rationality, thus creating real problems for rational people who now rightly experience much of Christianity as truly irrational and therefore impermissible. And maybe atheists can abandon attempts to disallow religious experience. They can start considering what religion comes to if taken as a form of experience comparable to no other, yet empirically belonging to the experience of an unimaginably vast majority of human beings past and present.

This could enable Christians to shift the burden of proof of the viability of their religion to changed lives rather than theology. It could also allow atheists to consider rationalism as a form of religion whose deepest origin may be the patriarchal impulse to control. If rationalism is a form of religion it may, paradoxically, also be a very primitive form of religion. As subconscious worship of an ordinary, relative, partial form of human experience, an unacknowledged hope in mythical powers, it would be a suppressed form of religion and hence not susceptible to criticism as a religion.

Perhaps one of our world's best known atheists, the British philosopher Sir Alfred Julius Ayer, provided an interesting empirical platform for a renewed discussion of religion in his account of what happened to him when he nearly died. "Near Death Experience" (NDE) is widely studied today and what Ayer experienced is common. The accounts are remarkably unified, though perhaps their interpretation is not. All experience something "out of" the ordinary, "extra-"ordinary, perhaps not infelicitously called "transcending" the boundaries of ordinary human experience. Religion is first and foremost the acceptance, as "fact of experience," of the irrationality of secularism and materialism. Religion confesses there is more to reality than meets the eye or yields to comprehension. Faith surrenders to this "more" rather than deny it in a fit of human autonomy. Ayer's NDE for him minimally opened the door—though very slightly—to rethinking religious reality; implausible though it remains for the inveterate empiricist-rationalst that he is. But he could not deny that he experienced something, nor that it slightly upset his certitude as an atheist.

My interpretation of the NDE is that it "reveals" in a flash—in many different forms—what all humans hope for: love, warmth, light, joy, trust, affirmation, healing. All of that is released because all defenses are given up. The impending reality of death has rendered impotent the ultimate fear of death. The dying person surrenders control. And with that, life becomes available in all of its reality. The person who returns from that NDE is "reborn" with a renewed energy to share the true forces of life. What psychiatrists take years to achieve and then only on a small scale is now made available in an instant and released in seemingly endless power: new life, healing. We can't all have NDE's. But the reality of what human beings encounter in the face of ultimate boundary conditions—guilt, death, evil, origins, destiny, hope—is also available outside of the NDE, namely in faith and religion. Faith is the practice of surrender to what transcends our own limits. The wisdom of ages concerning this extra-ordinary reality has through faith been collected in ancient traditions of myths, narratives, apocalypses, parables, legends, and poetry. All of this is not and cannot be assertive, explanatory, or informative in our modern rational sense. But we are no longer able to experience or acknowledge this. In the ancient rationality tradition reason was accepted as providing a more reliable access to the questions of ultimacy and boundaries. In time reason took the place of religion, i.e., itself took on the religious function of ultimacy and boundary. Thus was born the religion of faith in rational control, which denied the legitimacy of religion and managed to entice Christians to model themselves after the rational image.

What I am saying here is far from acceptable to moderns or postmoderns, Christians and atheists alike. But I hope that the conversations on the pages of this book have introduced these notions in a way that makes them worthy of serious discussion. And I hope that rationalism's respect for experience and reality will allow some adherents to take seriously the testimony of people who do have religious faith and who practice it. The judgment of rationalists about religious faith is not likely to be reliable, because it is foreign to them. But respect for reason might entice some rationalists to respect the experience of others and might even stimulate a critical openness to what underlies rationalism, namely a faith in the powers of autonomous criticism that far transcends our ordinary experience of human rationality.

In the withering tradition of the West we are threatened with an unprecedented loss of community. Christianity and Enlightenment Humanism, as a rational form of Biblical religion and as a search for rational human autonomy, shared a common rationality and on that basis experienced forms of community. But that shared basis is now eroding. That, however, need not lead to despair. Other forms of sharing suggest themselves. Many Marxian atheists and many postmodern Christians share a deep respect for the call to repent of our thirst for oppressive powers and an equally deep respect for the call to serve the renewal of creation and of human life. I hope the conversation on these pages may contribute to a more widely shared discussion among those who in mutual respect are willing to search for community in a withering tradition.

REFERENCES

Works cited in the chapters by Hendrik Hart
NB. The references are made as follows:
— Unspecified references to an author refer to that
author's work listed below.
— Specified references are as follows:
  = if the author has one work listed, the number
    refers to a page in that work,
  = if the author has more than one work listed,
    a single number refers to the entire work
    with that number, while two numbers sepa
    rated by a colon refer to a numbered work
    before the colon and to pages in that work
    after the colon.
— References to pages in this volume will have a
  number preceded by the letter v., both in Hart's
  and in Nielsen's essays.

Ayer, Sir Alfred Julius, "What I saw when I was dead ...", in
The Sunday Telegraph. London, August 28, 1988.

Belenky, Mary Field; Clinchy, Blythe McVicker; Gold-
berger, Nancy Rule; Tarule, Jill Mattuck, *Women's Ways of
Knowing: The Development of Self, Voice, and Mind*. New York, Basic
Books, 1986.

Bouwsma, William J., *John Calvin, A Sixteenth Century Por-
trait*. New York, Oxford University Press, 1988.

Code, Lorraine, *Epistemic Responsibility*. Hanover, University Press of New England, 1987.

Code, Lorraine; Mullett, Sheila; and Overall, Christine,
Feminist Perspectives: Philosophical Essays on Method and Morals.
Toronto, University of Toronto Press, 1988.

Davidson, Donald, "The Method of Truth in Metaphysics,"

in Baynes, K., Bohman, J., and McCarthy, Th., (editors) *After Philosophy, End or Transformation?* Cambridge, The MIT Press, 1987. Pp.166-183.

Derrida, Jacques, "The Ends of Man," in Baynes, K., Bohman, J., and McCarthy, Th., (editors) *After Philosophy, End or Transformation?* Cambridge, The MIT Press, 1987. Pp. 119-158.

Dewey, John, *How We Think, A Restatement of the Relation of Reflective Thinking to the Educative Process.* Boston, D.C. Heath and Company, 1933.

Dreyfus, Hubert L., "Why Studies of Human Capacities Modeled on Ideal Natural Science Can Never Achieve Their Goal," in Margolis, J., Krausz, M., and Burian, R.M., (editors) *Rationality, Relativism and the Human Sciences.* Dordrecht, M. Nijhoff Publishers, 1986. Pp. 3-22.

Eliade, Mircea, *Patterns in Comparative Religion.* New American Library, Meridian, 1958

Frei, Hans W. *The Eclipse of Biblical Narrative.* New Haven, Yale University Press, 1974.

Gadamer, Hans-Georg, *Truth and Method.* New York, Crossroad, 1984.

Govier, T., "Many Types of Trust and Distrust," paper read to the Canadian Philosophical Association, Victoria, May 24, 1990.

1. Hart, Hendrik, *Communal Certainty and Authorized Truth, An Examination of John Dewey's Philosophy of Verification.* Amsterdam, Swets & Zeitlinger, 1966.

2. _____, "Commitment as a Foundation for Rational Belief," in *Philosophy and Culture, Proceedings of the VIIth World Congress of Philosophy, Montreal, 1983.* Montreal, Éditions Montmorency, 1988. Vol. II, pp. 879-884.

3. _____, *Understanding Our World, Towards an Integral Ontology.* Lanham, University Press of America, 1984.

4. _____, *Setting Our Sights by the Morning Star, Reflections on the Role of the Bible in Postmodern Times.* Toronto, Patmos Press, 1989.

Havelock, Eric A., *The Muse Learns to Write: Reflections on Orality and Literacy from Antiquity to the Present.* New Haven, Yale University Press, 1986.

1. Hesse, Mary B., *Models and Analogies in Science.* Notre Dame, University of Notre Dame, 1966.

2._____, "The Cognitive Claims of Metaphor," in J.P. van Noppen, editor, *Metaphor and Religion: Theolinguistics 2.* Brussels, Vrije Universiteit, 1983. pp. 27-45.

Hawking, Stephen W., *A Brief History of Time: From The Big Bang to Black Holes.* New York, Toronto, Bantam Books, 1988.

Kant, Immanuel, *Critique of Pure Reason.*

Lashchyk, Eugene, "Models, Analogies, and Metaphors," in Margolis, J., Krausz, M., and Burian, R.M., (editors) *Rationality, Relativism and the Human Sciences.* Dordrecht, Martinus Nijhoff Publishers, 1986. Pp. 151-185.

Lloyd, Genevieve, *The Man of Reason: "Male" and "Female" in Western Philosophy.* Minneapolis, University of Minnesota Press, 1984.

MacIntyre, Alasdair, *Whose Justice? Which Rationality?* Notre Dame, University of Notre Dame Press, 1988.

0. Nielsen, Kai, "Critical Theory, Social Science, and Values." *In Liberal and Fine Arts Review,* 2, 1982.

1._____, *Philosophy and Atheism: In Defense of Atheism.* Buffalo, New York, Prometheus Books, 1985.

2._____, "On Finding One's Feet in Philosophy: From Wittgenstein to Marx." In *Metaphilosophy,* Vol. 16, No. 1, Jan. 1985. Pp. 1-11.

3._____, "On Sticking With Considered Judgments in Wide Reflective Equilibrium." In *Philosophia, Tidsskrift for Filisofi,* Denmark, Vol. 13, Nos. 3-4, 1985. Pp. 316-321.

4._____, "How To Be Sceptical About Philosophy." In *Philosophy,* Vol. 61, No. 235, January 1986. Pp. 83-93.

5._____, "Rorty And The Self-Image Of Philosophy." In *International Studies In Philosophy,* Vol. XVIII, No. 1, 1986. Pp. 19-28.

6._____, "Scientism, Pragmatism, and the Fate of Philosophy." In *Inquiry,.* Vol. 29, No. 3, 1986. Pp. 277-304.

7._____, "Can There Be Progress In Philosophy?" In *Metaphilosophy,* Vol. 18, No. 1, January 1987. Pp. 1-30.

8._____, "Philosophy as Critical Theory." In *Proceedings and Addresses of The American Philosophical Association,* supplement to Vol. 61, No. 1, September 1987. Pp. 89-108.

9. _____, "Cultural Identity and Self-Definition." In *Human Studies,* Dordrecht, Martinus Nijhof, 1987. 10, pp. 383-390.

10. _____, "Undistorted Discourse, Ethnicity, and the Problem of Self-definition." In *Ethnicity and Language,* The University of Wisconsin System Institute on Race and Ethnicity, Winston A. Van Horne, editor. 1987, pp. 15-36.

11._____, "Searching For An Emancipatory Perspective: Wide reflective Equilibrium And The Hermeneutical Circle." In Evan Simpson (editor) *Anti-Foundationalism and Practical Reasoning,* Edmonton, Alberta: Academic Printing and Publishing, 1987. Pp. 143-164.

12._____, "Legitimation und Ideologie." in *Ratio,* Vol. 29, no. 2, 1987, pp. 103-112.

13_____, "The Rational Knave: On The Link Between Morality And Rationality." In *Idealistic Studies,* XL, 4, June 1987. Pp. 10-18.

14._____, *Marxism and the Moral point of View.* Boulder, Colorado, Westview Press, 1988.

15._____, "Arguing about Justice: Marxist Immoralism and Marxist Moralism." In *Philosophy and Public Affairs,* Vol. 17, No. 3, Summer 1988. Pp. 212-234.

16._____, "Afterword: Feminist Theory—Some twistings and Turnings." In *Canadian Journal of Philosophy,* Supplementary Vol. 13, 1988. Pp. 383-418.

17._____, "The Withering Away Of The Tradition." In *Philosophia,* Vol. 18, Nos. 2-3, July 1988. Pp. 211-226.

18._____, "In Defense of Wide Reflective Equilibrium." In Odegard, Douglas, editor, *Ethics and Justification,* Edmonton, Alberta, Academic Printing & Publishing, 1988. Pp. 19-37.

19._____, "Reflective Equilibrium and the Transformation of Philosophy." In *Metaphilosophy,* 1989.

20._____, "Farewell To The Tradition: Doing Without Metaphysics and Epistemology." Typescript, 20 pp., 1989.

21._____, "On Transforming Philosophy." Typescript, 26 pp., *The Dalhousie Review,* Vol. 67, no. 4, 1989. Pp. 439-456.

22._____, "Indeterminacy Of Reference Without

Relativist Pain." Typescript, 14 pp., 1989.

23._____, "On Goldman's Resistance To Saying Goodbye To Epistemology." Typescript, 14 pp., 1989. Forthcoming in *Philosophia*.

24._____, "Intellectuals and Partisanship." Typescript, 12 pp., 1989. Forthcoming in *Interchange*.

25._____, "The Burden of Ideological Masks in *Ideologiekritik:* On Trying To View Faith Scientifically." Typescript, 1989, 19 pp.

26._____, "Wittgenstein, Wittgensteinians and The End of Philosophy." Typescript, 1989, 37 pp. Forthcoming in *Grazer Philosophische Studien*.

27._____, "The Confirmation of Critical Theory: The Role of Reflectiveness." Typescript, 1989, 20 pp.

28._____, "Meta-Comments on The Very Idea of A Critical Theory: Raymond Geuss and *The Idea of A Critical Theory*." Typescript, 1989, 28 pp.

29._____, *After The Demise of The Tradition*. Boulder, Colorado, Westview Press, 1989.

30._____, *God, Scepticism and Modernity*. Ottawa, The University of Ottawa Press, 1989.

31._____, "Foreword." In Parsons, Keith M., *God and the Burden of Proof: Plantinga, Swinburne, and the Analytic Defense of Atheism*. Buffalo, New York, Prometheus Books, 1989. Pp. 7-9.

32._____, "Defending The Tradition," in *Journal of Indian Council of Philosophical Research*, Vol. VI, No. 2, January-April 1989. Pp. 53-60.

33._____, and Campbell, Richmond, Exchange of letters, November 1988 and January 1990.

34._____, "Defending Atheism Again: Remarks on God and Coherence." In Moreland, J. P. and Nielsen, Kai, *Does God Exist?* Nashville, Tenn., Thomas Nelson Publishers, forthcoming 1990.

1. Rorty, Richard, *Philosophy and the Mirror of Nature*. Princeton, Princeton University Press, 1979.

2. _____, *Consequences of Pragmatism*. Minneapolis, University of Minnesota Press, 1982.

3._____, "Truth and Freedom: A Reply to Thomas

McCarthy," in *Critical Inquiry* 16, 1990, pp. 633-643.

Schaberg, Jane, *The Illegitimacy Of Jesus, A Feminist Interpretation of the Infancy Narratives.* San Fransisco, Harper And Row, 1987.

1. Schouls, Peter A., *The Imposition of Method: A Study of Descartes and Locke.* Oxford, Clarendon Press, 1980.

2._____, *Descartes and the Enlightenment.* Kingston and Montreal, McGill-Queen's University Press, 1989.

Smith, Wilfred Cantwell, *Faith and Belief.* Princeton, Princeton University Press, 1979.

Stout, Jeffrey, *Ethics After Babel: The Languages of Morals and Their Discontents.* Boston, Beacon Press, 1988.

Taylor, Charles, "Overcoming Epistemology," in Baynes, K., Bohman, J., and McCarthy, Th., (editors) *After Philosophy, End or Transformation?* Cambridge, The MIT Press, 1987. Pp. 464-488.

Colophon
Typesetting by Willem Hart for
University Press of America using
Aldus PageMaker on a Macintosh SE
in Adobe 11/13 New Baskerville
Roman and Italic with Bold Face
Cap heads and Italic u/l bylines.
Final printout was done on a
LaserWriter Plus at 300 dpi.
Printed in the U.S.A. by offset
lithography on acid-free paper.